Ancestral Roots and Descendants

of

Charles Robert Looney and LaVanchie Margaret Cool

and

the Families

of

Ackley, Bradford, Burbank, Cool, Crow, Dwight,
Fitch, Flint, Goodwin, Granger, Hoar, Kuhl, Looney,
Mason, Partridge, Peck, Wark, and Whiting

Revised

Ancestral Roots and Descendants

of

Charles Robert Looney and LaVanchie Margaret Cool

and

the Families

of

Ackley, Bradford, Burbank, Cool, Crow, Dwight,
Fitch, Flint, Goodwin, Granger, Hoar, Kuhl, Looney,
Mason, Partridge, Peck, Wark, and Whiting

Revised

RICHARD COLEMAN WITTERS

To order additional copies of this book, contact:
Xlibris Corporation
1-888-795-4274
www.Xlibris.com
Orders@Xlibris.com
57353

CONTENTS

To Maria, my loving wife, for without her patience, unselfishness, and utmost support, I would never have finished *Ancestral Roots and Descendants of Charles Robert Looney and LaVanchie Margaret Cool.*

PREFACE

The following pages contain a selection of my ancestors who graced the shores of America as early as 1620. In researching the history of these founders, I gained so much respect and admiration—I became so impressed with their religious belief, their integrity, their leadership, their unselfishness, their devotion to building a better world; and after much research, I came to the conclusion that they were very instrumental in the shaping of America.

This is my first attempt to write about our family history or anything else for that matter. I realize there may be imperfections, but please let me assure you, they are not intentional.

As for the facts contained herein, I have strived for as much accuracy as possible; however, I cannot guarantee that the information is correct or, for that matter, complete. I have used the best sources available to state the facts, sources both from here and abroad. I have not relied on the works of other genealogist with one exception, John W. Kuhl (see special acknowledgment). I have discovered that many so-called genealogists are just name and date accumulators and seem to be too much in a rush to add a new name without checking for sources or if a source is available, not verifying the facts pertaining to that particular name or fact—this has taught me to be patient and not be in a rush to move on to the next person or family. As for dates of births and deaths of females in the fifteenth, sixteenth, and seventeenth centuries, these dates were not recorded; but in later years, the dates became more available. And speaking of dates, one could conceivably check three of four good references and come up with perhaps three different dates of births. They may not be off by more than one or two years, but still, they differ.

Some of my references include the following: vital records from towns, cities, and states; probate records and copies of wills and family Bibles; records from genealogical societies; records from colleges both in America and England; and rare and out-of-date books dating as far back at the 1500s. There are a couple of cases where I have written and received information from a county medical examiner's office concerning the death of an individual. I have used as many sources as possible just to check one date or name. I have tried as hard to disprove a fact as much as I have to prove one. Various sources will differ in dates of birth or places of birth—headstones are not always correct, and town vital records will have errors. As hard as one tries, not all records are error free.

There will be, from time to time, words that the meaning may not be quite obvious; therefore, I have placed a glossary toward the end of the book for help in this area.

Not only is *Ancestral Roots and Descendants of Charles Robert Looney and LaVanchie Margaret Cool* about our ancestors, but it also describes the history and the way of life that surrounded them. Unfortunately, there will be just names with no dates and history about that person that could not be found. The Internet has been a tremendous help in correspondence with other genealogist, libraries, genealogical and historical societies, and universities. Just by typing a person's name or an event, you will discover many sites that have what you are looking for, but one must be careful not to rely on the information submitted by another genealogist unless he or she cites the source and then you verify the source. Some sources will just list another genealogist's name, and that is something you must stay clear of.

Ancestral Roots and Descendants of Charles Robert Looney and LaVanchie Margaret Cool is not a complete history of our ancestors, but rather an outline—a place to start for those who are interested in learning more about our family. I could never hope to duplicate the works of the many who have written about some of our ancestors.

Maria and I and, at times, my sister and her husband, Nancy and Ron Tietgen, have made many trips to Illinois, Indiana, Michigan, New Jersey, Connecticut, Massachusetts, Canada, England, Scotland, and the Isle of Man in search of information and the opportunity to take pictures of cemeteries and headstones of our ancestors. We have walked many cemeteries looking for our ancestors and waiting to hear one of us yell, "I found him" or "Here's one." The journey has been enjoyable, fun and at times, frustrating; but I wouldn't trade the experience for a million dollars.

Acknowledgment

Throughout the years, I have had so many people help me by directing me to a particular book or society. I wish that I had recorded all of their names so that I could give them proper recognition—to all of them I apologize but give a great big "thank you."

One person I want to give a special thanks is my Aunt Irene Cool (Wark) (Waddell) Coover who was the firstborn to Charles Robert Looney and LaVanchie Margaret Cool. Aunt Irene first introduced me to genealogy around 1991 when she asked me to help her organize the names and dates of all of those she had researched. I was able to assist her somewhat, but because of the aging process, Aunt Irene became unable to continue her work. Irene's two sons, Bob and Bill, boxed all of her material up and shipped it to me.

As I sifted through the material, I discovered several letters written by her asking for information. She would send checks for two or three dollars to pay copy fee or postage of anything sent back to her. For the time period, Irene did a lot of work—gathering names, dates, and places. She accumulated information that helped with my research. Had Aunt Irene had the Internet and the computer, her work would have been less cumbersome and probably more in detail. Irene, for the most part, did the same thing that our ancestors did—she and they planted the seeds and paved the way for others to follow and try to improve the paths that she and they carved. She planted the seed for me to cultivate. Aunt Irene did a fantastic job, and I wish that she were with us today so that I could thank her for getting me started in this wonderful world of genealogy.

John W. Kuhl has been tracing and recording the Kuhl/Cool family history for almost forty years. He has compiled more documented information about the Kuhls and their families. John was the consultant for the Kuhl families in

More Palatine Families by Henry Z. Jones Jr. Eighty percent of the chapter on the Kuhls can be attributed to John Kuhl and his dedicated and unselfish research.

I would like to give a special thanks to my wife Maria, my daughter Cherise, and my sister, Nancy and her husband Ron for taking the time to scrutinize and point out many errors—errors that have caused me to present a revised edition of *Ancestral Roots and Descendants of Charles Robert Looney and LaVanchie Margaret Cool.*

In recording the data in *Ancestral Roots and Descendants of Charles Robert Looney and LaVanchie Margaret Cool,* I discovered there is too much material for just one book and thus have begun volume 2. Hopefully, volume 2 will not take as long to publish. Having said that, there is plenty of information yet to be discovered, and I encourage others to take up genealogy and learn about your ancestors and the history that surrounds them. But be forewarned; it is time-consuming, expensive, and addictive.

As you will soon discover, *Ancestral Roots and Descendants of Charles Robert Looney and LaVanchie Margaret Cool* has very little information about the children of Charles and LaVanchie and the children of the children of Charles and LaVanchie. I have left that up to you to continue the story. I did, however, contact the grandchildren of Charles and LaVanchie and received replies from many, but not all.

It is with hopes that you will find *Ancestral Roots and Descendants of Charles Robert Looney and LaVanchie Margaret Cool* enjoyable, informative and at times, entertaining.

Enjoy the journey back in time.

Please e-mail me if you have any corrections, comments, or questions at rwitters@nc.rr.com or write me at Richard C. Witters, 106 Repton CT., Cary, NC 27519.

ONE

Charles Robert Looney and
LaVanchie Margaret Cool

———————◆◆◆———————

Charles Robert and John Thomas Looney were born 9 March 1877 in Kansas City, Missouri. The twins' parents were James H. Looney and Mary Kane. Twenty-one days later, Mary (Kane) Looney died. Records of her death, showing the cause, could not be located. She was buried in St. Mary's Cemetery in Kansas City, Missouri.

The 17 May 1877 edition of the *Porter County Vidette*,[sic] a newspaper in Valparaiso, Indiana, made the following report:

> *Mrs. John Wark has gone to Kansas City and brought back a pair of twin babies, children of her sister-in-law who lately died. She now has the children and intends bringing them up.*

In earlier days, allowing a relative or a close friend to care (without adoption) for the young child or children upon the death of the mother, was a common practice. John and Elizabeth (Looney) Wark had one child of their own. Robert Burns Wark was born in 1866, thus eleven years older than his cousins and, now, his new "brothers." Elizabeth was the sister of James H. Looney. John and Elizabeth never legally adopted the Looney twins, nor did Charles or John ever legally change their name to Wark. Throughout their childhood, the three boys were known as the Wark children. With the exception of some legal matters, Charles and John continued to use the name of Wark throughout their lives.

The June 1880 Federal Census for Valparaiso, Indiana, reflects the following:

> John Wark, age 46
> Lizzie Wark, age 43
> Robert Wark, son, age 14
> Charles Looney, nephew, age 3
> John Looney, nephew, age 3

According to the publication, *From Trumpet to Carillon*, outlining the 150th Anniversary of the First United Methodist Church of Valparaiso, Indiana, page 26, the Valparaiso Male and Female College (VMFC) was chartered in 1859 and began its first term on 21 September of that year. The college was under the control of the Methodist Episcopal Church. The first year's attendance was 157 students. As the town of Valparaiso was beginning to spread in a direction other than toward the school, the school was soon considered too far from the town and closed its doors in 1871. In September 1873, under the influence of the educator, Henry B. Brown of Ohio, the college reopened its doors and became known as Northern Indiana Normal School and Business Institute (NINS).

In an e-mail I received from Mel Doering of Valparaiso University, and that was later supported by copies of various directories, Charles Robert Wark (Charlie Wark of Porter County, Indiana) was enrolled (1891) in the Preparatory Department. He was thirteen years old when he enrolled. In the 1895 directory, he was enrolled in the NINS Commercial Department and in the Pharmacy Department in 1896-97. He was a pharmacy graduate in 1897.

There is also an alumni record card for 1897 pharmacy graduate Charles R. Wark of 705 Chicago Street, Valparaiso, Indiana, listing his occupation as hardware merchant; the date of the information was noted in 1938.

Mr. Doering located records on John Wark of Porter County, Indiana. John was listed in the 1893-1894 register of students and was enrolled in the telegraphic department. There were no other records for John Wark.

According to a photocopy of a marriage license, Charles Robert Looney and LaVanchie Margaret Cool were united in marriage on 26 January 1907 at Windsor, Ontario, Canada. The copy was signed by Rev. Thomas Manning; the original was said to have been in the family Bible and in the possession of their sixth child, James Wark.

In July 2003, I wrote to the Canadian Vital Records Department and requested a copy of the marriage application for Charles and LaVanchie. I had not received an answer by September when my wife Maria and I began a trip to Indiana, Michigan, Windsor, Ontario, Canada, and New York. Upon our arrival at Windsor, we found the church where they were married. We met with Virginia, the administrative assistant for the Central United Church, who helped us with our research. Virginia was kind enough to let us into the church to take pictures. When we finished, Virginia opened the original book of marriages. She and I searched the records for the month of December 1906 and January 1907, but could not find any listing of the marriage of Charles and LaVanchie Cool. All of the marriages listed were performed by Rev. Thomas Manning. Virginia dismissed this as just an oversight and said that since we have the original certificate, it should be proof enough. We thanked her, said our good-byes, and continued on our way.

On 4 January 1904, the church was destroyed by fire. Construction began almost immediately, and the new Sunday school building was completed in May 1906 before Manning became its minister. The sanctuary of the church was open for services on 10 December 1906 just after Rev. Thomas Manning had become its pastor. As late as 1923, the church was still known as Central Methodist Church. On 14 June 1925, the Central United Church held its inaugural services to celebrate the Union of three churches in Canada—the Presbyterian Church in Canada, the Congregational Churches of Canada, and the Methodist Church.

When we returned home almost two weeks later, among the pile of mail, there was a document from the Vital Records Department of Ontario, Canada. The records indicated that Charles Robert Looney and LaVanchie Margaret Cool were married on 3 July 1907. The marriage was recorded on 4 July 1907. I sent an e-mail to Virginia and asked her to look at the marriages for July 1907. She wrote back and said that she had found it under the date of 3 July 1907. So, instead of our grandparents being married 26 January 1907 as indicated on the copy of their marriage certificate, they indeed were married later that year, 3 July 1907. This was the beginning for us, the Looney-Wark cousins.

The following were taken from the street directories of Jackson, Michigan, and Valparaiso, Indiana. It shows when and where Charles and LaVanchie lived and, in some cases, the occupation of Charles.

(Living in Jackson, Michigan)

1907   Wark, Charles R., Salesman Jackson Paint and Wall Paper
        Co. bds. (Boarder) 125 2d.
1909   Wark, Charles R., broker, res. 911 Washington

(Living in Valparaiso, Indiana)

1898   Charles Wark, student—residence 9 E. Monroe
1902   Charles Wark, groceries, provisions and baker, 20 W. Wayne,
        residence 9 E. Monroe

1905	Charles Wark, residence 3 E. Monroe
1907	no listing for Charles Wark—see above Jackson, Michigan
1911	Charles and LaVanchie Wark builders' supplies, hardware and window glass, Phone 164 M—11 E. Main, residence 704 E. Erie
1920	Charles and LaVanchie Wark—705 E. Chicago
1921/2	Charles and LaVanchie Wark—15 E. Lincoln Way (Hardware store) tel 543-R
1921/2	Charles and LaVanchie Wark—705 E. Chicago tel 388-J
1924	Charles and LaVanchie Wark—Hardware 15 E Lincolnway, Tel 543-R, home 705 E. Chicago
1931	Charles and LaVanchie Wark hdw 15 E Lincolnway h705 E. Chicago
1938	Charles Wark, hdw 15 E Lincolnway h705 E Chicago 705 E. Chicago
1943	Charles Wark; 15 Lincoln Way

LaVanchie Margaret (Cool) Looney was born 11 May 1882 in Albion, Michigan, and was the only child of Crittenden Irelius Cool and Lydia Elizabeth Ackley (see Cool/Kuhl chapter) (see Ackley chapter).

LaVanchie graduated from Albion High in 1900. The directory of the Cleary Business College, Ypsilanti, Michigan, lists LaVanchie M. Cool in attendance from 1 July 1902 to 1 July 1904.

In a book published by the class of 1900, *Albionensis*, there is a letter from LaVanchie who was living in South Bend, Indiana, at that time.

After traveling around for several years, I have accepted a position in the toy department of a large city store. I wish I might write you a good long letter, but so far have had little excitement in my life, and know very little that is of interest to you, but want to relate an experience I had one day not long ago. A pleasant faced monk came in to purchase toys for some sick children, I waited upon him and thought I recognized his voice, and so looked at him closer. I found it to be our old friend Chas. O'Connor, who, being disappointed in love became disgusted with the world and gave it up for a life of quiet benevolence. Am sorry I can think of nothing more, but you know I was always abrupt. Best wishes for a pleasant reunion.

It was signed LeVanchie. [*sic*]

Following are three letters written to her daughter, Irene, just prior to LaVanchie's death:

(Note: I have copied the letters as written, with no corrections in spelling or grammar.)

Sunday Night—Feb. 24, 1935

Dear Irene,

 Thought you would like to know how I got home and how we all are!

 Daddy wasn't looking for me, but was glad to see me. Knobby, he was so excited, had the rug all up set!

 I packed John's cookies and took them to the Post Office; I got a few groceries and came home & rested.

 Frid.—I was on the davenport all the fore noon—I couldn't sit, but after dinner I felt better, there wasn't any school in the P.M. So Chas. washed and I made a "ginger bread"—I helped dry the cloths. Yesterday morn. I stayed in bed until about noon—then I got the car and took Speedy to the "Barber Shop"—

 I didn't feel so good last night but took some anacin. Ethel came up—& we played Rumie with Mary H. & Alene & had a lot of fun. Doc came up at 10—& we played bridge a little while, but Doc was so sleepy. Ethel & I beat them.

 Daddy had a nice dinner today—Roast beef—and it did hit the spot. Doc got a case of beer for me last night, $ 1.75—Its very good. First I've had since the two bottles you gave me. That was still ice cold & I opened a bottle soon after I got home—

 Betty & Alene got the ironing done yesterday and Betty has been a real good girl to help today.

 I don't know of any news—had thought of the nice time I had with you last week—

 I seem to have some temperature tonight but can't see why I should. Have been resting all day. I'll be glad when I can sit in some comfort, I thought after all those treatments I would be fine. I presume you are busy with your dinner about now—I know how nice it would be—

 This is my last sheet of paper—Everyone sends love to you & Bob

Love,
Mother

Feb. 28, 1935

Dear Irene,

 Well, the party was a real "success"—no one got "drunk"—Daddy went from down town at 6 o'clock we were to be there but I wasn't ready until 6:30.

 Daddy said P. L. never _____ when he says he is going to—& about 9:00—probably dinner would be ready. I was on the first floor landing when I heard someone coming down, & it was Daddy to call me—to make sure I was coming—I wasn't so keen about going but I am glad I went. Mr. & Mrs. George Dodger, Daddy & I & a cousin of Perry's—from New York were all there were. We had a nice quiet evening—tell you about his dinner Sunday.

This is another nice day & I want to get out, but was afraid that if I didn't write something now I wouldn't get a letter off to you so you get it Sat. P.M.—No, school tomorrow on acct' of Basket B at gym Charles will wash.

I've forgotten what I did write yesterday. I know I forgot to mention anything about your plants. How they must be growing, you better write so _____, _____ about the stuff you got. My ferns would enjoy a few doses.

I am asking Ethel & Doc up Sunday if they don't ask us down there. It's their third anniversary—Ethel is working at Beache's selling stockings & anything in the store—

Mrs. Jones had an operation—nothing serious I guess. She is delighted to have the job goes to work at 12 noon.

Did I say anything about beer? Yes I do want a case—I was sorry Bob didn't have the two bottles I brought home—instead of my bringing more home—

I found the death notice in the Trib of Richard so have Edith's address now & Daddy is writing to them today—I am sending Aunt Georgie a line. Was Dr. Poutuis his doctor?

Here is some good news—for the last four nights I have slept just fine—no night sweats, can't imagine what happened—I'm not gaining any weight but yesterday & today feel much better.

(Frid night) A busy day—Chas. Washed—& Betty & I hung the things outside. They are ready to iron. Wished I could have had more in the wash—it's been such a grand day—Hopes it's nice Sunday—we will be looking for you. All send love to you and Bob.

Lovingly,
Mother

Wed. Night 8 p.m. 6-12-35

Dear Irene,

Sorry you did not get a letter this morning but I spent the evening at Ethel's.

The Brave's played McGills last night and Ethel went with Alene, Mary H. Jeane, Speedy & I. Daddy had to stay at the store, Mac was here. So after the game, Ethel & I went to Sievers. We parked our car by the Palace. Harry was with his girl and friends & he had "Knobby." Alene & I gave him a bath after dinner yesterday and he looked so nice. When I stopped with the car, I tooted

*the horn & you should have seen him so excited. Harry wanted us to bring him
home, so when we went to Sievers we took Knobby. He sat up so nice beside of
Ethel & watched everything. We were so proud of him. I stayed at Ethel's until
10 o'clock—& when I got home I was to sleepy to write but I thought about
you if that will help any. The Braves won 8-2—a very good game.*

*I haven't worked all week—have been resting. I mended Tom's pants
yesterday. I didn't like that job. This morning I got some ice and washed
out a few things (Alene ringing them out). Then after dinner I rested at
3:30, went to get a shampoo _____ at Mary _____, got home at six; I do
rest but I'm not eating anything to put on weight; I have felt fine today.*

*Glad you had a good time Sunday—Don't bring straw berries or
cake—how silly—I don't like it warmed over. Received a letter from
my mother, yesterday I haven't asked her for money, but she said just as
soon as she had some money, she was sending some—& it would be quite
soon—Glad I didn't ask her for it.*

*Well dear, I can't think of anything else to write tonight. All send Love
Hope you get work soon—It's tiresome waiting.*

*Love
Mother*

*Grandmother's Salad Dressing
2 cup of Honey
2 cup Vinegar
2 cup Safflower Oil
2 teas salt
2 teas pepper
2 teas Worcestershire Sauce
2 teas Dry Mustard*

LaVanchie died 11 November 1935 in Valparaiso, Indiana, at the age of
fifty-three. She is buried in Graceland Cemetery. Charles Robert Looney died
15 March 1943 in Valparaiso, and is also buried in Graceland Cemetery, both
under the name of Wark.

Charles and LaVanchie had twelve children, six boys and six girls. These
children became our mothers and fathers—our aunts and uncles. Aunt Irene and
Uncle John were born in Jackson, Jackson County, Michigan. They were born with
the last name of Wark. The other ten children were born in Valparaiso, Indiana,
and were born with the last name of Looney. As far as I know, the fifth child, James
Cool Looney, was the only one to change his name from Looney to Wark. The
change was legally made after his marriage and the birth of their daughter, Mary

Helen. Again, to the best of my knowledge, the rest of the children continued to live under the name of Wark, except when legal documents needed to be signed.

In the probate file of James H. Looney, there is a letter requesting a transcript of the probate proceeding of James H. Looney. The letter was dated 27 September 1938 and was signed by Charles Robert Looney of 15 Lincolnway, [sic]Valparaiso, Indiana. This is just another indication that Charles never legally changed his name to Wark.

The children of Charles and LaVanchie Looney are the following:

I.   Irene Cool Wark   born 29 November 1907, Jackson County, Jackson, Michigan; married Robert Knox Waddell 4 November 1933, Valparaiso, Indiana; and had two children:

    1.   Robert Knox Waddell, Jr.,   born 13 November 1936, Chicago, Illinois
    2.   William Wark Waddell,   born 4 August 1938, Chicago, Illinois

Robert Sr. died 13 November 1970, Phoenix, Arizona. Irene married Richard Hoffman Coover 14 November 1975, Scottsdale, Arizona. Richard died in July 1993. Irene died 11 February 2008, Spokane, Washington.

1.   **Robert "Bob" Knox Waddell Jr.** married 27 May 1967, Sunnyside, Washington, Pamela Lee Shea, born 7 February 1945, Seattle, Washington. Bob and Pam had the following children:

   1a.   **Jennifer Lee Waddell,** born 5 January 1973, Newport Beach, California. Jennifer has one son, Cole Christopher Knox Waddell, born 4 December 1995, Vancouver, Washington. In May 2009, Meredith (Jennifer's sister) and her husband Cory McNair adopted Jennifer's son Christopher Knox Waddell. Christopher elected to retain his last name of Waddell. (see 1c below)

   1b.   **Christopher Knox Waddell,** born 13 January 1975 in Newport Beach, California, married 18 July 1998 Kristen Ruth (Norton). in Kooskia, Idaho. Kristen was born 13 January 1977 in Kooskia. They have three children—all born in Coeur d'Alene, Idaho; Connor Knox Waddell, born 29 October 2001, Brooklynn Ruth Waddell born 5 April 2003 and Kyle Christopher Waddell born 17 January 2007.

   1c.   **Meredith Tyler Waddell,** born 8 April 1977, Newport Beach, California. She married Cory Scott McNair 8 August 1998,

Vancouver, Washington. Cory was born 7 July 1976, Portland, Oregon. Meredith and Cory have the following children—all born in Vancouver, Washington: Caden Scott, born 17 June 2001; Jackson Tyler Knox, born 26 August 2003; Ella Rae, born 17 February 2005; and Brenton James, born 3 October 2006. In May 2009, Meredith and Cory adopted Jennifer's son Christopher Knox Waddell. Christopher elected to retain his last name of Waddell.

2. **William "Bill" Wark Waddell** married 29 May 1959, Riverdale, Illinois; Mary Jane Fritz born 7 May 1939, Blue Island, Illinois. Bill and Mary Jane are very much involved in ministry work. They have the following children:

2a. **William Ward Waddell Jr.**, born 9 July 1960, Waco, Texas, married Denise Davis born 24 January 1961, Denver, Colorado.

2b. **Whitney Ann Waddell**, born 23 November 1963, Harvey, Illinois; married Mark O. Cabrera, born 12 July 1962, Montgomery, Alabama.

2c. **Weston Scott Waddell**, born 1 September 1966, Harvey, Illinois; married Libby Laing born 18 November 1966, Detroit, Michigan.

2d. **Sarah Jean Waddell**, born 15 August 1965, Seoul, Korea; married Sympoph (Tom) Kongsynonh, born 18 October 1974, Suwana Ket, Laos

II. **John James Wark**   born 26 February 1909, Jackson County, Jackson, Michigan; married Wilma White, 4 July 1936, Miami, Florida; they had one child:

3. Ethel LaVanchie Wark born 29 July 1940, Tucson, Arizona

Wilma died 23 February 1987, La Mesa, California. John died 26 March 1992, El Centro, California.

3. **Ethel "Bunny" LaVanchie Wark** married (1) 10 October 1959 Earnest Studer and, (2) 4 July 1986, Rick Downing.

3a. **Lisa Irene Studer** was born 20 October 1962, El Centro, California.

3b. **Sam Studer** was born 14 August 1965, Brawley, California.

The other ten children of Charles and LaVanchie were all born with the last name of Looney in Valparaiso, Indiana.

III. Harry Crittenden Looney   born 8 November 1910; spent his entire life living in Valparaiso, Indiana; never married

IV. Ethel LaVanchie Looney   born 17 December 1911; married 3 March 1932 Aubrey Coleman "Doc" Witters, born 24 June 1909 Aden, Illinois; they had three children:

    4.   Nancy Jo Ann Witters   born 16 June 1936, Valparaiso, Indiana
    5.   Richard Coleman Witters born 2 May 1939, Valparaiso
    6.   John Charles Witters   born 29 August 1940, Valparaiso; died 15 July 1962 Miami, Florida; never married

Doc died 6 April 1953, Miami, Florida. Ethel married (2) 21 January 1961, North Miami, Florida, Raymond T. Moran who died 17 April 1963, North Miami. Ethel died 5 October 1991, Raleigh, North Carolina, and was buried in Graceland Cemetery, Valparaiso, Indiana.

    4.   **Nancy Jo Ann Witters** married 7 December 1956, N. Miami, Florida, Ronald Steven Tietgen, born 19 November 1934, New York, New York. They had two children:

      4a.   **Timothy "Tim" Hugh Tietgen,** born 11 May 1958, Miami, Florida, married 30 December 1978, Winston-Salem, North Carolina, Myra Kay Phillips, born 16 September 1957, Albuquerque, New Mexico. Their children are Laura Nicole, born 28 December 1985; Steven Taylor, born 3 November 1989; and Michael Carl, born 12 June 1993. All three children were born in Raleigh, North Carolina.

      4b.   **Kimberly "Kim" Lynn Tietgen,** born 30 December 1964, Miami, Florida; married 1 October 1988, Raleigh, North Carolina, Stuart Michael McCall, born 22 May 1959. Marion, North Carolina. They had the following children: Kendall Jo Ann, born 11 May 1991; Savannah Star, born 14 March 2002. Both were born in Santa Fe, New Mexico.

5. **Richard Coleman "Dick" Witters** married 2 July 1964, Folkston, Georgia, Maria Josephine Brancaleone, born 1 September 1941, Brooklyn, New York. They had two children:

    5a. **Michelle Marie Witters,** born 19 December 1965, N. Miami, Florida; her four children are Brandi Eden Tremblay, born 11 June 1989, Moore County, North Carolina; Megan LeeAnn Tremblay, born 31 August 1994, Bay County, Florida; Ryan William Tremblay, born 28 September 1996, Bay County, Florida and Joseph Yorke Tremblay, (adoption); born 6 March 1987, Pompano Beach, Florida; married 20 September 2008, Bithlo, Florida, Amanda Michelle Menard, born 3 November 1991, Orlando, Florida, daughter of Timothy Joseph and Susan Mary (Pulsifer) Menard.

    5b. **Cherise Lynn Witters,** born 14 June 1967, N. Miami; married 2 March 2002, Key West, Florida, Gregory "Greg" Mathew Dixon, born 8 January 1971, Cincinnati, Ohio. Their two children are Ava Coleman Dixon, born 25 May 2004, Winter Park, Florida and Andrew Biagio Dixon, born 28 October 2005, Wilmington, North Carolina.

V.   **James Cool Looney**   born 13 February 1914; married Eleanor Agnes Wagner 30 June 1945, Valparaiso; they had one child.

    7. Mary Helen   born 7 November 1947, Valparaiso, Indiana

On 27 September 1950, Jim, Eleanor, and their daughter legally changed their name from Looney to Wark. Eleanor died 14 July 1993. Jim continued to run Wark's Hardware in Valparaiso, up until his death 13 February 2001. Jim was buried in Graceland Cemetery in Valparaiso.

    7. Mary Helen married 29 June 1968, Chicago, Illinois, John George Petersen of Omaha, Nebraska. (No response to inquiries)

VI. **Lydia (Betty) Elizabeth Looney** born 15 May 1916; married William B. Forney 24 January 1936, San Marcos, Texas; they had one child:

    8. John Charles Forney   born 29 April 1936, Valparaiso

Betty married (2) Hugh L. Quinn 22 August 1946, Yuma, Arizona. Hugh died in Alpine, California. Jay's father, William, died in January 1999 while living in Texas. Betty died 8 February 1998, Louisville, Kentucky.

8.   **John "Jay" Charles Forney** married 2 June 1962, Huntsville, Alabama, Lynne Marie Coleman, born 1 December 1942, Philadelphia, Pennsylvania. They had the following children:

  8a.   **Elizabeth Marie Forney**, born 2 January 1963, San Diego, California, has one son, Chase Allan Forney born 14 August 2000, Louisville, Kentucky.

  8b.   **Stephanie Lynne Forney**, born 9 March 1964, San Diego, California; married 24 October 1987, Louisville, Kentucky, Robert Scott Bohnert born 21 November 1961, Louisville, Kentucky. They had three children all born in Louisville, Kentucky: Kirstin Rebecca, born 13 June 1991; Logan Dominic, born 3 May 1994; and Nathan Joseph, born 24 May 1996.

  8c.   **Christopher Sean Forney,** born 12 March 1967, Louisville, Kentucky, married on 18 June 1994 in Cocoa Beach, Florida, Ramona Beatriz "Bea" Alfonso who was born on 12 July 1963 in Matanzas, Cuba. They have the following children: Jessenia Katherine Forney, born on 30 November 1994, Titusville, Florida; twin boys born on 18 May 1999, Cocoa Beach, Florida, Nicholas Alexander and Zachary Daniel Forney; children from a previous marriage: Gabriela Nicole Pena, born on 7 October 1989, Hollywood, Florida; Natalia Kristina Pena, born on 28 July 1991, Long Island, New York.

VII. Charles Robert Looney   born 6 June 1917; married Mable Pauline "Polly" Cober 15 October 1938, River Forest, Illinois; they had three daughters:

9. Margaret Ann Wark   born 18 September 1942, Chicago, Illinois
10. Pauline Cober Wark   born 19 April 1946, Chicago, Illinois
11. Mary Ruth Wark   born 14 July 1952, Chicago, Illinois

Charles "Chuck" died 11 January 1999 in Maui, Hawaii. Polly died 14 April 2003, Maui.

9. **Margaret Ann "Peggy" Wark** married 5 September 1964, Flossmoor, Illinois, William Wyman "Bill" Hoffman, born 25 March 1939, Chicago. They had the following children:

   9a. **Marjorie Ann "Margie" Hoffman,** born 6 July 1966, St. Louis, Missouri; married 23 May 1987, Grand Rapids, Michigan, Richard Dean Robert, born 8 July 1964, Bangor, Maine. Their children are Jeffrey Scott Robert, born 26 December 1990 and Jessica Laura Robert, born 17 October 1992. Both children were born in Peoria, Illinois.

   9b. **Laura Kay Hoffman,** born 1 May 1970, Beloit, Wisconsin, married 30 May 1992 Grand Rapids, Michigan; Brent Raymond Mitten born 8 April 1969, Edmonton, Alberta, Canada. Their children are Samuel William Mitten, born 1 July 1997 Birmingham, Alabama; Joseph Brent Mitten, born 1 June 2000, Birmingham, Alabama; Thomas Raymond Mitten, born 23 September 2002, San Francisco, California; Tabitha Joy Mitten, born 20 November 2007, Santa Rosa, California.

   9c. **Jeffrey Scott Hoffman,** born 14 May 1973, Beloit, Wisconsin, died 26 September 1973 Caledonia, Illinois, of sudden infant death syndrome.

10. **Pauline "Penny" Cober Wark** married 15 April 1978 on board the *Judy Ann* between the islands of Maui, Molokai, and Lanai, Hawaii, Frank Kamauoha Hoopai Jr., born 10 April 1946; died 21 December 1994, Lahaina, Hawaii.

11. **Mary "Pat" Ruth Wark**, married 18 November 1972, San Diego, California, Monte Gene Nelson, born 22 May 1951, San Diego. Pat and Monte have two children:

    11a. Monte Gene Nelson II, born 2 October 1980, San Diego, California.

    11b. Mark Charles Nelson, born 6 July 1992, Maui, Hawaii

VIII. Rhoda Alene Looney	born 19 July 1918; died 2 February 1992; buried Graceland Cemetery, Valparaiso, Indiana; never married
IX. Thomas Frederick Looney	born 16 August 1919, Valparaiso, Indiana; married 9 October 1948, New Castle,

NSW, Australia, Catherine Blanch; Tom and Katie had two children through adoption:

12. Charles Henry Wark	born 4 October 1957, Sydney, Australia
13. Virginia Ruth Wark	born 9 September 1960, Sydney, Australia

Tom died on 13 May 1998 at St. George Hospital, Kew, Victoria, Australia.

12. Charles Henry Wark (no response)

13. Virginia Ruth Wark worked as a professional model, now living with her spouse Yvonne Burke, born 16 March 1965, New York City, New York.

X. Ruth Marie Looney	born 12 September 1921; married Dr. Philip Heller 28 April 1945, St. Luke's Hospital Chapel, Chicago, IL; Ruth and Phil had five children:

14. Jeanne Heller	born 18 July 1947, Chicago, Illinois; never married
15. Philip Henri Heller Jr.	born 27 April 1949, Chicago, Illinois
16. Nancy Lynn Heller	born 26 February 1951, Chicago, Illinois
17. Patricia Lee Heller	born 11 August 1954, Evanston, Illinois
18. Mary Elizabeth Heller	born 26 August 1959, Evanston, Illinois; married 1 October 1983 William Burton Taber, born 6 July 1957

Dr. Philip Heller died 10 January 1991, Hilton Head, South Carolina.

15. Philip "Phil" Henri Heller Jr. married 23 December 1977, Long Grove, Illinois, Elizabeth Ann Von Lehe, born 10 August 1950, Chicago. They had two children:

15a. Kimberly Nicole Heller, born 25 January 1981, N. Canton, Ohio, married 19 August 2006, Cincinnati, Ohio, Robert Thurlow, born 1 November 1978, Buffalo, New York.

15b. Caroline "Cari" Marie Heller, born 20 July 1983, Des Moines; married 21 February 2008 Cincinnati, Ohio, Joshua Carleton

McEnaney, born 25 February 1983, Charlotte, North Carolina. Because Cari's father was an only son and because he had no sons of his own, Joshua changed his last name to Heller just after marriage in order to carry on the Heller name

16. **Nancy Lynn Heller** married 20 August 1977, Waukesha, Wisconsin, Joseph John Boppre, born 20 May 1948, Milwaukee, Wisconsin. They had two children:

    16a. **Ryan Joseph Boppre**, born 6 February 1979, Waukesha; married 21 August 2004 in Waukesha, Daina Marie Moretti, born 13 January 1980, Waukesha. They have one daughter, Katelynn Marie Boppre, born 11 April 2006, Waukesha.

    16b. **Shaun Philip Boppre**, born 22 January 1982, Waukesha; married 8 June 2008, Germantown, Wisconsin, Katie Ellen Nefstead, born 16 October 1982, Waukesha, Wisconsin.

17. **Patricia "Pat" Lee Heller** married (1) 21 May 1982, Dallas, Texas, Paul Michael Hines, born 27 April 1953; divorced 13 October 1995. Their children are Meghan Elizabeth Hines, born 29 August 1983, Dallas, Texas, and Daniel Lucas Hines, born 24 January 1986, McKinney, Texas. Pat married (2) 5 February 1998, Las Vegas, Jack Steven Bolowskie, born 13 March 1948, Syracuse, New York.

XI.	Mary Helen Looney	born 14 October 1925; married Fred F. Keller 11 April 1948 in Brawley, California; Mary and Fred had four children:
19.	Frederick Francis Keller	born 31 July 1949, Brawley, California
20.	Patricia Ann Keller	born 21 February 1953, Brawley, California
21.	Jeanne Marie Keller	born 1 March 1956, Brawley, California
22.	Betty Sue Keller	born 31 December 1957, Brawley

Frederick F. Keller was born on 28 December 1921 and died on 13 January 1996.

19. **Frederick Francis Keller** (no response)

20. **Patricia Ann "Trish" Keller** married 7 January 1978, Adrian, Michigan; Michael Lloyd Kiley, born 31 December 1944, Adrian, Michigan. They had four children:

20a. Erin Ya Sook Kiley, born 9 September 1981, Seoul, Korea (adoption); married 6 November 2004, Campbell, California, Jeffrey Moffet, born 25 August 1980, Corona, California.

20b. Judah Ben Michael Kiley, born 23 February 1984, San Jose, California.

20c. Caleb Michael Kiley, born 20 April 1988, San Jose

20d. Kaitlyn Elizabeth Kiley, born 26 May 1993, San Jose

21. Jeanne Marie Keller (no response)

22. Betty Sue Keller married 19 August 1989, Little Falls, New Jersey, Glenn Nicholas Gorab, born 24 April 1955, Hackensack, Bergen, New Jersey; they had three children:

22a. Lauren Jean Gorab, born 18 May 1992, Glen Ridge, New Jersey

22b. Nicholas James Gorab, born 6 January 1995, Glen Ridge

22c. Matthew Frederick Gorab, born 10 June 1998, Glen Ridge

XII. Edward Louis Looney,   born 8 January 1927, Valparaiso; married in 1951 Odella Brown. They had one child born of this marriage and one adopted:

23. Debbie Lynn Wark   born December 1952, Valparaiso, Indiana; died three days later

24. Kathryn Jean Wark   born 19 December 1954, Valparaiso

24. Charles (Chuck) Wark   born about 1957 and was adopted around the age of two. No other information.

Speedy served in the U.S. Army and was a policeman for the Valparaiso Police Department. He died 16 November 1987 and is buried in Graceland Cemetery in Valparaiso, Indiana.

Elizabeth Looney and John Wark

This story and this book would not have been possible had it not been for Elizabeth and John. Just think—if our great-grandmother (Mary Kane) had lived to raise her sons, then Elizabeth and John would not have taken on the role as parents and, therefore, Charles Robert and John Thomas would have been raised in Kansas City, Missouri, instead of Valparaiso, Indiana, and we would be writing a whole different accounting of our history—or there wouldn't be a history for us to write or read about.

Elizabeth Looney, sister of our great-grandfather, James H. Looney, came to America in 1855. According to the Federal Census for Valparaiso, Indiana, Elizabeth married John Wark in 1866 and settled in Valparaiso. According to the same census, John was from Scotland and came to America in 1856. Elizabeth was christened on 28 May 1837 on the Isle of Man. Her death certificate shows a date of birth of 27 March 1836. Her obituary and tombstone show 27 May 1837. The 1880 census shows John at age forty-six and Lizzie at age forty-three, a three-year difference in age. The 1900 census shows John at age sixty-six and born in August 1833. The same census shows Elizabeth at age sixty-one, now a five-year difference and being born in March 1839. John was born in 1833 and was from Scotland. His tombstone shows 21 August 1834. Is any of this important? Probably not, but I thought I would mention it just the same.

The 1890 census shows John Wark as a tanner, according to George Neeley, the author of the book, *City of Valparaiso, A Pictorial History*, in the celebration of the 125th anniversary of the city of Valparaiso, Indiana. John had been in the hardware business since 1899, having bought the store from Mr. Hiram Brickford. Mr. Brickford founded the hardware store in 1856. It had changed hands seven times before our grandfather became the owner. Charles Robert Wark held his grand opening on 9 September 1919. The store was at 15 Lincolnway, which is the main street in Valparaiso. The second floor of the store was the residence of Charles R. Wark and his family.

The 1885-86 Valparaiso street directory shows "Wark, John, hides and leather e Mechanic, res. 15 e Monroe." This means his business was on East Mechanic Street and their residence on East Monroe.

> 1890-1893 Valparaiso Street Directory—Wark, John, a resident of this city since 1865, wholesale and retail dealer in leather and findings, also dealer in hides and tallow and director State Bank of Valparaiso, 6 E. Mechanic, res. 3 E. Monroe.
>
> 1898   Wark, Charles student r 9 e Monroe
> Wark, John hide and leather 6 e Mechanic r 3 Monroe
> John W clk r 3 w Monroe

1902	Wark Chas, groceries, provisions and baker, 20 W. Main tel 331, r 9 East Monroe
	Wark, John (Elizabeth wife) hides, 6 E Mechanics, r 9 E Monroe
1905	Wark Chas r 3 E Monroe
	Wark Elizabeth Mrs. r 3 E. Monroe
	Wark Robert (Hattie, wife) farmer, r 54 W Institute

I have given you these addresses in the event your travels take you to Valparaiso and just in case you want to take a tour through town and see where some of our ancestors once lived.

John Wark died on 28 March 1904. The following was reported in the *Valparaiso Messenger*, Valparaiso, Indiana, 31 March 1904.

Monday's Daily

JOHN WARK DEAD
Passed Away This Morning at His
Home in This City

John Wark, one of Valparaiso's most prominent retired business men, died this morning at his home on Monroe street of stomach trouble. He had been in poor health for the past year and only recently returned from a trip to Hot Springs, Ark., where he spent several months taking treatment. He came home little improved in health. Last Friday, while down town he was taken ill and had to be removed to his home in a carriage. He had been unconscious most of the time since Saturday.

The deceased was born in Beith, Ayershire, Scotland, and came to this country in the 60's, coming to this city in 1865, where he had since resided. For thirty-five years he was engaged in the hide and leather business.

Mr. Wark was a member of Masonic order of this city. He was a member of the board of directors of the Valparaiso National Bank; the State Bank; and the Thrift Trust Company.

The deceased leaves a wife, one son Robert, and two nephews, Charles and John Wark.

In the death of Mr. Wark, Valparaiso loses one of its most substantial citizens. He was an upright and honest man, and enjoyed the confidence of everyone in the community.

The funeral will be held Wednesday at 2 o'clock from the Presbyterian Church.

The Evening Messenger, Valparaiso, Indiana, Tuesday, 19 August 1924

MRS. WARK DIED TODAY

Mrs. Elizabeth Wark, age 87 years died at 4:30 this morning at the home of her son Robert Wark 504 E. Lincoln Way. Being in good health until Tuesday morning when she was stricken with acute indigestion. Funeral Services will be conducted from the Robert Wark home Friday afternoon at 2 o'clock, with interment following in Graceland cemetery.

Mrs. Wark was born in Ramsey, Isle of Man, on May 27, 1837, the daughter of Mr. & Mrs. Looney. The Isle of Man is in the Irish Sea. Mrs. Wark came to this country when very young. In the year of 1864, she married John Wark, who predeceased her in death twenty years. After marriage, the couple moved to Valparaiso, and has been residing here ever since.

Mrs. Wark is survived by one son, Robert, with whom she was making her home, and two nephews: John and Charles Wark. The late Mrs. Wark raised the two boys, John and Charles as her own sons. John and Charles Wark are the two sons of Mrs. Wark's brother. She is survived by fourteen grandchildren.

Mrs. Wark's death came very suddenly, as she was out riding Monday afternoon and calling on some of her many friends. She became seriously ill Tuesday morning at nine o'clock.

Deceased had been living in Valparaiso for the past sixty years and during this time made many friends among the city people. She has always been a member of the local Methodist church and a willing and ardent attendant of her church, of which she thought so much. Mrs. Wark will be sorely missed, not only by her immediate relatives, but by old and young who knew this congenial well meaning lady.

Vidette Messenger, Monday, 29 November 1937
ROBERT WARK, CITY PIONEER, PASSES TODAY
End Comes in Early Morning Hours After Wark's Critical Illness; Falling for Three years.
MEMORIAL RITES HELD WEDNESDAY

Robert B. Wark, age 71 years, former business man and identified with the banking business in this city for thirty years, died this morning at 4 o'clock at his home 504 East Lincolnway.

Though he had been in ill health for the last three years, his condition did not become critical until last Wednesday night.

Mr. Wark was born in Valparaiso on April 21, 1866. He was the son of John and Elizabeth (Looney) Wark the former pioneer business man of this city.

When a young man he engaged in the merchandising business in Kansas City, Mo., where he was located for a number of years. Returning to Valparaiso, he operated a grocery business here, later disposing of his interest to look after his farm properties.

On June 14, 1893, he was united in marriage to Harriet Aln Summer, who survives together with three children, Robert C. Wark, and Miss Dorothy Wark of Chicago, and Mrs. J. G. Smith of Bartlesville, Okla.

For the last thirty years, Mr. Wark has been a director and officer of the First State Bank of Valparaiso. He was also a member and officer of Methodist Episcopal church.

Memorial services will be held Wednesday afternoon at 2 o'clock at the Stinchfield funeral home, conducted by Rev. Russell B. Kern of the Methodist Episcopal church. Burial will be at Graceland cemetery.

In an attempt to find a living descendant of John and Elizabeth Wark, with hopes that we might learn more about our ancestors (Looney), I have discovered the following:

Robert Burns Wark (1866-1937) was born on 21 April 1866 in Valparaiso, Indiana. He married Harriet Ann Summer 14 June 1893 in Kansas City, Missouri. Harriet was born 18 July 1863, Valparaiso. She died 23 April 1954, Bartlesville, Oklahoma and was transported back to Valparaiso, for burial next to her husband, Robert in Graceland Cemetery. Harriet "Hattie" was the daughter of John and Sabrina (Ritter) Summer.

John Summer, father of Harriet, was born in Canada 12 June 1836 and died 16 April 1903 at the age of sixty-six. His wife, Sabrina M. Ritter, was born 13 May 1823 and died 28 October 1905. Both are buried in Graceland Cemetery in Valparaiso, Indiana.

Robert and Harriet had the following children:

Robert C. Wark was born 6 September 1894, Kansas City, Missouri. He died 6 June 1947, Valparaiso and is buried in Graceland Cemetery. Robert married Rachelle Lemay who was born in Tomahawk, Wisconsin.

Helen Sabina Wark was born 27 July 1899, Valparaiso. Helen was in nursing and moved to Bartlesville, Oklahoma, where she met and married Dr. Joseph Green Smith (his second marriage) who was twenty-eight years her senior. Helen died 23 May 1956, just seventeen days after her husband passed away. Her obituary indicates that she was survived by one son, Robert, who attended Oklahoma A&M College in Sweetwater and who was graduating "this month."

Helen is buried next to her husband in Memorial Park Cemetery in Bartlesville. Dr. Smith purchased six cemetery plots in the 1930s; however, only space 1 and 2 are used (Dr. Smith and Helen)—the other four are still empty.

Dr. Smith was born 8 December 1870 in Newburg, Arkansas, and died 6 May 1956, Bartlesville. His obituary indicates that he left the following children: Terry, a son living in Chicago at that time; Robert, a son who was graduating from Oklahoma A&M College in Sweetwater, Oklahoma (now know as Oklahoma State University), on May 1956, the same month as Dr. Smith passed away. Dr. Smith also mentioned a daughter, Margaret Frances Smith of Chicago. Terry and Margaret were from Dr. Smith's first marriage.

Dorothy Wark was born in Valparaiso, Indiana. She married Robert Booker and—lived in Dewey, Oklahoma.

In trying to find Robert Alexander Smith, son of Helen (Wark) and Joseph G. Smith, I learned from Shirilyn Dehis of the Office of Registrar at Oklahoma State University that Robert Alexander Smith transferred from Panhandle State University (in Goodwell, Oklahoma) and attended Oklahoma A&M from fall 1948 through summer 1951 and from fall 1955 through spring 1956. He received a Bachelor of Science degree in the College of Agriculture majoring in Dairy Production. The degree was conferred 27 May 1956.

To date, I cannot find any living family members in John Wark's line.

TWO

Joseph Ackley and Hannah Archer

Joseph Ackley Sr. was born about 1741 and died in Reading, Windsor County, Vermont, 17 July 1824 at the age of eighty-two. Hannah or Anna Archer died 11 July 1792. Following Hannah's death, Joseph Sr. married Martha (last name not known). Martha died 4 March 1825. Joseph, Hannah, and Martha are buried in Sawyer Cemetery. In 1999, I received the following transcript, (typed) with a copy of the original agreement (very poor penmanship).[5]

> *Known all men by these presents [sic] that I Joseph Ackley of Reading in the county of Windsor and state of Vermont for the consideration of fifty dollars paid me in hand by Joseph Ackley, Jr., of Granville in the County of Washington and the State of New York the receipt whereof I acknowledge do by these presents [sic] grant bargain and sell to the said Joseph Ackley, Jr. a certain tract or parcel of land lying in Plymouth containing ninety acres of land being of the original William Willard to have and to hold the above granted and bargained premises with all the privileges and appurtenances thereunto [sic] belonging to him the said Joseph Ackley, Jr. his heirs and assignees forever against all claims and demands whatsoever and I also agree that until the ensealing [sic] of these presents [sic] I am a lawful owner of the above premises and have a good right to bargain and sell the same in manner and form as above and further I the Said Joseph Ackley do by these presents [sic] bind myself and heirs and administrators to warrant and secure and Defend the same against all lawful claims of any person or persons whatever.*

In witness whereof I have hereunto set my hand and seal this third
Day of June A.D. one thousand seven hundred and Ninety Nine. [Sic]
Signed Sealed and in the presence of
Elisha Bigelow   (Signed)
Joseph Ackley [Seal]

State of Vermont
Windsor County
Reading, June ye 3rd 1799 personally appeared Joseph Ackley Signer and
sealer of the above instrument and acknowledged the same to be his free
act and deed before me, Elisha Bigelow, Justice of the peace.
Recorded July ye 10th 1801   Moses Priest, Town Clerk[2b]

Granville, Washington County is located in the upper portion of New York, just west of Poultney and Pawlet, Vermont. The town is divided into four sections: Granville, South Granville, Middle Granville and North Granville. Just west of North Granville is Fort Ann, also in Washington County, New York.

Joseph Ackley Jr. and Phebe Chandler

Joseph Ackley, son of Joseph Ackley Sr. and Hannah Archer, was born 28 October 1777. His birth record was found in Reading, Vermont; however, at the bottom of his record card is the notation, "Born in East Haddam, Conn." The record also shows that his parents were Joseph and Hannah Ackley. Hannah's last name is not listed.[2a]

The New York census taken on or about 4 August 1800 shows the name of the "head of house" and then breaks down those living in the household by sex and "between ages." Joseph Ackley was listed as head of house and living in the town of Granville. The oldest male living in the household was between the age of twenty-six and forty-four, indicating he was born between the years 1756 and 1774. He was too young to be Joseph Sr., beside the fact that Joseph Sr. was on the 1800 Vermont census, so we can't be sure who he was. The next oldest male was between sixteen and twenty-six, which would indicate that he was born between the years 1774 and 1784. This would probably be Joseph Ackley Jr. There was one other male between the ages of ten to fifteen, which gives us a date of birth of 1785 to 1790. As for the females, there were two under the age of ten (1790-1800), one between sixteen and twenty-five (1775 to 1784). The two younger girls would be Sarah and Frances, both of whom are mentioned in the will of Joseph Chandler, their grandfather and the father of Phebe Chandler. The one family member between the age of sixteen and twenty-five would of course be Phebe Chandler, who was born in 1780. The next name on the 1800 census is Joseph Chandler, father of Phebe, Joseph's wife.

The following is found in the book *1737 History of Washington County*, page 196.[1]

> *Joseph Ackley, step-father of George N. Bates, of Middle Granville, came to this town about 1806. He was a builder; erected at North Granville the hotel, the academy, and other buildings. About 1816, in the company with Mr. Oliphant, he built and afterwards carried on the old brewery that was on the grounds of the present military school.*

Note the date of the will of Joseph Ackley Sr. (10 July 1801) and the date in the above history book (1806). The book has a list of those who contributed to the information contained. George N. Bates was one of those listed. One must assume that the date 1806 was obtained from him. I mention this because another source shows Joseph moved to Granville in 1812.[1a]

There is a small cemetery located on County Road 17, also known as Dewey Bridge Road. County Road 17 intersects with State Highway 22 and runs between Granville and Fort Ann. Over the years, this cemetery has been known as Dewey Bridge Cemetery, Fort Ann Burial Grounds, and Otis Cemetery. The official name is Otis Cemetery.[21]

On 7 October 2000 while on a trip with my wife, Maria, and my sister and brother-in-law, Nancy and Ronald Tietgen; and in search of Otis Cemetery, we stopped at a farmhouse to ask if they knew of Otis Cemetery. They did not! While backing up the car, we glanced to our left; and there, standing right in front of a cemetery, was the headstone of Ann Burbank, the author's fourth great-grandmother and the wife of Shem Burbank. Her headstone read:

Sacred
To Memory of
Ann Burbank
Relict of Shem
Burbank who died
February 4, 1813 in the 76 year of her Age

After parking the car, we started our walk through the cemetery in search of our Ackley family. The cemetery was old and run-down. There was farmland on one side, a house on the other side, and a pasture in the rear. We had found what we had driven almost 1,500 miles for. This, what I have been led to believe, was the oldest cemetery in the Fort Ann/Granville area. Occasionally, someone would come by and cut the grass; but for the most part, it is completely run-down. There were several headstones lying on the ground, some in just two pieces and others in many pieces. One could only imagine that cattle were the cause of the destruction of the headstones, as there were no fences or walls to keep them out. Most of the headstones were made of limestone, and over the years, the inscriptions became illegible because of the weather. The oldest headstone was dated 1797, and the newest headstone was dated 1908, according to the cemetery records published by Historical Data Services in Glens Falls. Most of the grave sites, at least the earlier ones, had footstones. A footstone is a small man-made piece of limestone (in this case) that measures about three inches in thickness and five inches in width. The length could not be determined as they were embedded into the ground. On top of the footstones are initials, and in this case, they were J. A. and P. A. Both headstones were toppled over, but because of the proximity, we felt that we had found where Joseph and Phebe Ackley are buried. Next to the footstones were other headstones that told us we had found the Ackley family and therefore Otis Cemetery, so out came the cameras and clipboards. We were able to read a couple of the headstones:

Mary Ackley, wife of Ellis Bank—the rest was either broken off or buried.

Another headstone read:

Mary J., daughter of E&M Banker, born January 6, 1858, age 12 days

Still another read:

In memory of Laura, daughter of Mr. Joseph and Mrs. Phebe Ackley, born June 3, 1812, in the 2nd year of her age

Another headstone had the name of Henry.
There was another headstone that read, "Phebe, daughter of Joseph and Ann Ackley, died February 7, 1830, age 13 months."[10]

We also discovered the burial plots of some of our Osborn family. According to the 1840 and 1860 censuses, and now the headstones, Osborn is without an *e*.

Lydia Osborn, wife of Robert O. Ackley, died 6 April 1857, Age 27 yrs & 18 Days.
Isaac Osborn died 11 March. 1870, Age 70 years.
Sarah Ann, wife of Isaac Osborn.
Jacob Son of Isaac and Sarah Ann Osborn, died 20 January 1842 in the [?] year of his age.
Jonathan, Son of Isaac and Sarah Ann Osborn, 30 June 1841 in the 12th year of his age

According to a booklet titled *Cemetery Records Town of Fort Ann Washington County New York*, indexed and compiled by Charles B. Moore, Historical Data Services, Glens Falls, NY, the following are buried in the Otis Cemetery:

George Ackley	1810-1812 son of Joseph and Phebe
Henry Ackley	1803-22 December 1856 age 53y 6m
Joseph Ackley	1777-1849 married Phebe Chandler
Laura Ackley	13 June 1812-7 November 1813, daughter of Joseph and Phebe
Mary Ackley	1830-1 October 1868, married Elisa Banker
(a) Phebe Ackley*	1829-7 November 1830, daughter of Joseph and Phebe
Mary J. Banker	1858-18 January 1858, daughter of Elisa and Mary
Ann Burbank	1737-14 February 1813, 76 years; relict of Shem Burbank
Captain Joseph Chandler	1748-26 December 1828, age 81y; married Esther
Esther Chandler	1758-1 February 1818; wife of Capt. Joseph
Esther Chandler	1757-17 September 1823, age 66y; wife of Capt. Joseph
Esther Chandler	daughter of Capt. Joseph Chandler
Lydia Osborn	1830-6 April 1857 age 27 y-18d, married Robert O. Ackley
Sarah Ann Osborn	No dates-stone broken
Jacob Osborn	1833-20 January 1842, age 9y, son of Isaac and Sarah Ann
Jonathan Osborn	1824-20 January 1841, age 17y, son of Isaac and Sarah Ann
Isaac Osborn**	born about 1800, died 11 March 1870 age 70

---

*   At the time of Joseph Ackley's death, he was married to Ann Burbank, his third wife, therefore Phebe (a) Ackley could not have been the daughter of Joseph and his first wife Phebe who as you will soon discover died in 1813. The information in the book was a typo as I have a picture of the headstone that indicates her parents were Joseph and Ann Ackley.

** Isaac Osborn was not listed in the above mentioned book, however there is a headstone indicating the "Isaac Osborn died 11 March 1870, age 70y"

In the spring of 2003, after several phone calls, I found a person who was willing to help me with the Ackley headstones. Jennifer worked for a monument company in Granville. I explained to her what I needed. She said she knew the cemetery as her folks lived right next to it (the same family that did not know where Otis Cemetery was). She said that she would be there that weekend and would see if her brothers would turn the headstone, by the footstone with the initials P. A., over. Fortunately, it was lying face down. A couple of days later, I called Jennifer, and she read the following:

> "Sacred to the
> Memory of Mrs.
> Phebe Ackley
> Consort of Mr.
> Joseph Ackley
> who died March 14
> 1815, in the 33d
> year of her age
> Ah' Yes tis she who once like you
> Did stand such monuments to view,
> But soon with me you here must be
> and others stand and read of thee.
> Sleep on dear wife and take your rest,
> in this cold bed of clay.
> I hope your sole forever blest
> in Heavens eternal day."

The one thing that did not make sense was Phebe's date of death. In September 2003, Maria and I went to Fort Ann and paid another visit to Otis Cemetery. We took more pictures, one of which was the headstone of Phebe Ackley. Her date of death was 1813, not 1815. The engraving was as if it were written yesterday, not almost two hundred years ago. As for the headstone for Joseph, we were not as fortunate. In June 2005 while traveling with our granddaughters, Brandi and Megan, and with tools and water (to wash the headstone) in the trunk, we went to the cemetery and turned Joseph's headstone over. Unfortunately, the headstone had been lying face up, and therefore the inscription had been washed away.

In the late 1700s and early 1800s, record keeping was not at its best. Some records, you just stumbled across; and other records, no matter how hard you looked, just couldn't be found. Because Phebe died in the earlier years of census taking, her name never appeared in those records. Also, the marriage records of Joseph and Phebe could not be found. It was not until February 2005 that I had the good fortune of stumbling across the name Lois (Loudon) Cutler. Lois lived in Texas, and during our phone conversation, I learned that she was a descendant of Captain Joseph Chandler. Lois sent me copies of two wills written by Joseph Chandler, one dated 18 March 1824 and the other 28 October 1826. In the first will, it states, 'I also give and bequeath unto my granddaughters, Sarah Gray and Francis Ackley, daughters of Phebe Ackley, deceased, the sum of four dollars and to be paid out of my personal estate." In the second will, Joseph makes no mention of either granddaughter. Joseph Chandler died in February 1829 in Granville, Washington County, New York, and is buried in Otis Cemetery.

Lois also sent a list of the children that were born to Captain Joseph and Esther Chandler. The list was found in the Chandler Bible, and among that list is the following:

Phebe Chandler was born 16 Mar 1780 in the morning.

In parenthesis, someone had inserted *(died 14 March 1813).*

Over the years, I have learned that in the early years, couples would marry and never have their marriages recorded. Children born at home may never have had their births recorded. The same thing held true for their deaths.

Joseph and Phebe (Chandler) Ackley were married about 1799 (unable to locate records).

Joseph was born on 28 October 1777 and died between 22 June 1847 and 20 July 1850.

Joseph and Phebe (Chandler) Ackley had the following children:

1.	Sarah Ackley	born about 1799; died 15 July 1881, age eighty-two[22]
2.	Frances Ackley	mentioned in the 1824 will of Joseph Chandler, but not in his 1826 will
3.	Henry Ackley	born 1803 (unable to locate a birth certificate and the headstone is too worn to read)
4.	Phebe Ackley	born 27 June 1806 [6]
5.	Charles Thompson	born 2 October 1808 [6,7]
6.	George Ackley	born 1810[8] (unable to read the headstone)
7.	Laura Ackley	born 13 June 1812; died 7 November 1813[10]

1.   **Sarah Ackley** married Rubin Gray who died on 12 October 1831 at the age of thirty-eight.[22] Sarah and Rubin had one child, Mary H. Gray, who was born about 1828 and died on 19 September 1851 at the age of twenty-three.[22] All three are buried in the Granville Cemetery.

Joseph and Second Wife Nancy (Burbank) Bates

Joseph married (2) Nancy (Burbank) Bates 6 September 1813 [18] this was Nancy's second marriage.[9] Nancy Burbank first married Nathaniel Bates 23 January 1803 in Granville, Massachusetts.[13] Nathaniel died 1 September 1804 at the age of twenty-eight. He is buried in the Granville Cemetery in Granville, Massachusetts (not to be confused with Granville, New York). Nathaniel never got to meet his son, George N. Bates, who was born 13 April 1805 in Granville, Hampden County, Massachusetts, six months after Nathaniel's death.

When or why Nancy and her young son moved to Granville, New York, is a mystery—and I have yet to discover who her parents were. I have not learned whether Joseph met Nancy in Massachusetts or New York. Nancy must have died before 13 April 1817 because according to the *Book of Deeds at Washington County* of the New York Archives, Grantor book 1, page 570, this was the date of the first recording of a deed owned jointly by Joseph Ackley and Ann Burbank (his third wife). Joseph and Nancy did not have any children of this marriage. Upon the death of Nancy, George N. Bates remained with Joseph and was raised and cared for by Joseph and his third wife, Ann.

George N. Bates was almost eight years old when his mother married Joseph Ackley in 1813. He was nine or ten years old when his mother died and his stepfather married Ann (Burbank). Based on the following, there must have been a lot of love in this family as evidenced by the fact that in later years, several male members were named after George N. Bates. When George reached adulthood, he became very successful as a businessman.

He was one of the first five elders chosen under the ministry of Rev. Charles Doolittle of the First Presbyterian Church of Granville.

1853—He was the treasurer of the Middle Granville Slate Company.

1853—The Bank of Salem was first organized in 1853, and George N. Bates was elected one of the first directors.

1861 and 1862—He was town clerk of Granville, New York.

1866—He was president of the Washington County Agricultural Society in Granville. George was one of the contributors of the publication of the *History of Washington County.*

George N. Bates married Janet Allen, the sister of William H. Allen. William and George were merchants in Granville and operated under the name of Bates, Allen & Company, according to the Gazetteer and Business Directory of Washington County for 1871, page 187.

George and Janet had one child, Sarah Ann, who died 29 April 1844 at the age of thirteen. George died 28 March 1883 (age of seventy-eight) and was followed by Janet 29 August 1895 (age of eighty-five). George, Janet, and Sarah are buried in Elmwood Cemetery in Middle Granville, New York.

It was through George's will and probate records that I was able to learn how large the Joseph Ackley family really was. In his will, George refers to Robert O. Ackley and George Ackley as his half brothers rather than stepbrothers. The probate record of George N. Bates also mentions Cretoria (Ackley) Smith (youngest daughter of John B. Ackley) and M. Helen Ackley of Poughkeepsie, New York.

The Chicago 1870-1871 street directory shows John B. Ackley, insurance agent, living at 624 W. Washington. The 1872 Chicago street directory had John living at 504 W. Washington. His business address was 95 S. Clinton, and he was listed as an insurance agent. John was not listed in the 1873 Chicago street directory. Cretoria Caroline Ackley was born in 1853 in Lorain, Ohio. She married James W. Smith 25 December 1871 in Cook County, Illinois. James Smith was a farmer. They were living on the farm of Leander Smith, James's father in Pine Plains, Dutchess County, New York.

Mary Helene Ackley was found in the Poughkeepsie, New York, 1890-97 directory. She was working for the Smith Brothers' restaurant as a foreman.

Joseph and Third Wife Anne Burbank

Anne (Ann) was the daughter of Shem Burbank and Anne Fitch. I have been unable to learn of the relationship of Nancy (Burbank) (Bates) Ackley and Anne Burbank. I do know that Anne and Nancy were not sisters; but there has to be a connection somewhere as Ann lived with her parents in Granville, Massachusetts, which is where Nancy Burbank married Nathaniel Bates.

As for when Joseph and Ann were married, again, we cannot find a marriage record. However, in the Index of Deeds, Washington County, the first entry where Ann's name appears is 13 April 1817. This was when Joseph and Ann Ackley sold a piece of land to Duncan Oliphant.

The exact date of death for Joseph Ackley is not known. According to the Records of Deeds, for Washington County, book 16, page 567, property was sold to George and Janet Bates by Ann Ackley, wife of Joseph Ackley. The indenture was dated 10 June 1847 and recorded 1 July 1847. For some reason,

Ann sold the property without Joseph—in the indenture, she indicated that she was the "*wife* of Joseph."

In book 23, page 198, Ann made her first mention that she was the relict of Joseph Ackley. At the time, "relict" was used in place of "widow." This land sale was made on 20 July 1850 and recorded on 20 August of the same year. One might conclude that Joseph died between 10 June 1847 and 20 July 1850.

Joseph and Ann (Burbank) Ackley had the following children:

8.	John B.[24]	born 1824 New York
9.	George[23]	
10	Robert O.	born 21 January 1826 (see narrative below)
11.	Phebe	born January 1829; died 7 February 1830
12.	Mary	born 1822, Fort Ann, New York

8.   **John B. Ackley**, according to the 1860 and 1870 censuses, was born in 1824 in New York. He married Janet Bodfish of Sudbury, Vermont, on 8 January 1848.[25] The 1850 Vermont census indicates that Janet was living with Truman and Harriet Bodfish (probably parents) in Sudbury, Vermont. She is listed as Janeth Ackley, age twenty-two, which puts her date of birth at 1828. Also listed is Mary H. Ackley, age one. There is also a Helen C. Bodfish, whom I suspect was Janeth's sister. Janeth's name is spelled several ways on the various censuses and their marriage certificate. John was not listed on the 1850 Vermont census. John left his wife and daughter behind and went to Ohio, looking for work. The 1860 and 1870 Chicago, Illinois, census show John Ackley, age thirty-six, with wife, Janet, age thirty-four; Mary H., age eleven; and Cretoria, age seven. Cretoria was born in Ohio in 1853. John's occupation is listed as "Insurance." The 1870 census shows him as "Fire ins. Agent."

In 1870, there were two John B. Ackleys living in Chicago. One was a stonemason, the other, an insurance agent. One record, recorded by another genealogist, has the two confused and has the stonemason Ackley in the Ackley line outlined in this chapter. The stonemason Ackley was killed 30 October 1877 in an accident when he was assisting the setting of a three-ton stone in place at the corner of a courthouse being built at that time. There was an inquest performed that same day.

Dr. Holden, County Physician

> *Inquest on John Ackley at Ds. 6 Seymour Street in the city of Chicago on 30th Day of October 1877, Verdict: That the said John Ackley now lying dead at 6 Seymour Street in the City of Chicago, County of Cook and State of Illinois, came to his death on the 30th of October 1877. From injuries received by being crushed by a heavy stone of three tons weight while he*

was in the act of setting said stone at the South East corner of the new County Courthouse and we the jury, find that this occurred accidentally and therefore we have nobody to blame.

The obituary for this John Ackley shows he was at the age of fifty-two and left a surviving wife named Annie. The 1878-79 Chicago street directory shows, "Annie Ackley, wid. John, house rear, 8 Seymour Av." Again, this proved that this was not the John B. Ackley, son of Robert O. Ackley and his wife Ann. The last Chicago directory that John B. Ackley, insurance agent, appears was in 1872. The 1873 directory does not show John, Jannett, Mary H., or Cretoria.

John B. and Jannett Ackley had the following children:

13.	Mary H. Ackley	born Vermont, about 1849
14.	Cretoria Ackley	born Lorain, Ohio, 1853; married James W. Smith, 25 December 1871; living 1880, Dutchess County, New York

11. **Phebe** was buried in the Otis Cemetery. According to the book, *Cemetery Records, Town of Fort Ann,*[8] Phebe was born in 1829 and died on 7 November 1830. Phebe's headstone reads, "Phebe, daughter of Joseph & Ann Ackley died 7 February 1830 at the age of 13 months."[13]

12. **Mary Ackley** married Elias Banker, a farmer, and lived in North Granville and had the following children:

15.	Joseph Banker	born 1849
16.	John W. Banker	born 1854
17.	Mary J. Banker	born 6 January 1858; died 18 January 1858, age 8 days[10]

13. **Mary H. Ackley**, daughter of John B. and Jannett, was born in Vermont, about 1849. She is listed in the New York street directory for the years 1890-97 as M. Helene Ackley (no address), foreman, Smith Brothers' restaurant.

14. **Cretoria Ackley**, daughter of John B. and Jannett Ackley, according to the 1880 census, was married to James W. Smith 25 December 1871 in Cook County, Illinois. In 1880, according to the census of Pine Plains, Dutchess County, New York, Cretoria and her family were living with James's father, Leander Smith, head of household and a retired farmer. Also listed on the census are the following (relationships are as they relate to the head of the house, Leander Smith):

James W. Smith, son, age 32, Cretoria's husband, born in Michigan
Cretoria, Daughter-in law age 26, born in Ohio, housekeeper
Jennie S. Granddaughter age 6, born in Michigan
Helene C. Granddaughter age 4, born in Michigan
James B. Grandson, age 3, born in New York Maggie M.
Granddaughter age 8m, born in New York

Robert Ackley and Lydia Osborn

10. **Robert O.** was the son of Joseph and Ann (Burbank) Ackley and was born in Granville, Washington County, New York, 21 January 1826. He married Lydia, daughter of Isaac and Sarah Ann (Hunt) Osborn. Lydia was born in 1830, in Pittstown, Rensselaer County, New York. Isaac, Sarah, and their family later moved to Fort Ann, Washington County, New York, where they were farmers.[11] The 1850 Federal Census shows Robert, Lydia, and either Henry or Harry, at the age of forty-seven (which makes his year of birth 1803), and therefore the son of Joseph and Phebe Ackley and, thus, Robert's half brother. Also living with Robert and Lydia was Robert's mother, age sixty-six, Anna, daughter of Shem and Anna (Fitch) Burbank. Lydia died 6 April 1857 and was buried in Otis Cemetery.

The following were children of Robert O. and Lydia (Osborn) Ackley:

18.	Charles H. Ackley	born 15 October 1851, Fort Ann, New York
19.	Robert Andrew Ackley	born 9 July 1853, Fort Ann
20.	George Osborn Ackley	born 5 February 1855, Fort Ann
21.	Lydia Elizabeth Ackley	born 3 August 1856, Fort Ann

18. **Charles H. Ackley** was born 15 October 1851 in Fort Ann, Washington County, New York. He was the oldest of the four children born of this marriage and was around the age of thirteen when his family moved to Albion. He married Louise M. Newton 3 March 1874. They were farmers in Calhoun County, Michigan. According to the Permit for Burial, Robert died 22 December 1917. The cause listed on the Permit for Burial was Paralysis. According to Riverside cemetery records, Louise died in 1902. Both Charles and Louise are buried at Riverside.

Charles H. and Louise M. (Newton) Ackley had one child:

22.	Grace Mae Ackley	born 14 December 1876

22.   Grace Mae Ackley, born 14 December 1876, Albion, Michigan; died 18 February 1950, Detroit, Michigan, age seventy-three; buried Riverside Cemetery Albion; never married[15] Her occupation was listed as a secretary. According to the death certificate the cause of death was cancer to the lungs and breast, however, the cause was written by a doctor and you know what their handwriting looks like. This is my best guess.

The "Informant" on Grace's death certificate was Harriet (Ackley) Kull, daughter of Nathaniel Bates and Grace (Waterman) Ackley and cousin of Louise died in 1902. Charles died 22 December 1917.[16]

19.   Robert Andrew Ackley was born 9 July 1853 in Fort Ann. He married Elizabeth Pauline Loder 18 August 1880—he was twenty-seven, she was nineteen. Robert Andrew Ackley died 13 November 1925. Robert and Pauline had one daughter.

23.   Pearl   born 1880; died 1881[15]

This was reported in the *Albion Evening Recorder* on Friday, 13 November 1925, page 1.

ROBT. A. ACKLEY TAKES OWN LIFE THIS AFTERNOON

South Albion Farmer, Despondent Because of Ill health, Shoots Self with revolver at His Home, Dies at Hospital

Despondent because of ill health, Robert Andrew Ackley, 73 years old, a well known South Albion farmer, shot himself with a revolver at his home about 12:45 this afternoon, his death occurring a few minutes later at Sheldon Memorial Hospital.

Mr. Ackley, who had been a sufferer from heart disease for the past three or four years, got up from the dinner table, secured a 32-caliber revolver which had been in possession of the family for some time and had been used for killing rats and other purposes around the farm, went out upon the back porch and turned the gun on himself. Mrs. Ackley, who told relatives she did not realize what her husband was almost [sic] to do, said she heard three shots fired. One bullet took effect in the left breast, just over the heart, and another went through the right temple close to the ear. The third evidently did not strike him.

A physician was called and the Marsh ambulance was summoned to take Ackley to the hospital. He died in the elevator at the hospital as he was being taken to the operating room.

Coroner Harold H. Weeks, after investigating, decided an inquest was unnecessary, declaring the tragedy a clear case of suicide. Relatives of the dead man informed the coroner that Ackley had often hinted that he might take his own life, because of ill health.

Mr. Ackley came to Albion when he was a boy of eleven years and had lived in the country near here since that time. He is survived by his widow, one brother George A. Ackley, of South Albion, one sister, Mrs. C. I. Cool of Albion, and a half brother, Bates N. Ackley of Detroit.

Arrangements for the funeral have not been completed.

On 19 November 1925, page 5 of the *Albion Evening Reporter* ran the following notice:

OBITUARY
Robert A. Ackley

Robert A. Ackley died at the Sheldon Memorial Hospital Friday, November 13, 1925, having been in poor health for a number of months.

He was born at Fort Ann, Washington Co., N. Y., July 9, 1853, coming to Albion with his parents in 1864, and has been a resident of South Albion ever since.

He was united in marriage to Pauline E. Loder August 18, 1880, who survives him; he also leaves two brothers, George O. Ackley of Albion and N. Bates Ackley of Detroit, and one sister, Mrs. C. I. Cool of Albion.

Mr. Ackley had a kind and loving disposition and was highly respected by all who knew him. He leaves a wider circle of friends who will mourn his loss.

Funeral services will be held at his late home Monday afternoon November 16, conducted by Rev. M. J. Weaver. Interment will be made in Riverside's cemetery.

Pauline died in 1927 and is buried next to Robert in the Riverside Cemetery.[15]

20. **George Osborn Ackley** was born 5 February 1855 in Fort Ann, New York. He married (1) 19 March 1879 Purley E. Crane of Calhoun County, who was born 9 February 1856, daughter of Lewis D. Crane and Ursula Bidwell. Purley died 28 April 1887 and was buried in Riverside Cemetery.[15] George married (2) Mary Elizabeth Snelgrove of Albion 3 October 1888,

and like the rest of their family, they were farmers. Mary Elizabeth was affectionately known as Libbie. She was born 19 March 1856 in Homer Township, Michigan. Libbie died 30 December 1938 in Albion, Michigan. George Osborn Ackley died 9 October 1940.

George and Mary Elizabeth had one son:

24. George Bates Ackley   born 27 June 1892

21. **Lydia Elizabeth Ackley** was born 3 August 1856 in Fort Ann, New York, and was eight years old when her family moved to Albion. Lydia married 25 February 1880, Crittenden Irelius Cool, who was born 8 May 1849, Blairstown, Warren County, New Jersey and who moved to Albion with his family at an early age (see Cool chapter). Sometime around 1881, Crittenden and Lydia were considering a move out west, perhaps influenced by an uncle (Sam Cool) who had moved his family to Huron, South Dakota. Sam was the older brother of Crittenden. Robert O. Ackley was not going to let his little girl go without a fight.

The following letter was written by R. O. Ackley to his son-in-law Crittenden Cool. I have tried to copy it as it was written, without changing spelling or punctuation.

Albion, May 26, 1881

>   *Son Crit,*
>   *I all most think you would be as well suited in Michigan, and if so you can have my place for the price I was to get from Mr. Sefer say (11,000) (Eleven thousand dollars) and, the 145 acres at home & 20 acres wood land for that amt. The personal property we will have appraised by three men and I will deduct five hundred dollars from there [sic] price. I have sewed of clover, timothy & plaster 40.00 dollars worth. Also have the 25 acre lot planted to corn which was not put in until last Friday like many others and cannot expect to come up until it rains. My oats are looking well and I will enclose the papers of agreement made with Mr. Sefer, you will see by that that [sic] I deduct 100. on the sale and 500 on the appraisal making (600) six hundred dollars. as Charles H. has gone to work for Willis the house is empty but Geo. will work what you want I had a chance to sell the large Sorrel horse that I bought and will keep Dale so you would not get but Dan and Bill, the Sorrel horse is gone. The price of the farm 165 acres*

11100.00 Dollars
Deduct _ 600.00_ on appraisal
10500.00

With wheat, corn, oats, Clover, plaster, posts, Hay fork and some other things. Now do not let this influence you from the west.

Yours truly, R. O. Ackley

(Note: Charles H., age thirty, and George, age twenty-six, were sons of Robert O. Ackley. Dan and Bill are the names of two horses.)

Lucky for us that Crittenden and Lydia accepted the very generous offer. One year later, on 11 May 1882, Lydia gave birth to LaVanchie Margaret Cool who married Charles Robert Looney (see Looney-Wark chapter). Crittenden "Crit" and Lydia were farmers. Around 1913, they retired from farming and moved to the city of Albion where they lived at 900 South Superior Street. (The obituary of Crittenden shows 903 S. Superior)

When I transcribed the above letter, there were certain words and meanings I could not make out, so I sent a scanned copy to a "Roots Webb mail list" and asked for help. With the help of several on the list, I was able to complete the letter. One thing that puzzled me was, why would a farmer be interested in plaster? I received a letter from Darryl Warncke, professor, Soil Fertility, Michigan State University, East Lansing, Michigan, explaining the purpose:

Your request regarding plaster as fertilizer has been forward to me. There are two aspects to your question. In the early 1800's limestone was first being used in Virginia to neutralize soil acidity. As a result of the great improvement in crop productivity of acid soils some may have viewed limestone as a fertilizer—actually it was improving the availability of the essential nutrients in the soil and reducing aluminum availability as well as supplying additional calcium and sometimes magnesium, if dolomite lime was used. Since large quantities of lime were being applied, the surface of the ground became white; looking like it had been plastered. Therefore, some referred to the practice of liming the soil as "land plastering," and lime as "land plaster."

Wallboard (plaster board) and plaster are made of gypsum, calcium sulfate. Gypsum has been used effectively to improve the structure and infiltration capacity of high sodium soils, predominantly, in the western U.S. Today there is a lot of interest in using ground up recycled or by-product wallboards rather than the mined gypsum. Gypsum is most beneficial for supplying sulfur in low organic matter soil or calcium in sandy soil where

available levels are low. As mentioned it can also be used for improving
soil structure primarily in soils with high sodium levels.

From time to time, I have seen the name Robert O. Ackley referred to as Robert Osborn (sometimes with an *e*) Ackley; however, I have yet to find any documentation as to the name Osborn being Robert's middle name. The marriage license between Robert and Lydia Osborn cannot be found. Robert's birth certificate cannot be found. The marriage license between Robert and Maria Wright shows Robert O. Ackley. His death certificate shows Robert O. The cemetery records (not the original) show Robert Osborne; however, the name Osborne was added long after Robert died. So far I have found nothing official, indicating that his middle name was Osborn. My best guess, but only a guess, since Robert was born in 1826 (four years before Lydia Osborn was born) and since his father Joseph Ackley was working with a partner named Duncan Oliphant, Robert stands a better chance of having a middle name of Oliphant, but again, nothing official. Of course there is always the possibility that the *O* stands for nothing more but *O*.

Robert Ackley and Maria Wright

Robert married (2) 10 December 1857 Maria Wright of Granville, New York. This was Maria's first marriage.[14] The 7 August 1860 census shows Robert was living in Fort Ann with his wife Maria, sons—Charles H., age eight; Robert A., age six; George, age five—and daughter Lydia, age four. Robert's mother was now living with her daughter, Mary Banker, as indicated on page 290 of Town of Granville census dated 8 August 1860. The value of Robert's real estate was $9,000. His personal property was valued at $2,000.[13]

In 1864, Robert, Maria, the children, and Robert's mother, Ann (Burbank), moved to Albion, Calhoun County, Michigan, where they continued making their living as farmers. On 29 March 1872, Anne, daughter of Shem and Ann (Fitch) Burbank, widow of Joseph Ackley Jr., and the mother of Robert O. Ackley, died and was buried in Riverside Cemetery, in Albion. [15] Riverside Cemetery is the resting place for many of the Ackley families.

Robert O. Ackley died 17 November 1882, just two months before his fifty-seventh birthday and four months prior to George N. Bates's death. According to George's probate record, in a codicil to his will, Robert's share of the inheritance was to be paid to his children: Charles H., Robert Andrew, George Osborne, Lydia Elizabeth, and Nathaniel Bates Ackley.

Maria (Wright) Ackley—according to death records, book 2, page 237, record number 284, in Detroit—died 4 October 1895. The cause of her death was suicide. The record shows her name to be Mrs. M. D. Ackley (should read

M. L.). They also show her age as sixty-five when it should read age sixty-two. The obituary from the *Albion Review* dated 5 October 1895 reported her death:

> *Mrs. M. L. Ackley, a lady long and favorably known here, died at 1:30 a.m. Friday in Detroit and will be brought here for burial. Arrangements are not yet completed, but the funeral will probably be held in the Baptist church at 3:30 Sunday afternoon. Ackley—October 4, 1895 at the residence of her son N. B. Ackley, 727 Forth ave., Maria L. Ackley, age 62 years, Burial at Albion, Mich.*

The October 5, 1895 Detroit News reported Maria's death:

> *Ackley- October 4, 1895 at the residence of her son N. B. Ackley, 727 Forth Ave., Maria L. Ackley, age 62 years, Burial at Albion, Mich.*

Robert and Maria had one child.

22.   Nathaniel Bates Ackley   born 29 November 1868

22.   Nathaniel Bates Ackley was the only child of Robert O. and Maria (Wright) Ackley. Bates was born on 29 November 1868 in Albion, Michigan. He attended and graduated from Albion High School in 1885.[20] Bates married on 23 November 1893 Grace Waterman. Grace was born in Missouri. According to a newspaper article, they were married in New York.

Nathaniel Bates and Grace (Waterman) Ackley had the following children:

23.   Marion Ackley   married (first name unknown) Chenowith. Marion committed suicide in November 1967.
24.   Betrice Ackley   married Emmet C. Kull
25.   Robert W. Ackley

The *Albion Evening Reporter* (18 January 1955) reported Bates's death.

> *A native of Albion, N. Bates Ackley, 86, who was one of Detroit's senior financiers and executives, died Saturday (January 15th) at his summer home in Tecumseh, Ont. His residence was at 954 Nottingham, Grosse Pointe Park.*

Mr. Ackley lived with his parents at Irvin Ave and South Clinton Street here, it is recalled by O. H. Gale, and after attending school here went to Detroit as a young man of 20. He was with the Michigan Central railroad from 1885 until 1912, serving as assistant general auditor. At various times, he was the assistant treasurer of Studebaker Corp., treasurer of the Peninsular Engraving Co., and vice president of Bankers Trust Co. From 1918 to 1950, he was associated with the Detroit office of the Equitable Life Assurance Society, being its group department supervisor.

A Baptist, he was treasurer for 15 years and a trustee of Kalamazoo College.

Surviving are two daughters, Mrs. Marion A. Chenoweth and Mrs. Emmett C. Kull; a son Robert W. Ackley and a granddaughter, Mrs. Ralph A. Hileman of Laurel, Md.

Services will be Wednesday at 11 a.m. in the William R. Hamilton Co., chapel 3975 Case in Chicago. Burial will be in Woodmere Cemetery.

Another report of 18 January 1955 reads:

N. Bates Ackley, 86, a pioneer Detroit financier and executive who lived at 954 Nottingham, Gross Point Park, died Sunday at his summer home in Tecumseh, Ont.

A native of Albion, he had lived in Detroit 65 years. He retired in 1950 as group department supervisor of the Equitable Life Assurance Society of the United States. He has been associated with the organization since 1918.

Mr. Ackley began his career in 1885 with the Michigan Central Railroad, serving as assistant general auditor until 1912.

He also served as assistant treasurer of the Studebaker Corp. and treasurer of the Peninsular Engraving Co. He was for 15 years treasurer and a member of the board of trustees of Kalamazoo College.

Mr. Ackley was active in Baptist affairs and was a member of the First Baptist Church of Detroit.

Surviving are two daughters: Mrs. Marion A. Chenoweth and Mrs. Emmet C. Kull; a son Robert W. Ackley and a granddaughter, Mrs. Ralph Hileman.

Services will be at 11:a.m. Wednesday in the William R. Hamilton Co., 3975 Cass. Burial will be in Woodmere Cemetery.

24. **George Bates Ackley** was born on 27 June 1892 in Albion, Michigan. He was the son of George Osborn and Mary (Snelgrove) Ackley. George married on 31 October 1917, in Homer, Michigan, Marian Alliene Cook, who was born on 8 March 1897. She was the daughter of George Cook

and Mary Overy. Marian died on 22 January 1989 in Marshall, Michigan.
George Bates Ackley died on 20 May 1972. Both are buried in Riverside
Cemetery in Albion, Michigan.[15]

George and Marian had the following children:

25.	Helen Ackley	born 1920
26.	Robert James Ackley	born 1923, Homer, Michigan
27.	Francis Louise Ackley	born 1928, Homer, Michigan

27. **Francis Louise Ackley** was born in 1928 in Homer, Michigan. She was
the daughter of George and Marian Ackley. Francis married in 1954 Victor
Earl Frendt, who was born on 3 December 1903 in Hungary. Victor came
to America in around 1905.

Francis and Victor had the following children:

28.	Martin Jay Frendt	born 1958
29.	Joel Michael Frendt	born 1960
30.	Janet Kay Frendt	born 1964; married Steven Martz

Notes

1.   Evert & Ensign, Philadelphia, Publisher, *1737 History of Washington CO.,
     New York*, 1878 with Illustrations and Biographical Sketches of some of the
     Prominent Men and Pioneers. (George N. Bates and William H. Allen as two
     of the many citizens who contributed toward the publication of this book).

1a. Hiel Hollister, *Pawlet (VT) One Hundred Years*, 1867.

2a. Birth Certificate from the Town of Reading, Vermont

2b. Transcript of deed from Joseph Ackley to Joseph Ackley Jr., in Vol. 2 of the
     3rd book, page 290, Town Clerk's Office, Plymouth, Windsor Co., Vermont.

3.   *Vital records of Granville, Massachusetts To The Year 1850*, published by the
     New England Historic Genealogical Society, Boston, Mass., 1914.

4.   Picture of Headstone of Nathaniel Bates.

5.   Copy of "Sale of Property" from Nancy Pitcher Nobel October 5, 1999.

6.   *Marriages, Births and Death Records*, of Pawlet, Vermont, Book 1, Page 6.

7.   Birth Certificate from Pawlet, Vermont

8.   Charles B. Moore, indexer and compiler, *Cemetery Records Town of Fort Ann,
     Washington County, New York*, Historical Data Services, Glens Falls, NY

9.   *The New York Genealogical and Biographical Record*, Volume LXXI, 1940, page 83.

10. Photo of Headstone.

11. *1850 Federal Census* Fort Ann, Washington County, New York.

12. *1870 Federal Census* Albion, Calhoun County, Michigan.

13. *1860 Federal Census* Fort Ann, Washington County, New York.

14. Actual Marriage Certificate.

15. *Riverside Cemetery Records*, Albion, Michigan

16. Permit for Burial, issued by Calhoun County, Michigan.

17. Death Certificate issued by the Department of Health for the State of Michigan.

18. *Marriages in The Reformed Dutch Church, New York City,* pg. 81.

19. *1984 Albion (Michigan) Area Historical Architectural Survey.*

20. Frank Passic, *A History of the Albion Public Schools* 1991, E. Weil Publishing Services, Albion, Michigan.

21. *An Introduction to Historic Resources in Washington County, N. Y. 1976* Washington County Planning Department, for the Washington County Planning Board

22. Margaret Jenks, *Granville Cemetery Inscriptions, Washington County, New York*

23. George N. Bates "Last Will and Testament" dated October 21, 1883.

24. George N. Bates "Probate Records" dated April 18, 1883.

THREE

John Looney and Margaret Kelvie

(See Appendix B)

Our Looney ancestors came from the Isle of Man—a small Great Britain island (227 square miles) located in the north Irish Sea. It sits between Ireland and England, just south of Scotland. The island measures 12 miles across at its widest point, and 30 miles from top to bottom. The coastline measures just over 100 miles[1] and was occupied in the ninth century by the Vikings. It passed from Norway to Scotland in 1266 and to three earls of Salisbury and of Derby in the fourteenth century. Parliament purchased the island in 1765, and it remained an autonomous possession of the British crown.[2]

The Isle of Man is divided into divisions (sheadings): Ayre, Garff, Glenfaba, Michael, Middle, and Rushen. Politically and historically, Maughold belongs to the sheading [*sic*] of Garff. A tithing or division, in the Isle of Man, in which there is a coroner or a chief constable. These sheadings (divisions) were imposed on the island by the Vikings. Each sheading is then divided into parishes. Up until 1796, Garff consisted of three parishes: Maughold, Lonan, and Onchan. However, in that same year, Onchan was joined to Middle, leaving Garff with only the parishes of Loan and Maughold.

Every parish is divided into treens. In theory, each treen consists of four quarterlands with each of them being used as farms or Balla. In practice, some treens contain only three quarters, e.g., Ballafayle. Some contain five quarters, e.g., Corna beg; and some contain only one, e.g., Rencullen, later known as Ballig.

Intacks were areas of land not originally forming part of the treens and quarterlands. They tend to be lands of inferior quality, being situated on higher or lower grounds than the farms.

Some common words in Manx place names:

balla	"a farm or homestead"
cronk	"a hill or mountain"
keeil	"a church"
creg	"a rock"
slieu	"a mountain"
knock	"a hill or mound"

Often, the place-name is a combination of one of the above words plus the family surname. All farms, houses, etc., are known by a name. In case you are interested, the Bee Gees were born on the Isle of Man.

The name Looney, also spelled Lowny, is found in the Maughold register from the beginning (1647).[3] Records of 1748 show that John Looney was of the town "of Ramsey." There is no record of his baptism in Maughold; however, this is where he called home.

John (Yack) was married to Margaret Kelvin (Kelvie) who was of Scottish descent and who came to Ramsey in the eighteen century. John Looney died on 28 July 1769. On 10 February 1770, Margaret married William Creetch (Creech) of Ballachrink, whom she also survived. William Creetch of Ballachrink was the son of Robert and Margaret Creetch. William's marriage to Margaret Looney was his second marriage. He was first married to Isabal Cottaraugh who died in 1751. He had no children by either marriage. Upon William's death, he left to his wife Margaret "the corn in the haggard, the dressed and undressed corn within and without, and all his part of the crop that is to be in Ballacrinck this year."

In 1791, Margaret gave all of her property to her youngest son, Ewan, and his wife, Mary Taggart, who were happy to have her live with them. The agreement between the three was for Ewan and Mary to provide Margaret "a decent living as be cometh a loving mother in her old age". This agreement was accepted as part of Margaret's will in 1798; and as part of the will, there was a clause that if Evan and Mary disagreed with Margaret, she would go anywhere else she pleased and that she would take her goods with her.[3]

Margaret and John Looney had nine sons and one daughter, and from six of those sons are descended all of the Looneys in Maughold at the time of the 1841 census and subsequently.[3] The parish register often refers to them as "Yack" (Jack) after their original ancestor.

The will of John Looney
Dated 14 July 1769

In the name of God Amen

*I John Looney of Crowcreen in the parish of K. K. (Kirk) Maughold being
weak and infirm in body, but of perfect mind and memory for which I
praise God, and for calling to mind the uncertainty of life, do make this
my last will and testament in the manner following:*

First, I commit my sole to God and my body to Christian burial.

*Item Forasmuch as I John Looney and Margaret Looney my wife who did
on or about the 25th day of March 1769 settle and [sic] estate upon our son
Daniel Looney and Isabel Looney then Cashen his wife the half of their parcel
of intack land lately purchased from William Callow of Ballagilley commonly
called and know by the name of Talloo >Gob ne Scoote and understanding
that our purchased lands of the Crowcreen would be more commodious and
convenient for said Daniel Looney and his said wife they consenting that our
purchased lands of Gob ne Scoote and Crowcreen should be disposed of the
following manner it being my will and pleasure so to do, that is to say, that
they are to possess and enjoy the one half of Gob ne Scoote land as mentioned
in their marriage agreement settled during the natural life of me and my wife
and after the decease of the survivor of us John Looney and Margaret my wife
that then all of our purchase lands of Crowcreen together with the houses erected
thereon are to fall to our said son Daniel and said wife which I bequeath unto
him, and in want or failure of lawful issues the said Daniel to his next of
kin, the said Daniel Looney and his wife consenting to pay after the death of
us his father and mother ten pounds on account (?) of said lands to his eldest
brother William Looney and also agreeing to acquit and give up the half of
Gob ne Scoote which he had in settlement to his brother John Looney in lieu of
Crowcreen lands at the decease of the survivor of us together with our other half
of Gob ne Scoote which I leave and bequeath to my son John after the decease of
the longer liver of us he also paying ten pounds (10) to his eldest brother William
Looney on account of the whole of Gob ne Scoot's purchased land.*

*Daniel Looney promising to till and labour [sic] wholly the lands of Gob
ne Scoote during our life except what shall be laid out thereon and also to
plow the parcels of Crowcreen and Gob ne Scoote together Daniel Looney
putting two beasts in the plow and so to continue till at our decease (?),
and it is the meaning of the above bequest of the ten pounds apiece that
Daniel Looney and John Looney my sons are each of them to pay to their*

brother William Looney that the twenty pounds are to be paid by them to my daughter Jane as the said William is a poor pitiable object in case she takes care of him and maintains him after our death during his life, but if she refuses to maintain and take care of him after the decease of me and my said wife that then my two sons Daniel and John are to maintain and take care of him during his life without paying the said money and if the said William is dead before the survivor of us, that is me and my wife, that then the said twenty pounds is not to be paid by my sons to the said William, or to Jane, or any other persons whatsoever.

I leave and bequeath to my daughter Jane Looney ten pounds when she arrives at the age of 24 years.

Two—I leave and bequeath all my concerns of houses and gardens belonging to me in the town of Ramsey to my two sons Thomas and Robert Looney my wife consenting that they are to have her part of shares of the land (?) whenever they will have occasion for them, the whole equally between and four pounds to the aforesaid Robert to bind him to a trade.

I leave and bequeath to my three sons James, Patrick and Ewan Looney twenty pounds equally between them when they come to the age of 20 years, and if either of them three die before they come to that age, that their legacy is to fall to the survivor or survivors of them.

Lastly I nominate constitute and appoint my dear and loving wife Margaret Looney sole executrix of all the rest of my goods moveable and immoveable of what kind or nature and six pence legacy to all cravers and I do also commit the care and tuition of the children under age unto their mother (?) She the said Margaret Looney consenting thereto and the said Daniel Looney and Isabel Looney alias Cashen his wife and John Looney the Testator's son do all of them bind and oblige themselves to abide by the contents of this will and perform the same that in the penalty and forfeiture of one hundred pounds to be levied and paid according to law. In Testimony whereof they have hereunto set their names and marks to their names the 14 day of July 1769.

Ewan Kissack	John Looney my mark X
	Margaret Looney my mark X
Robert Lowey my mark X	Daniel Looney
	Isabel Looney
	John Looney (Junior) my mark X

At a Court of Correction Holden at Lezayre

Ewan Kissack and Robert Looney the witness to the forgoing will have sworn? On the holy Evangelist that the Testator John Looney being of sound and (?) mind and memory made, declare and sign said will in their presence—as also that Isabel Looney one of the subscribing Parties thereto signed and duly executed the same in their presence and whereas Margaret (the widow of the Testator) now wife of William Creetch with her said present husband have (?) consented and agreed to this will in every respect and that Daniel Looney and John Looney have also acknowledge and consented thereto—William Creetch aforesaid is now sworn duly to execute the last Will and Testament of the Testator, he undertakes the tuition and maintenance of Robert, James, Patrick and Ewan Looney the Testator's children who are under age and hath Daniel, Thomas and John Looney three of the Testator's who are of the lawful age, are sworn supervisors of those underage in form of law.

Probatum est
Ja. Wilks and Joh Moore

According to the book A *History of Kirk Maughold* and the will of John Looney, the list below were the children of John and Margaret (Kelvie) Looney. This information is also found in the registry of christening, marriages, and burials. Dates of births are difficult, if not impossible to locate since the births took place at home. It was customary for a child to be christened at least one year after the child's birth;[4] however, I have noticed that of the few dates of birth that I have obtained, baptism took place shortly after birth.

John and Margaret (Kelvie) Looney had the following children:

1.	William Looney	described in his father's will as a "poor pitiable object"
2.	Daniel Looney	baptized 4 August 1745; married Isabel Cashen; lived in Crowcreen after his parents' deaths
3.	John Looney	born 1748
4.	Thomas Looney	baptized 1750; married Isabel Moore
5.	Jane Looney	baptized 3 March 1754
6.	Robert Looney	baptized 3 July 1757
7.	James Looney	baptized 7 September 1760
8.	Patrick Looney	baptized 25 March 1764
9.	Ewan Looney	baptized 3 August 1764

2.   **Daniel** was born in 1745 and was christened on 4 August 1745. He married
     Isabel Cashen. Daniel lived in Crowcreen after his parents' deaths. Daniel
     died in 1826.

Daniel and Isabel had the following children:

10.	John Looney	baptized 14 January 1770
11.	Robert Looney	baptized 14 March 1773
12.	Margaret Looney	baptized 31 December 1775
13.	William Looney	baptized 17 January 1779
14.	Mary Looney	baptized 17 March 1782
15.	Thomas Looney	baptized 20 February 1785
16.	Jane Looney	baptized 9 August 1789; married Caley
17.	Esther Looney	baptized 6 May 1792; married Quayle

3.   **John (nicknamed Yack)**, son of John Looney and Margaret Kelvie, was
     born in 1748; but it was not until 3 March 1835 that he was christened.
     On 17 September 1788, John married Isabel Camaish. Isabel died in 1817.
     John died in 1835.

John and Isabel (Camaish) Looney had the following children:

18.	John Looney Jr.	baptized 21 September 1788; married Rachael Redhead
19.	Elizabeth Looney	baptized 9 February 1794
20.	Margaret Looney	baptized 14 August 1796; married Stowell
21.	Robert Looney	baptized 2 April 1799; married Isabella Lewin

4.   **Thomas** was born in 1750 and, on 2 December 1775, married Isabel
     Moore. Thomas was a shoemaker; he bought part of Ballagilly.

22.	John Looney	baptized 29 December 1783
23.	Ewan Looney	baptized 27 November 1785
24.	William Looney	baptized 1 December 1787
25.	Catharine Looney	baptized 8 January 1794

5.   **Jane** was the daughter of John and Margaret Looney. Jane married Ewan Moore
     (date unknown). On 29 May 1795, Ewan signed the following statement:

I Ewan Moore husband of Jane Moore, alias Looney daughter of the Testator do acknowledge to have received from Margaret Looney the executrix the sum of ten pounds being the Legacy bequeathed unto my said wife in the annexed will and exonerate acquit and discharge the said executrix and every other person of the same and every part thereof. As witness my mark annexed to my name the day and date above written. Signed Ewan Moore my mark X

7.   **James Looney and 8. Patrick Looney** signed the statement below on 29 May 1895:

We James Looney and Patrick Looney Legatees in the annexed Will of John Looney do acknowledge to have received from Margaret Looney the Executrix the sum of six pounds thirteen shillings and four pence each being the legacy bequeathed unto me by the said John Looney our Father and exonerate acquit and discharge the said executrix and every other person of the same and every part thereof. As witnessed our Marks subscribed by our names the day and date above written.
Patrick Looney mark X James Looney my mark X

The statement was signed before John Crellin.

9.   **Ewan,** the youngest son of John Looney and Margaret Kelvie, was born in 1766 and was christened on 3 August 1766. He married Mary Taggart on 26 June 1790. Mary was born in 1766 and died at the age of eighty-five on 6 February 1851.

Ewan and Mary (Taggart) Looney had the following children:

26.	Joseph Looney	baptized 10 April 1791; owner of Crowcreen and Magher e Kew; died 19 April 1877
27.	Margaret (1) Looney	baptized 30 September 1792; died before 7 December 1800
28.	John (1) Looney	baptized 7 September 1794; died before 26 March 1796
29.	John (2) Looney	baptized 25 March 1796; they were farmers
30.	George Looney	baptized 2 September 1798; they were farmers
31.	Margaret (2) Looney	baptized 7 December 1800; died 13 November 1819
32.	Daniel Looney	baptized 13 March 1803

33.	Hugh Looney	baptized 5 May 1805
34.	Catherine Looney	baptized 16 August 1807; married John Kerruish 20 January 35
35.	Robert Looney	baptized 22 August 1813

On 3 June 1790, Ewan Looney (9 above) signed the following statement:

> *I Ewan Looney one of the legatees mentioned in the beforegoing [sic] Will of John Looney do acknowledge to have received from Margaret Looney the Executrix the sum of six pounds thirteen shillings and four pence being the legacy bequeathed unto me by the testator and do hereby exonerate acquit and discharge the said executrix and every other person of the same and every part thereof. Witness my Mark to my name this 3rd July 1790. Ewan*
> *Looney my mark X*

The statement was prepared and witnessed by John Crellin.

18. **John Looney Jr.** was born in 1788. He married Rachel Redhead before 1810. She was the daughter of Isaac and Mary (Kneale) Redhead. In 1813, John Looney Jr. purchased the house and garden that he and Rachel occupied, along with a small field adjoining Cronk Barre Noa. Sometime around 1839, the house was turned into an inn. Because Rachel was of Irish descent, John named the inn the Hibernian. The Hibernian was first mentioned in *Pigot's Directory* of 1837. The licensee was the most famous of all the Maughold innkeepers, the redoubtable Rachel Looney.[3] A description of her in 1834 when she was about forty-seven reads:

> *She was an odd figure, dressed in a blue petticoat of some sort of cloth or flannel, surmounted by a man's pilot jacket a good deal too long in the sleeves. To obviate the inconvenience this would have caused, the cuffs were turned back, displaying a pair of large muscular hands and wrists quite out of proportion to her size, as she was considerably below the middle height . . . When going in Ramsey she rode a large raw-boned carthorse on which what did duty for a saddle was a sack thrown across the animal's back from which straw might be seen sticking out. I then saw her come out exactly as before except that instead of a sunbonnet on her head, she wore a man's hat of tough beaver.[3, 3a]*

The Hibernian became the first of several inns, which came into existence for the improvement of the main road from Ramsey to Douglas.[3] Although the Hibernian existed prior to the 1841 census, for some reason, it was not included in that census. The 1851 census, again, was published with no mention of the Hibernian, perhaps because Rachel had sold the inn in 1843, and thus it became nonexistent.

Rachel Looney was described as "a vigorous, determined, sometimes even a violent woman, well-known throughout the Isle of Man." She brewed her own ale, and it was even rumored that she had an illicit still with which she made whisky, using the peaty flavoured [*sic*] water from a stream on North Barrule. (North Barrule is a mountain on the Isle of Man.) This still was supposedly hidden in an old grandfather clock. Tradition has it that Rachel would push her customers out into the curragh (flat open plain sandy soil) behind the inn when the local constabulary made an unwelcome after-hours visit.

One Friday, during the building of some outhouses, the workmen complained of a lack of stone for building material. Rachel told them that by the time they came back on Monday, they would find they had enough. It is said that during the weekend, she herself carried down from the hillside sufficient stone for them to finish their work. Rachel came in possession of a number of various objects and documents of interest; these form the basis of the museum and library at the inn. John emigrated to either Australia or New Zealand and was followed, sometime later, by Rachel.

Mrs. B. L. Humphreys, who bought the Hibernian and restored it to the delightful old house it was when it had a tea garden at the turn of the century (twentieth century), had been told by its previous owners that it was haunted by Rachel Looney. Being skeptical about this, as Rachel had died on the other side of the world; she was surprised to find what was possibly the sole of her shoe deep inside one of the walls. This she duly gave a decent burial in order that her "sole" may rest in peace.[11, 12]

In addition to being able to do a man's job around the inn and running a still, "Rachel was also an excellent caterer," according to Ms. Mona Douglas of *Mona's Herald* (a Manx newspaper which started in 1833). Here is what Mona had to say:

> But if costume was of the country style at the Hibernian, amenities were exceptionally good for the period. The inn had its own brewery and also a museum and excellent library for residence.
>
> Weddings were occasions of great gaiety, in those days and often included a party of anything from 50 to 100 folks. The only honeymoon was usually the wedding day itself, on which the whole party went for a long drive after the morning ceremony and then had dinner at the inn.
>
> At the Hibernian, Rachel, as she was called generally, would be in her element providing for a wedding party arriving from Ramsey or Kirk Maughold or even from Laxey or Douglas.
>
> She would serve a substantial meal which often included such delicacies as fresh salmon, pigeon pie, lobster salad, roast ducklings, lamb and beef,

*succulent vegetables grown by herself, puddings, light pastries, jellies and
fresh fruit (all of these from an actual menu).*

One source indicates that in 1841, because of poor economy on the Isle of
Man, John Looney immigrated to Australia. A letter printed in *Mona's Herald*
from Thomas Cain, South Adelaide, Currie Street (Australia), dated 10 January
1840, stated that "John Looney has been working for me for some time." In
1843, Rachel left the Isle of Man and joined John in Australia.

According to the *Register*, an Australian newspaper dated 29 August 1863,
"On 24 August. at Noarlunga, Mrs. Rachel Looney, farmer in her 88th year, after
a very short illness, greatly regretted." Another accounting shows that Rachel died
on the twenty-fifth of August. Rachel is buried at Willunga Cemetery, South
Australia. John died on 9 September 1872 at Sea View at the age of eighty-four.

John and Rachel (Redhead) Looney had the following children:

36.	Sara Looney	baptized 21 January 1810
37.	Isabella Looney	baptized 11 July 1813
38.	Margaret Looney	
39.	John Joseph Looney	baptized 11 September 1819
40.	Sarah Looney	baptized 1821

21. **Robert** married Isabella Lewin on 10 February 1828.[5] Robert was a
    shoemaker. He died in March 1853 at the age of fifty-five.[7] In a letter dated
    19 September 1978 from Constance K. Radcliffe, the author of the book
    A History of Kirk Maughold,[3] she writes, "The father Robert (1799-1853)
    met a sad end. He hanged himself in a fit of depression after his wife's
    death; although a contemporary newspaper said that he was in comfortable
    circumstances." Isabella died on 17 July 1850 at the age of 47.[7]

Robert and Isabella (Lewin) Looney had the following children:

41.	Isabella Looney	baptized 22 February 1829
42.	Margaret Looney	baptized 13 March 1831; married Robert Kermeen
43.	Robert Looney	baptized 10 November 1833; married Elinor Corkill
44.	Elizabeth Looney	baptized 28 May 1837
45.	John Looney	born 13 February 1840;[7] baptized 1 March 1840
46.	James H. Looney	baptized 26 February 1843

42. **Margaret Looney** married Robert Kermeen, son of John Kermeen. The registry shows Robert as being of age and Margaret as being a minor. They were married on 1 October 1850.

43. **Robert Looney** was the elder son of Robert and Isabella. Robert Looney came to America before March 1851, as he is not mentioned on the March 1851 Isle of Man census. Upon arriving, he traveled to Brimfield, Peoria County, Illinois, to visit with friends from the Isle of Man. He worked at his trade (carpentry) in Peoria County for nearly four years. Sometime in 1854, Robert returned to the Isle of Man to marry his childhood sweetheart.[10]

According to the General Registry of the Isle of Man, page 54, Robert married Elinor Corkill, daughter of William (farmer) and Isabella (Jochan) Corkill, 2 September 1854 in the parish church in Maughold, Isle of Man. Their daughter was born in December 1854. Another source says that William Corkill was a banker.[10]

In the spring of 1855 Robert, Elinor, and their daughter Alice returned to America.[10] Accompanying Robert were his siblings: Elizabeth, John, and James H. They stopped at Brimfield, Illinois, for a couple of weeks to visit friends and then traveled to Galva, Illinois, where they would spend the rest of their lives. Robert had previously purchased forty acres and later purchased an additional 140 acres for farming. Robert farmed the entire 180 acres up until his death 22 January 1874. The story that has passed down through the years is that Robert was killed by a team of runaway horses while working in the field. I have been unable to find documentation to support this accident.

Robert Looney applied for citizenship to the United States of America 22 October 1860. On coming to this country, Robert was "poor in purse, but rich in will power and ambition, and his life from the time he first located in Peoria County until the time of his death was one of continual activity and labor."

The following declaration was submitted to the Circuit Court of Henry County, Illinois, on 7 October 1858:

> *Robert Looney, a free white man, and a native of the Isle of man, comes, and being duly sworn, deposes and says it is bona fide his intentions to become a citizen of the United States, and to renounce all allegiance to any foreign, Prince, Potentate, State or Sovereignty whatever, and particularly to Victoria, Queen of England whereof he is a subject.*
> *Subscribed and sworn to in an open Court this 7th day of October 1858*
> *Signed Robert Looney*

Robert Looney became a citizen of the United States of America on 22 October 1860.

The will of Robert Looney was dated 22 December 1873. He died just one month later on 22 January 1874.

> *Known all men by these presents, that I, Robert Looney, aged forty and a resident of Galva Township, in the County of Henry and the State of Illinois, do hereby make, declare and publish this to be my last will and testament, hereby revoking all former wills if any, which I may have made. As to my estate, both real and personal or mixed of which I shall die, seized and possessed, or to which I shall be entitled to at the time of my decease, I devise, bequeath and dispose of in the manner following: viz.*

1st   *My will is that all my just debts and funeral charges shall, by my executors herein after named, be paid out of my estate, as soon after my decease as shall by them be found convenient.*

2nd   *I give, devise and bequeath to my wife Eleanor Looney for and during her natural life, all my estate, both real and personal as well as mixed, subject nevertheless to the following bequest and conditions.*

3rd   *It is my will that my said wife Eleanor Looney, shall pay or consent to be paid to each of my children Alice, Isabelle, Harriet, Robert Henry, Frederick, Fanny, Elizabeth and Florence when they shall arrive at the age of twenty-two (22) years respectfully the just and full sum of five hundred dollars ($500) each, to be paid out of my personal estate and the income from my real and personal estate, after the maintenance of my said children shall be provided for and secured by her.*

4th   *In the event of the remarriage of my said wife, Eleanor Looney, it is my will that two-thirds (2/3) of my estate, both real and personal shall be equally divided among my said children, deducting the amount of five hundred dollars from the shares of those to whom it shall have been paid in accordance with this my said will.*

5th   *I hereby appoint and my wife, Eleanor Looney and John G. Emory of Lynn Township, Knox County, Illinois, sole executors of this my last will and testament.*

6th   *It is my desire that my said wife, Eleanor Looney be appointed Guardian of my said children who may be minors at my decease.*

> *In testimony whereof, I hereunto set my hand and seal, and publish and declare this to be my last will and testament in the presence of the witnesses named below:*
>
> *This 22 day of December in the year A.D. one thousand eight hundred and seventy three.*
>
> *Signed Robert Looney (seal)*

*Signed, sealed and published and declared by the said Robert Looney
as his last will and testament in the presence of us, who in the presence
of each other and at his request have subscribed our names as witnesses
hereunto?*

December 1873   *J. M. Sipes*
O. P. Emory

Elinor (Corkill) Looney was born 8 November 1835 and died 6 April 1903.
The *Galva Weekly News*, Thursday, 9 April 1903 edition gave this report:

Old Citizen Dead

*Mrs. Eleanor Looney died at her house southeast of Galva last Monday
on the 68th year of her age. She had been afflicted for many months with
cancer of the throat and mouth and had submitted to a heroic operation
at a Chicago hospital last winter, from the effects of which she came near
dying. She was brought home about two months ago and made a brave
battle for life, but to no avail.*

    *The funeral was from the Methodist church Wednesday afternoon
and the interment was in Galva cemetery.*

Robert and Elinor (Corkill) Looney had the following children:

47.	Alice Looney	born December 1854, Island of Man; died 23 October 1927; married Americus Nichols 2 July 1875
48.	Isabella Looney	born August 1856, Galva, Illinois; married John Meikle 4 July 1877
49.	Harriet (Hattie) Looney	born 1 February 1859, Galva, Illinois; married Thomas A. Costain 19 July 1886
50.	Robert H Looney	No Information
51.	Frederick Looney	born 1865, Galva, Illinois; married Neva
52.	Fanny Looney	born 30 April 1866, Galva, Illinois; died 15 May 1890; married William E. Snyder 25 January 1890
53.	Elizabeth (Lizzie) Looney	born 1869, Galva, Illinois; died 22 October 1892
54.	Florence Looney	born January 1873, Galva, Illinois; died 1960; married 21 September 1898 to Peter W. May

55.	Eleanor Looney	born 1857, Galva, Illinois; died 1857
56.	John T Looney	born 1863, Galva, Illinois; died 1864
57.	Robert Henry Looney	born January 1860, Galva, Illinois; died 11 February1923, California; married Margaret "Maggie" Kermeen

The follow is a transcript of the will of Eleanor Looney, filed with the Henry County Courthouse on 26 June 1903 in book 222, pages 330, 331, 332, 333 at 2:00 PM.

I, Eleanor Looney of Galva Henry County Illinois, being this eleventh (11) day of November, A.D. 1902 of sound mind and memory and desiring to dispose of my property do hereby make publish and declare the following to be my last will and testament.

First—I declare that my debts be paid.

Second—I will and devise to Florence May, my beloved daughter the following described real property: Commencing on the South line of the South West quarter of Section thirty six (36) Township fourteen (14) North of Range four (4) East, Henry County Illinois, twenty rods West from the South East corner of said quarter section, thence North parallel with the East line of said quarter section to North line of said quarter section thence West forty rods (40) to land owned by Robert Looney's heirs on the 21 day of October A.D. 1878, thence South along East line of said Looney land to South line of said quarter section, thence East to place of beginning containing forty acres being the same land which I bought from William L. Wiley on the 21st day of October A.D. 1878. This devise is chargeable with the following bequest:

To Fred Looney, my beloved son six hundred fifty (650) dollars; to Belle Meikel, my beloved daughter six hundred fifty (650) dollars; to Alice Nichols, my beloved daughter, six hundred fifty (650) dollars; to Nellie May Costain, my beloved granddaughter, six hundred fifty (650) dollars; to Henry Looney, my beloved son, I will and bequeath as a charge on said devise of said forty acre track the sum of Thirty nine (39) dollars to be paid to him yearly during his natural life and after his death I will and bequeath that the sum of six hundred fifty (650) dollars shall be paid to his children then living, and in default of each children, said sum of money shall be equally divided among my then living children and their issue, such issue to take a parent's share, said sum of six hundred fifty (650) dollars being likewise a charge on said forty acre track.

By will from my daughter Fannie Snyder, I am the owner of one-eighth interest in fee in the estate of Robert Looney, deceased, my husband, I will and devise said undivided one eighth interest in fee to my beloved daughter Florence May, and it is my earnest wish and desire that the balance of the heirs of the Robert Looney estate in the division award said interest to Florence May in such a way that it may include the dwelling house and out buildings where I now live; and if partition in court shall be necessary to effect a division it is my earnest wish that the court and commissioners appointed to make the division carry out these desire. On said undivided one eighth interest I make the following charges of three hundred (300) dollars each: To Fred Looney, my beloved son, that amount; To Belle Meikle, my beloved daughter, that amount; To Alice Nichols, my beloved daughter, that amount; To Nellie May Costain, my beloved granddaughter, that amount, and I will and bequeath the sum of eighteen (18) dollars per year to Henry Looney, my beloved son, to be paid to him during his natural life and after his death, the sum of three hundred (300) dollars shall be paid to his children then living and in default of such children, said sum shall be equally divided among my then living children and their issue, such issue to take a parents share: and said bequest for Henry Looney and his children are likewise to be a charge on this interest, it being my intention that the bequests in favor of Henry Looney's children shall remain in both the forty acre track and in the undivided one-eighth until they are entitled to receive it. All of the six hundred fifty (650) dollars bequests and all of the three hundred (300) bequests which are by their terms payable to the legatees, other than Henry Looney and his children shall be paid as follows: one fifth thereof every year beginning on the first day of the first year after the probate of this will until the bequest are paid together with interest thereon at the rate of six per cent, the interest to commence one year after the probate of this will.

Third I give and devise to my children and Nellie May Costain the following described real property, share and share alike: The North West quarter of section five (5) Township fourteen (14) North of Range twenty four (24) West of the sixth Principal Meridian, Trego County Kansas. Also lot one (1) in Block seventy seven (77) in the original Town of Galva, Henry County, Illinois; also lot two (2) block six (6) of the original Town of Kewanee, Henry County, Illinois.

Fourth I give and devise W. J. Kelley, who for so many years has been my faithful servant and assistant, the following described real property: Lot one (1) Block twenty six (26) in the original Town of Galva, Henry County, Illinois said property being the same property bought by me from William M. Elroy, whether the description above given is correct or not.

Fifth give and bequeath to John Lipp, sometimes known as John Looney the sum of five hundred (500) dollars to be paid out of my personal property. I give and bequeath to my granddaughter Estella Meikle the sum of five hundred (500) dollars to be paid out of my personal property. Of the rest, residue and remainder of my personal property I give and bequeath to Fred Looney, Henry Looney, Florence May, Belle Meikle, Alice Nichols, and Nellie May Costain the entire balance to be equally divided among them share and share alike.

Lastly, I nominate my son-in-law Peter May to be the executor of this my last will and testament, hereby revoking any and all former wills by me made.

(Signed) Eleanor Looney

Signed published and declared as and for the last will and testament of Eleanor Looney who in our presence subscribed her name to said will, at the time declaring to be her last will and Testament; and we at her request and in her presence and in the presence of each other have subscribed our names as witnesses thereto, consisting of five pages of writing.

(Signed) S. Thompson
N. F. Anderson

Within will held duly proven and admitted to probate and ordered recorded

June 1, 1903.
(Signed) T. H. Chesley Co. Judge

45. **John Looney,** the son of Robert and Isabella Lewin, was born in the Isle of Man on 13 February 1840.[7] John was about fourteen years of age when he came to America with his older brother, Robert; his older sister, Elizabeth; and his younger brother, James H. Looney. John became a citizen of the United States on 22 October 1860. He was schooled in Galva, Illinois, and worked on his brother's farm until he enlisted on 15 August 1862 and fought in the Civil War for the Union. He was assigned to Company G, 112th Regiment, Illinois Infantry. John served until 20 June 1865 when he "mustard out" at Greensboro, North Carolina. John's

Declaration for Pension shows that he was five feet seven inches tall and had light complexion, gray eyes, and brown hair. On 15 April 1908, it was reported in the Galva newspaper, *Galva Standard*, that John had been visiting his brother James, in Kansas City, Missouri. During his visit, the illness he had for some time was getting worst; so James returned him to his home in Kewanee, Illinois, just outside of Galva. According to his Civil War pensions papers, he had angina pectoris. John passed away on 19 April 1908 and was buried in the Galva cemetery.

FUNERAL TOMORROW
Remains of John Looney Interred at Galva

John Looney, whose death was reported in yesterday's paper, was born in Kirk Maughold, Ramsey, Isle of Man, 13 February.1840 and came to Galva, Ill., in 1855. He was a member of Co. G., 112 Illinois Infantry under Col. Henderson. He joined the army in 1862, and served until the close of the war. He died at the home of his niece, Mrs. Isabelle Meikle, 207 West Fifth Street, Kewanee, Ill., Sunday at 9:50 o'clock. Beside his brother and sister, he leaves a number of other sorrowing relatives. A short funeral review will be held at the home of Mrs. Meikle Wednesday at 12 o'clock. The remains will then be taken to Galva at 12:56 o'clock. The funeral will be in charge of the Galva. I.O.O.F The funeral party will go to Galva on a special car. An old soldier and friend of Mr. Looney speaking of him says, "He was a brave and gallant solider ever ready to do his duty no difference what the danger might be." Six old soldiers from Kewanee will be the honorary pall bearers and will accompany their departed comrade to Galva.

John was never married, nor did he have any children. In the will of Eleanor Looney (shown above), John is also referred to as John Lipp; however, I have yet to determine why.

46. **James H. Looney** was born on 31 January 1842 and christened on 26 February 1843.[8,9] The 1851 census for Maughold, Isle of Man, shows that Robert Looney (father of James H. Looney) was at the age of fifty-one and a widower. His occupation is that of a master shoemaker. It shows the following children living in his household: Margaret Kermeen, Elizabeth, John, and James.

Shortly after the death of James H. Looney's father, James, his brother John and their sister Elizabeth journeyed to America with their brother Robert and his wife Elinor and their daughter Alice. After visiting with friends in Brimfield, Illinois, they went to Galva, also in Illinois, where they would begin their lives in America.

On 4 June 1862, James, at the age of twenty, joined Company D, Sixty-ninth Regiment, Illinois Volunteer Infantry as did almost one hundred other men from Henry County and the surrounding areas. This was the first of two enlistments for James, which seemed to be common at that time. The first was a three-month enlistment, probably a basic training type enlistment. All of these volunteers were mustered out on 6 October 1862. A certificate from the adjutant general's office, issued on 21 November 1912, indicated that at the time of James's discharge on 6 October 1862 he was twenty years old and five feet and four inches tall. He had light hair, blue eyes, and was of a light complexion. His occupation listed was that of a student.

On 1 October 1862 (just prior to the discharge stated above), James enlisted at Peoria, Illinois, and was assigned to Company K, Fourteenth Illinois Cavalry. He was mustered out on 31 July 1865 in Pulaski, Tennessee. He made his way back to Galva where, according to one of the military forms he completed, he "stayed a month or more" and then went to Kansas City, Missouri, to work in the coal and wood industry.

James married Mary Kane on 17 August 1873.[11] Mary was the daughter of Thomas and Mary Ellen (Russell) Kane (Cain). Ellen was the daughter of Patrick Russell and Bridget Kane of Ireland. Mary Ellen was born in 1835. The 1870 census of Kansas City, First Ward, Jackson County, Missouri, shows Thomas Cain's age as fifty and Ellen's age as forty. Both indicated that their place of birth was Ireland. Their children's ages and places of birth were listed:

Mary Kane, 16	Kentucky
Patrick Kane, 13	Missouri
Charles Kane, 9	Missouri
Willie Kane, 7	Missouri
Thomas Kane, 5	Missouri
Katy Kane, 3	Missouri

Kansas City Star, Sunday, 25 February 1917, has this report:

Mrs. Mary Ellen Kane, 80 years old died yesterday at the home of her daughter, Mrs. J. P. Sullivan, 408 Waverly Way. Two sons, Patrick J. Kane, Kansas City, and Thomas F. Kane, Los Angeles also survive. The funeral will be at 8:30 o'clock Monday morning at 408 Waverly Way.

Mary Ellen was living in a home known as Little Sisters of the Poor. She is buried in Mt. St. Mary's cemetery.
From the Kansas City Star, Saturday, February 8, 1919:

Patrick J. Kane, *age 63 years, chartered member of the Musician's Union died early Saturday morning. 7 February 1919. He is survived by one brother, Thomas F. Kane of St. Louis Missouri, one sister, Mrs. J. P. Sullivan of 709 W. 32nd Street. Funeral from the residence of his sister at 8:30 Monday morning. Services at Redemptorist Church, Hunter ave. and Broadway at 9 o'clock. Interment family lot, Mount St. Mary Cemetery. Quirk & Tobin funeral directure in charge.*

The informant on his death certificate was Little Sisters of the Poor. Patrick is buried in Mt. St. Mary's cemetery.

The *Kansas City Star*, Monday, 12 April 1934, also shows this information:

Mrs. Katie (Kane) Sullivan, age 66 years died at her home 701 West 32nd Street, Sunday afternoon. She is survived by her husband, Jerry P. Sullivan and her daughter Miss Helen Sullivan and her brother Thomas F. Kane, Los Angeles. She was buried in the family interment lot at St. Mary's cemetery.

Kansas City Star, 29 December 1940, page 6B, shows this report:

Jerry Sullivan, husband of Katie (Kane) Sullivan died 27 December 1940, at his home 702 W. 33rd Street. He is survived by his daughter, Miss Helen Sullivan. He was also buried at St. Mary's cemetery.

On 12 April 1882, James H. Looney purchased from Mount St. Mary's Cemetery, six grave sites (1, 2, 3, 10, 11, and 12) of St. Matthew, lot 330, section B and three grave sites (1, 2, and 3) of lot 31, section B. The following are buried at the said graves:

Lot 330	Grave # 1	Lotti May Looney*	buried September 1883
	Grave # 1	Jerry P. Sullivan	buried 30 December 1940
	Grave # 2	Charles Kane	buried 28 June 1886

---

*   Lotti May Looney was the daughter of James H. Looney and his second wife Hilda A. Nelson.

	Grave # 3	Mary (Kane) Looney	buried 1 April 1877
	Grave # 10	Kate Sullivan	buried 4 September 1934
	Grave # 11	Empty	N/A
	Grave # 12	Patrick Kane	buried 10 February 1919
Lot 331	Grave # 1	Thomas Kane	buried 3 August 1881
	Grave # 1	Mary Ellen Kane	buried 26 February 1917
	Grave # 2	Empty	
	Grave # 3	Eugene Sullivan	buried 20 April 1915
	Grave # 4	William Kane	buried 5 May 1890

On 9 March 1877, Mary (Kane) Looney gave birth to twin sons, Charles Robert and John Thomas.[12] Twenty-one days later, 30 March 1877, Mary (Kane) Looney died and, on 1 April 1877, was buried in Mount St. Mary's Cemetery, Kansas City, Missouri.

The *Porter County Vidette* of Valparaiso, Indiana, reported in its 17 May 1877 edition the following:

> *Mrs. John Wark has gone to Kansas City and brought back a pair of twin babies, children of her sister-in-law who lately died. She now has the children and intends on bringing them up.*

On 19 July 1882, James married Hilda A. Nelson; and on 1 July 1883, the first of their two children was born. Lottie Mary Looney died 12 September 1883, just two months after her birth. Lottie Mary was buried in Mount St. Mary's Cemetery with her Uncle Jerry P. Sullivan, husband of Katie K. Kane (sister of Mary Kane). Their second child, Harry Roy Looney, was born 13 June 1885 in Kansas City, Missouri.

James H. Looney died 15 January 1917 and is buried in Elmwood Cemetery, next to Hilda Nelson Looney, in Kansas City, Missouri. The *Kansas City Star* for Monday, 15 January 1917, reported the following:

> ### Death of James H. Looney
> #### The Pioneer Business Man came to Kansas City in 1866
>
> *James H. Looney died at his home 3422 St. John Avenue, today. Mr. Looney, one of Kansas City's oldest pioneer business men, was born on the Isle of Man in 1843 and came to Kansas City in 1866. He early engaged in the coal, wood and seed business, being the first to transport wood on barges on the Missouri River. To get the Missouri Pacific and the Chicago*

& Alton railroads to build stations here he gave the land at First Street and Grand Avenue. Forty-eight years ago, Mr. Looney was the proprietor of Looney's Hotel, then one of the best known hotels in the North End.

Mr. Looney is survived by his widow, Hilda Looney, a sister Mrs. John Wark, and three sons, Harry Looney, this city; John Looney, Detroit, and Charles Looney, Valparaiso, Ind.

A search has been made concerning the "Looney Hotel," and so far, there is no record of our James Looney ever being in the hotel business. However, a William J. Looney was living in Kansas City and indeed was in the hotel business around the same time.

James's will was admitted into probate 16 February 1917, and an inventory of all assets was presented to the court. In his will, James named John Kennish as executor. The notice of "Letters Granted" was published in the *Daily Record*, a newspaper published in Kansas City, Missouri. The application for letters testamentary listed these people as recipients: Hilda Looney, widow, 3422 St. John Avenue, Kansas City, Missouri; John Looney, son, Detroit, Michigan; Charles Looney, son, Valparaiso, Indiana; and Harry Looney, son, 3422 St. John Avenue, Kansas City, Missouri. The application valued James's estate as $1,000 personal property and $15,000 real property. As this form was produced on 16 February 1917, the just-mentioned figures had to have been estimates as an inventory had not yet been taken.

Earnest A. Johnson, James's partner in Looney Coal Company, stated in a petition to the court that the interest of the Looney Coal Company amounted to $3,042.83; and it was ordered that John Kennish, executor, release the interest of James H. Looney (deceased) to Earnest A. Johnson, the surviving partner, for the sum of $3,042.83, less $60.00 to be paid to the attorney for his part in this transaction as well as a 3 percent commission to be paid to the surviving partner, with the remainder to be paid to John Kennish, executor, after payment of the probate fees. The surviving partner agreed to assume all debts against the partnership.

On 22 March 1917, a bill was submitted by Leo J. Stewart Undertaking Company for the cost of services as listed below:

Casket	$250.00
Steel Vault	80.00
Embalming	15.00
Black suit	25.00
16 pr. gloves	4.00 (25¢ per pair)
Publications	5.65
Grave	7.50 (must have been to open and close)

| Hearse (auto) | 10.00 |
| Automobiles | 52.50 (7—seven passenger automobiles at $7.50 each) |

The cost of the above funeral service for James H. Looney was $449.65. On 4 April 1917, a bill was presented to the estate of James H. Looney by Elmwood Cemetery Society for the grave site (lot 284, block 4) at a cost of $100.00.

On 23 March 1917, a request was made by Hilda Looney (widow):

> *On this 23rd day of March 1917, comes Hilda Looney, widow of James H. Looney, deceased, and reports to the court that at the time of the death of the deceased, there were no grains, meats, vegetables, groceries, or other provisions on hand, providing for the sustenance of this widow.*
>
> *Therefore she prays that the court, make an allowance for her, in lieu of provisions not on hand, as aforesaid, as provided by law, out of the estate or estates of the said deceased; and she believes that the sum of six hundred seventy five Dollars, ($675.00) would be a reasonable allowance for that purpose.*
>
> *The party further represents to the court that, in addition to the above and under section 116 of the General Statutes of the State of Missouri, for 1909, she asks that Four Hundred Dollars ($400.00) be allowed her under the aforesaid Section.*

This request was signed by Hilda Looney.

The sum of $1,075 was paid to Hilda by John Kennish, executor, on 23 April 1917.

The inventory showed cash in the bank in the amount of $902.66. Also, there was a family Bible and an old edition of *Encyclopedia Britannica.* There was also household goods and kitchen furniture, which consisted of a gas stove, rugs, chairs, and bedroom set. There was a deed to lots 116 and 117, Melrose Avenue, Kansas City, Missouri, and also a one-half interest in the Looney Coal Company composed of James H. Looney and Ernest A. Johnson, now being administered by the surviving partner.

The final settlement and closing of the probate records were completed on 18 February 1918. Copies of the final settlement are found at the end of this chapter. A search of the probate records and Missouri archives has been made for the will. However, one cannot be found.

On 27 September 1938, a letter was written by Charles R. Looney, requesting certain information pertaining to the probate records and proceedings of the estate of James H. Looney. On 5 October 1938, a reply was sent from the chief deputy clerk stating that the cost of these documents would be $10.50 and, as soon as this amount was received, copies would be mailed.

The History of Jackson County, Missouri, printed in 1881, has a short biographical sketch on page 806 about James H. Looney:

J. H. Looney

> *Dealer in cool and wood, is a native of the Isle of Man, Great Britain, born January 31, 1848, and was there reared to manhood. In 1855 he came to the United States, landing at New York, and immediately removed to Galva, Ill., remaining until 1863. In the spring of 1866 he became a residence of Kansas City and has been actively engaged in the wood business since. He at first had to transport the wood on barges on the Missouri River, and this industry has been much appreciated by citizens of this place. His marriage occurred in August 1872, to Miss Mary Kane. She died in 1876, [sic] leaving two children; John and Charlie. Mr. Looney commenced life in a very moderate circumstances, and by hard work, good judgment and economy, he has secured a comfortable competency.*

Even though the above is a published biographical sketch, it is still not error free. For example, James was born in 1842, not 1848. Mary Kane died on 30 March 1877, not 1876 as printed above.

Hilda Nelson Looney was born 29 March 1865 in Stockholm, Sweden. Hilda came to Kansas City, Missouri, with her parents as a child. Hilda died 6 March 1939 and is buried in Elmwood Cemetery.

The *Kansas City Times* dated March 7, 1939, has this information:

> *LOONEY; Mrs. Hilda Looney, 73, widow of James H. Looney, early-day coal and wood dealer here, died yesterday at the home of her son, Harry Looney 5601 Euclid Avenue. Mrs. Looney lived at 3422 St. Johns avenue. Born in Stockholm, Sweden, she came to Kansas City with her parents as a child. Surviving also are two other sons, John T. Looney, Galva, Illinois and Charles R. Looney, Valparaiso, Indiana and a niece, Mrs. D. K. Spellman, Tulsa, OK.*

James H. and Mary (Kane) Looney had the following children:

58. Charles Robert Looney born 9 March 1877, Kansas City, Missouri
59. John Thomas Looney born 9 March 1877, Kansas City, Missouri

(Note: Both Charles and John were raised by their aunt and uncle—John and Elizabeth (Looney) Wark.)

James H. and Hilda (Nelson) Looney had the following children:

60.	Lotti May Looney	born July 1883, Kansas City, Missouri; died 12 September 1883
61.	Harry Roy Looney	born 13 June 1885, Kansas City, Missouri; died 12 August 1946

58. Charles Robert Looney was the son of James H. and Mary (Kane) Looney and was the twin brother of John Thomas Looney (see Looney-Wark chapter).

59. John Thomas Looney was the son of James H. and Mary (Kane) Looney and twin brother of Charles Robert Looney. John is listed in the 1894 directory of the Northern Indiana Normal School on page 5, under the Telegraphic Department, class of 1894-5. This was the only year that John was listed. Sometime before 24 November 1901, John married Ruth Kingsley. They lived in the Detroit area for a while as John either owned or worked in a confectionary store in Detroit. I am uncertain whether the marriage was ended by divorce, or death, but I do know that John's second marriage was to Evelyn (Glick) Wark who died on 15 June 1941 and is buried in the Galva cemetery. John died in San Diego, California, on 14 November 1957. He was cremated at the Cypressview [*sic*] Crematory. His ashes were sent to Galva and placed in lot 68N1/2, block 12, grave no. 1. Grave no. 2 shows John Looney, buried 4/08 (1908), age sixty-eight. Grave 3 shows Evelyn Wark, age forty-eight, died 6/18/44 (1944).[14]

John and Ruth (Kingsley) Looney-Wark had one child.

62.	Charles Kingsley Wark	born 24 November 1901

62. Charles Kingsley, the son of John Thomas and Ruth (Kingsley) Wark, was born 24 November 1901, probably in Detroit, Michigan. He married Francis H. and lived in Rancho Santa Fe, California. Charles was a medical doctor and had been for thirty years prior to his death on 1 March 1983. To the best of my knowledge, they did not have any children.[15]

61. Harry Roy Looney, born 13 June 1885 in Kansas City, Missouri, was the son of James H. Looney and Hilda (Nelson). From all indication, Harry spent his entire life in Kansas City and, according to a city directory dated

1916, at the age of thirty-one, was still living with his parents at 3422 St. John Avenue. The same directory shows Harry in business with Frank DeMayo (Looney and DeMayo) running a poolroom at 1024 Baltimore Avenue.

Harry married Mary M. Long, and at the time of his death, they were living at 5601 Euclid Avenue. On 12 August 1946, Harry was involved in an automobile accident and died the same day in the receiving ward of Research Medical Center. The cause of his death was listed as skull fractures—auto trauma. His death certificate shows him as a tavern owner. His death was recorded in the *Kansas City Times* on 13 August 1946, pages 7 and 13. It was also reported in the *Kansas City Star*, also on page 13. Harry was buried in Elmwood Cemetery.

At the time of Harry's death, the *Kansas City Times*, Tuesday, 13 August 1946, page 10, wrote about Harry's earlier days as a gambler. He was also a partner with Frank DeMayo, King of Kansas City Bootleggers, in the prohibition days. Harry later on became partners with Fred Wedow, another gambler in Kansas City. Harry was also a part owner of the Green Hills club as well as having operated several saloons in the area.

In 1931, Harry paid $12,000 for a collection of minerals that he used to build four fishponds behind his home on Euclid Avenue. An estimated thirty-five thousand mineral specimens were used in the pools, which housed Harry's collection of veil-tailed fish.

Sometime after Harry's death, Mary remarried Gus Lanio and lived at 4340 Highland. Mary died on 11 April 1965 and is buried next to Harry Roy Looney. As far as I can determine, Harry and Mary did not have children.

Harry R. Looney Rites
(Kansas City Times)

Services for Harry R. Looney, age 61 of 5601 Euclid Avenue, will be held at 2:30 o'clock Thursday at the Quirk & Tobin chapel. Burial will be in the Elm wood cemetery. The pallbearers will be Al Unser, B. T. Bishop, Frank M. Flory, Bernie Goldstein, Bernard Lukehart and Joseph Murphy.

(Kansas City Star) Looney—Harry—R., 61 years died August 12, 1946. He is survived by his wife Mrs. Mary Looney, of the home, 5601 Euclid. Services will be held at The Parlors, Linwood and Main, 2:30 Thursday afternoon. Interment Elmwood Cemetery.

Quirk & Tobin, WE. 1777

Notes

1.   Gordon N. Kniveton, *The Story of Mann*, pg 62.

2.   The Wikipedia Encyclopedia, information on the Isle of Man.

3.   William and Constance Radcliff, *A History of Kirk Maughold* The Manx Museum and National Trust 1979,

4.   James H. Looney "A written statement" January 23, 1913.

5.   "Certified copy of marriage records" General Registry of The Isle of Man,

6.   "Certified copy of marriage records." General Registry of The Isle of Man,

7.   "Certified copy of death records." General Registry of The Isle of Man,

8.   James H. Looney, (signed by) "Declaration for Pension" February 12, 1907.

9.   James H. Looney (signed by) "Department of the Interior, Bureau of Pensions", April 3, 1915.

10. *Portrait and Biographical Album,* Henry County, Illinois, 1885.

11. "Certified copy of Marriage Certificate," Church of St. Patrick, Kansas City, Missouri, dated May 16, 1970.

12. "Baptism Records" Church of St. Patrick, Kansas City, Missouri.

13. James H. Looney, "Civil War military records."

14. "Cemetery records" Galva, Illinois.

15. Charles Kingsley Wark "Death Certificate"

FOUR

Paul Kuhl and Eva Marya Kaes

(See Appendix C)

―――――●◆◄――――

In a letter dated 2 June 1997 to John W. Kuhl of Pittstown, New Jersey, from *The Palatine Families of New York* (A Genealogical and Historic Study, by Hank Jones, our Kuhl (Cool) ancestors were located and found on the census of Maxsain for the hamlet (small village) of Zurbach. The information was retrieved by Mr. Hank Jones's researcher, Frau Carla Mittelstaedt-Kubaseck, an eighteenth-century German handwriting specialist. According to the letter, "Carla went village-to-village looking" for the family of Paul Kuhl. The earliest direct forefather of the branch of this chapter is Johannes Kuhl.

Naturalization in the colonial period was not a requirement of settlers who came from England, Ireland, or Scotland as they made no change of their allegiance. Many from Germany, Holland, and France first located on Long Island, New Amsterdam (New York). This was where they took their oath of loyalty to the British government. Some of those moved to New Jersey and settled in Essex and Monmouth counties. On 4 April 1709, by the Act of Assembly, owners of at least one hundred acres of land or a possessor of an estate of at least fifty were given the right to vote for public officers. This was known as naturalization. The names of all of those who were naturalized in the colonial period were compiled from Allison's Acts of the General Assembly. The list starts with the date of 11 March 1713-14 and ends 26 September 1772.[8] On 8 July 1730, Johan Philip Kaes and Paul Kole were naturalized. On 21 October 1754, Christian Kule was naturalized.

The history of the Knowlton Presbyterian Church starts in 1766. In 1775, it was under the care of the New Brunswick Presbytery under the title of *The First English and German Congregation of Knowlton*.[10] Up until 1802, the congregation consisted of Presbyterians, Dutch, Calvinists, and Episcopalians. They worshiped in an old stone church south of the village of Delaware. However, the church was inconvenient for many who attended; so in 1802-03, a larger church was built in the center of the township, and it was then that the congregation became a truly Presbyterian church. The Kuhl name has many variations of spellings—such as Kaul, Kuehl, Kole, Kool, Kehl, Kule, Cuell, Cool, and Cuhl—as does one's given name. Names like Maria can be spelled Maria or Myra or at times recorded as Mary. Christopher at times will be referred to as Chris, Christ, or Crest. Kaes has often been spelled Case. All of these variations make search and connecting the proper children to the correct family quite difficult. Just imagine coming from a country and not speaking the language of the country you have just entered—attempting to communicate with a person unable to speak your language and having them ask your name. They then wrote down what sounded correct to them. You say Kuhl, and they spell it one of five different ways. I am sure this didn't happen in every case, but I am sure this happened at times. The variation of Kuhl wasn't always the fault of translation; it was just the way that some decided to spell it Cool rather than Kuhl—perhaps to distinguish the difference from one family and another, especially since so many men were named Johann or Wilhelm or Paul or Peter or Adam.

The Kuhl family was of Germanic origin and arrived on the shores of America in the 1720's and 1730's. Some soon changed the spelling from Kuhl to Cool. The Kuhls living in Hunterdon were ones that switched to Cool but by the time of the Civil War, they had reverted back to the Kuhl spelling.[1] One of the sources used for this chapter was the birth and baptismal records of Knowlton Church. In those records, the name Kuhl and Cool are used interchangeably.

This Kuhl family has been traced back to 1694 where an Inhabitant List at Zurbach records Johannes Kuhl, Sendschoffen. He and his wife Veronica Lentz had two sons and two daughters.

I. **Leonhard Kuhl,** son of Johannes Kuhl the Sendschoffen at Zurbach, married 14 October 1696 Anna Veronica Staats, daughter of the late Adam Staats, formerly inhabitant at Maxsain. Leonhard Kuhl at Zurbach died 6 February 1721 at the age of fifty-six. Anna Veronica (Staats) Kuhl died 12 December 1734. Anna was fifty-eight years old. Her death was the result of an accident one day earlier. They had the following children:

    (a). Veronica Christina, married 28 April 1727 Johannes Dorner.
    (b). Johann Paul, born 24 March 1700; confirmed 1717 at Maxsain.

(c).   Johann Peter, confirmed in 1722, age 16.

(d).   Johann Christian, confirmed 1731, age 16 (went by the name Crest).

(e).   Maria, confirmed in 1735, age 16.

II.   **Johann Jacob Kuhl** was confirmed in 1695 at the age of sixteen. He married 30 November 1701, Maria Eva, daughter of Peter Zeitz, who was the parish leader and inhabitant at Zurbach.

III.   **Anna Maria Kuhl** was confirmed in 1699 at the age of sixteen.

IV.   **"A daughter"** appears in the 1694 Inhabitant List (probably died young).

(I-b). Johann Paul Kuhl (went by the name of Paul), son of Leonhard and Anna Veronica (Staats) Kuhl, was born 24 March 1700. Paul was the first Kuhl of record in this country and was naturalized 8 July 1730.[11]

Records at Trenton, New Jersey, show several deeds concerning Paul: William Burge to Paul Cool and Henry Dilts in 1742; John Reading to Paul Koul and Henry Dilts, 20 April 1743; Paul Coul to Henry Dilts, 21 January 1745 (West Jersey Deed Book G—H, pages 80+, 289, 293+, etc.). There is a deed dated 25 January 1759 indicating that William Kase, Henry Winter and his wife Frona Catherina, Philip Dilts and Henry Dilts Jr., the children of Anna Dilts (late widow of Henry Dilts), Peter Aller and wife Elizabeth, all of Amwell Township (children and grandchildren of John Philip Kase) gave twenty-nine acres in Amwell Township to Paul Coul and his wife Eva Maria (Kaes). In an indenture dated 14 January 1779, Paul Cool gave this same twenty-nine acres to his four sons: Philip (2), William (2), Christopher (2), and Leonard (2).

Paul married Eva Maria Kaes before 1735 in Hunterdon County, New Jersey. Eva was the daughter of John Philip Case (Kaes) who settled in the Flemington area in 1732.[9] Paul had a brother, Crest Kuhl, who was the fourth great-grandfather of the main source of this chapter, John W. Kuhl of Pittstown, New Jersey.

Paul lived on the Plantation in King Wood, Amwell Township, Hunterdon County, New Jersey. He died in 1784 and is buried in the Kuhl Burial Ground on the fifteenth fairway of Copper Hill Golf Course. He married Eva Maria/ Marya/Mary Kaes, the daughter of Johann Phillip and Anna Elizabeth (Jung) Kaes. Eva Mary Kaes died in 1783 and is also buried in the Kuhl Burial Ground. According to the Web site for Case Family History by Russell S. Pickett of the Hunterdon, New Jersey area, Johann Kaes changed his name from Johann Phillip De Casse (Case) to John Philip Kaes "to make it more American." Mr. Pickett goes on to report that Johann Phillip Kaes came to America with his two brothers in 1728, following the death of Johann's first wife, Anna Elizabeth Jung. He further states that Johann was the son of Duke Karl De Kasse (Case), and he was born 1680 in Hausen, Germany.

Paul and Eva Mary (Kaes) Kuhl had the following children: [11b]

1. Philip (2) Kuhl
2. William (Wilhelm) (2) Kuhl died 6 November 1815
3. Christopher (2) Kuhl born 1739; died 1827
4. Leonard (2) Kuhl died 27 August 1793
5. Paul (2) Kuhl born 1742; died 26 November 1825
6. Elizabeth (2) Kuhl married Henry (Henrich) Young; died before 1825
7. Frances (Frankey) (2) Kuhl
8. Mary (2) Kuhl married Daniel Feit (Fite) 6 March 1770, Greenwich Township, Sussex (Warren) County, New Jersey; died after 1825

(I-d). Johann Christian Kuhl (Crest), son of Leonhard and Anna Veronica (Staats) Kuhl, was confirmed in 1731 at the age of sixteen (went by the names Crest, Johann, and Christ). He was the brother of (b) Johann Paul Cool. He emigrated from Germany and was naturalized in 1754 as "Christian Kuhl" Crest Cool of Amwell Township, Hunterdon County, New Jersey. His will, dated 10 April 1770, was proved 27 August 1770. Those named in his will were his wife, children, and his nephews, Crest Cool and Paul Cool Jr. Crest and Paul Jr. were named as executors.[16] Crest married Maria Hummer (date unknown)

Crest and Maria (Hummer) Kuhl had the following children:[1, 11]

9.	Johannes Cool	baptized 9 April 1745; not in his father's will
10.	Peter Cool	baptized with Johannes, 9 April 1745; called eldest son in father's will
11.	Wilhelm Cool	baptized 14 June 1746; died October 1823 at Knowlton Township, Warren County, New Jersey
12.	Philip Cool	baptized 24 April 1748; married 1762, Eva Hummer (1742-1836); Eva married (2) Adam Hummer
13.	Christian/Christopher	Cool born about 1747; married (1) Maria Case and (2) 10 November 1810 Catherine Case; died 29 October 1841, age 94 years
14.	Paul Cool	according to land records—married Elizabeth Case
15.	Catharina Cool	born 25 March 1755; married Philip Jager/Yager; died 20 July 1832, Union Springs, New York

16. Maria Cool   no information
17. Elisabetha   married 18 November 1784, Barnet Cruise; died April 1844, Cayuga Junction, New York

The will of (b) Paul Kuhl includes a codicil dated 22 May 1783 and was proved 20 April 1784. Below is a summary of the will of Paul Cool, of Amwell Township, Hunterdon County[6] (Hunterdon County Will # 1238J). A notation included in this report says, "John W. Kuhl of Pittstown, New Jersey a researcher on his family for over thirty years, has greatly assisted me in gathering date on the ch. of (Johann) Paul (1) Kuhl and his wife Eva Maria." This was a quote from Henry Z. Jones Jr.[11]

The below summary of the will of Johann Paul Cool, was copied from New Jersey Colonial Documents—Calendar of Wills—1781-1785 pages 92-93. At the time the currency being used was still British, thus the £ symbol, meaning British pound.

> *Being old, Wife, Eve M, household good; To son Leonard, the care of my wife. Son Paul Cool is to help. Son, Christopher also to help. Son and heir Phillip, 53. and the plantation where he lives in Kingwood. Son William, the plantation in Sussex Co., where he lives. Son Christ, the plantation where he lives in Amwell Township. Son Paul, the farm I live on. Son Leonard, ½ of Paul's farm. Son Paul, 42 acres I bought of Joacam Greggs, formerly belonging to George Reading, joining Herbert Trimmer. Daughter Elizabeth Yong, £ 250, daughter Frankey Fisher, £ 250, daughter Mary Fite £ 250. ExecutorsCsons, Phillip and Christ. WitnessesCSamuel Maxwell, Charity Glick, Jonathon Higgins.*
>
> *May 22, 1783, Codicil, My Executors are to survey ½ acre of ground joining lands of Henry Dils for a burying ground and to be in that part bequeathed to son Leonard. Proved April 20, 1784.*
>
> *April 20, 1784, Inventory, £ 874.10.0, made by Samuel Maxwell and Jonathan Higgins.*
>
> *May 2, 1792, Account by Christopher Cool, one of the Executors, paid legacy to Philip, £ 50; to Daniel Feit and wife Mary, £ 270, to Henry Young and wife Elizabeth, £ 270, to John Fisher and wife Frankey, £ 270.*
>
> *April 20, 1826, Sale of real estate, a track of land in Amwell Township, joining Peter Dilts and John Laquer, of 196 acres, to William Kuhl, of $5,495.14. Woodland, joining Frederick Still, George Crouse and others, 42 acres, was sold in two lots; one to John E. Trimmer and the other to Paul Kuhl. One other lot sold to Francis Trimmer, one to William E. Case, one to Elijah Carman, one to John Higgins, two to Leonard Kuhl and one to John Crouse.*

July 20, 1826, Account by Christopher Cool, surviving Executor
(Lib. 26, 198).

The following is a summary of the will for Johan Kaes, father of Eva Marya, wife of Paul Cool, dated 27 November 1754:

Johan Pilipus (Phillip) Kaes of Amwell Township, Hunterdon Co., yeoman. Former wife Anna Elizabeth, present wife Rachael. ChildrenBWilliam, Eva Marya, (wife of Paul Koul) Frona Catherina (wife of Henry Winter) Elizabeth (wife of Peter Aller), Ann (deceased, who left children Philip and Headrick Dilts), children by present wife, Headrick, Peter, Philipp and Catherine, all four under age. Real and personal estate. Executors-Brother Peter Young, and son-in-law Peter Allar, both of said county, yeoman and William Poppelsdorph, of New York City, banker. Witnesses DirekSchuyler, Theodor us van Wyck, Adolph Bras, Jr. Proved February 12, 1756. (The testator signed in German) Lib. 8, p 426

February 16, 1756-Inventory, £ 256.4 incl. 3 servant men, and one "garl" [sic] (girl).

October 20, 1772, Inventory "of the money arrising [sic] of the sale of land of Philip Case, desc'd,", £ 464.8; made by James Stout and Samuel Furman

On 8 July 1730, the Legislative Act of the Royal Colony of New Jersey was enacted, therefore enabling inhabitants of the province of New Jersey to hold lands and invest them with privileges of natural-born subjects of said province. Among the list of inhabitants were Johan Phillip Kaes, Willem Kaes, and Paul Kole. Paul Kole was also known as Paul Kuhl. Mr. Pickett has recorded a few deaths, among them being "Eva Marie (Case) Kahl" [sic], "Paul Kahl" [sic], and "Leonard Kahl" [sic]. He has indicated that they are buried in the Case Burial Ground, when in fact they are buried in the Kuhl Burial Ground, which is a part of the land purchased by Paul Kuhl and, later became and still is, the Copper Hill Country Club. A section of approximately forty feet by forty feet just to the left of the 14th green contains twenty-four upright headstones that range in height of about six inches to the tallest being about three feet. There were only two in the three-foot range. There could be, and probably are, more of our ancestors buried there; but their headstones are either missing or buried into the earth. The grass is being maintained by the groundskeeper of the golf course, so it was in excellent condition—that is with the exception of the headstones. On Wednesday, 30 October 2000, Maria (my wife) and I, along with my sister and her husband, Nancy and Ronald Tietgen, and our cousin John Kuhl walked the course and took pictures and notes of the burial ground.

Unfortunately, because of weather, age, and material, most of the information could not be read.

Those buried in Kuhl Burial Ground are in this list:

(Note: The numbers in parentheses represent age, i.e. years, months, days. Also the notes in parentheses are from additional research.)

Sarah Cool,	died 10 April 1814 (1-0-06); daughter of Paul and Hanna
Leonard,	died 27 August 1793
Christopher Cool	
Philip Kuhl	(married Eva Hummer)
William Kuhl	(married Mary ___)
Mary Kuhl	(married Daniel Feit)
Elizabeth Kuhl	(married Henry Young)
Frankie Kuhl	(married John Fisher)
Mary Cool,	died 20 January 1799 (0-4-8); daughter of Paul
and Hanna	
George Kuhl,	died January 1806, age 26
Ann Kuhl,	died 22 February 22, 1837 (56-02-06)
C. K.,	died August 1795
A. S.	
C. T.	
E. M. K.	(Prob. Eva Mary Kaes)
Paul Kuhl,	born 24 May 1700; died 1784
Eva Mary,	born 27 July 1704; died 1783

1. **Philip (2)**, son of Paul Kuhl and Eva Maria Kaes, married in April 1755 Catherine, daughter of Herbert Hummer. Catherine was born 17 May 1737 and died 19 April 1812. They lived in Kingwood Township, Hunterdon, New Jersey, until 1790, when they moved to Virginia (now W. Virginia).[11a] This information was shared with John W. Kuhl by Edith Culp of Youngstown, Ohio, who was in possession of the Philip (2) family Bible.[11]

Philip and Catherine (Hummer) Kuhlhad the following children:

9. **Paul Kuhl**, son of Philip and Catherine Kuhl, was single in 1793 and no mention of him during a family probate hearing in 1828.[7]

18. **Jacob Kuhl**, son of Philip and Catherine Kuhl, married Elizabeth Aller [7]

19. **Philip Kuhl**, son of Philip and Catherine Kuhl, was single in 1793 and no mention of him during a family probate hearing in 1828.[7]

20. **Herbert Kuhl,** son of Philip and Catherine Kuhl, married Ann ___.
    Herbert died in 1834.[7]

21. **Lydia Kuhl,** daughter of Philip and Catherine Kuhl, married Luther
    Colvin.[7]

22. **Anna Eva Kuhl,** daughter of Philip and Catherine Kuhl, was baptized
    on 23 May 1764 and died at a young age.[7]

2. **Wilhelm (2),** also known as William Cool, son of Paul Kuhl and Eva Maria
    Kaes, died in November 1815 in Knowlton Township, Sussex (Warren)
    County, New Jersey. He married Marie (last name unknown) who died 7
    July 1825 at the age of eighty-seven. Both are buried in Knowlton Frame
    Cemetery.[11]

Wilhelm (2) and Maria (last name unknown) Cool had the following
children:[7]

23.	Anna Cool	born 18 July 1759; married Michael Raub before 1785 (Michael was born in 1754 and died in the spring of 1833); died August 1854[5]
24.	Mary Cool	born about 1761; married Conrad Linnabury before 1785
25.	Elizabeth Cool	born 18 October 1763; married Andrew Teel; died 12 May 1849, in Knowlton
26.	William Cool	born 17 December 1765; died 7 October 1824, Knowlton (no record of marriage or children)
27.	Paul Cool	born 6 May 1768; married Susannah Raub; died 6 March 1845, Knowlton.[5]
28.	Adam Cool	baptized 9 May 1771; married Abigail Green; died 14 April 1834, Mt. Herman
29.	Christian Cool	born 9 May 1771; died young
30.	Catherine Cool	born 28 March 1773; married William Swayze before 1796 (children: Barnabas, born 13 April 1794, baptized 3 August 1794; Mary, born 3 July 1797, baptized 26 September 1797); died 10 May 1860, buried in Swayze cemetery
31.	Margaretta (1) Cool	born 25 September 1777; died young
32.	Christina Cool	born 7 July 1780; married Charles Beatty bet. 1815-1825; died 22 May 1856

33.	Margaretta Scharlotta Cool	born 28 February 1783; baptized 27 April 1783; married John Frees

3. **Christopher (2),Kuhl** son of Paul and Eva Maria Kuhl, was born in the year 1735[11b] and died 22 December 1827 at the age of ninety-two. He lived in Amwell, Hunterdon County, and was a farmer. He first married Anna, daughter of Peter Fischer. Anna died before 1789. Christopher married (2) the widow Phoebe Chamberlain who died before October 1836.[11]

4. **Leonard (2), Kuhl** son of Paul and Eva Maria Kuhl, was born in Hunterdon County and died 27 August 1793. He is buried in the Kuhl Burial Ground at Larson's Corner (Bible Record #2128 of the Genealogy Society of New Jersey at Rutgers University has this family's details). He married (1) Margaretha, daughter of William Jung. Margaretha was born 26 July 1751 and died 14 January 1775. Leonard married(2) 4 August 1777 Catharina, daughter of George Trimmer.[11] She died 17 November 1812 and was buried in the Kuhl Cemetery at Larson's Corner.

5. **Paul (2), Kuhl** son of Johann Paul Kuhl and Eva Maria Kaes, married Anna Dilts who died 2 June 1815. Paul died 26 November 1825 at the age of eighty-three. They are both buried in the Kuhl Burial Ground at Larson's Corner.

6. **Elizabeth (2) Kuhl**, daughter of John Paul Kuhl and Eva Maria Kaes, married Henrich Jung/Young. There is no other information.

7. **Frances "Frankey" Kuhl** was the daughter of John Paul Kuhl and Eva Maria Kaes (date of birth unknown). Frankey married John Fisher of Hunterdon, New Jersey, about 1760 in John Fisher, Bethel Township, Bedford County, Pennsylvania. Frankey was buried in 1830 in the Bethel Cemetery, Fulton, Pennsylvania.

John and Frances "Frankey" (Kuhl) Fisher had the following children:

34. Peter Fisher
35. Mary Fisher
36. Paul Fisher
37. John Fisher Jr.
38. Ann Fisher
39. Margaret Fisher
40. Jacob Fisher
41. Ruhamah Fisher

8. **Maria Kuhl (2)**, daughter of John Paul Kuhl and Eva Maria Kaes, married 6 March 1770 Daniel Feit.[11]

Below is a summary of William's (Wilhelm) (2) will written 6 January 1815 and proved 21 December 1815:

> *In the name of God, amen I William cool of the Township of Knowlton, county of Sussex, & State of New Jersey, being weak in body yet of perfect (?) sound mind and memory & calling to mind the mortality of my body & knowing that it is appointed unto all men once (?) to die do make and ordain this my last will and testament in form and manner following (that is) first it is my will and order that all my just debts and funeral expenses be paid as soon as may be convenient after my decease. Secondly, I give and bequeath unto my three sons William Cool, Adam Cool, & Paul Cool, one dollar each. Thirdly I give and bequeath unto my six daughters, that is, Anna Raub, Mary Linnaburey, Catherine Swayzy, Christina Cool, Elizabeth Teel & Margaret Frees, one dollar each. Fourthly, I give and bequeath unto my beloved wife Mary Cool the residue of all my personal estate that is not above mentioned of every kind and description whatever in whom lands are found, to her & her use during her natural life, & for her to dispose of it, as she shall see cause or think proper. Lastly, I nominate & appoint my son Adam Cool & my son-in-law Andrew Teel executors of this my last will & testament, revoking & annulling all other wills by me before made. In witness whereof I have set my hand & seal this sixth day of January in the year of our Lord one thousand eight hundred and fifteen.*

This will was signed William Cool (with an *X* between William and Cool and the words "his mark").

23.   **Ann Kuhl,** daughter of William Cool and Mary Ann, born 18 July 1759 and died in August 1854. She married Michael Raub before 1785. Michael was born in 1754 and died in the spring of 1833.[5]

Ann Kuhl and Michael Raub had the following children:

42.	Andreas	born 29 March 1783; baptized 27 April 1783
43.	Maria	born 24 January 1785; baptized 18 May 1785
44.	Elisabeth	born February 1794
45.	Anna	born February 1797; baptized 19 March 1797
46.	Sarah	born December 1801

27. **Paul Cool**, son of William "Wilhelm Kuhl Sr. (Cool)," born 6 May 1768 and baptized 24 April 1768 in Knowlton Township, New Jersey; he died 6 March 1845 at the age of seventy-seven. Paul married Susannah Raub, daughter of Andrew Raub Sr. and granddaughter of Michael Raub. Susannah born 23 December 1773 and died in July 1839.[5] In the Knowlton Church records their name was recorded as Kuhl but later they were known as Cool. Both Paul and Susannah are buried in the Knowlton Cemetery.

Paul and Susannah (Raub) Cool had the following children:[2]

47.	William Cool	born 28 August 1793; married Catherine White 1 November 1821who died 23 March 1885; William died April 1835
48.	Andreas (Andrew) Cool	born 20 January 1795; baptized 22 March 1799
49.	Maria Cool	born 12 October 1797; married Robert Clayton
50.	Margaret Cool	born 23 October 1799; married ___ Angle in 1823 (Poss. Samuel Angle)
51.	Jacob Cool	born 20 March 1802
52.	Sarah Cool	born 14 January 1805; married David Kinney and lived in Albion, Michigan; died 15 July 1885.
53.	Charlotte Cool	born 1 July 1807; married Lewis Smith
54.	Elizabeth Cool	born 25 May 1810; married 19 January 1836 Powell Grover (born 2 November 1806, died 18 October 1881, Albion, Michigan); Elizabeth died 20 October 1881
55.	John Friese Cool	born 27 August 1815; married Sarah Ann Snover 6 December 1845 who died in 1904, Albion, Michigan; John died 29 April 1863

51. **Jacob Cool**, son of Paul Cool and Susannah Raub, born 20 March 1802 in Knowlton, Warren County, New Jersey. Here he lived the first thirty years of his life. Jacob married Mary H. Wooliver 20 November 1828. Mary was also born in Knowlton, New Jersey. In 1835, Jacob and his family moved to Homer, Michigan, and lived in a cabin owned by a relative of his, Powell Grover—until Jacob had purchased a farm on section 22 of Homer Township, where he spent the rest of his life. Mary died 27 July 1868. Jacob died 5 December 1881.[4]

Jacob and Mary (Wooliver) Cool had the following children:[3, 4]

56.	Caroline	
57.	Nelson	
58.	Susan	married Morris who had two children: Mary and Nettie
59.	John	no information
60.	Andrew	married Francena Thorington September 1868 and continued to live on the farm; had two children: Bryon J. and Irwin
61.	Charlotte	married L. H. Hovey of Rochester, New York in June 1864
62.	Jehiel	married Fanny J. Lacey, 9 November 1869[14] had one daughter, Gertie
63.	Henrietta	married M. O. Robertson 10 April 1869; moved to Ashton, South Dakota; children: Ada, Clarence, Orval, Eddy, and Ray

28. **Adam Cool,** son of William Cool and Mary (last name unknown), baptized 9 May 1771; he married Abigail Green. Adam died 14 April 1834 in Mt. Herman.

Adam and Abigail (Green) Cool had the following children and probably more:

64.	William	born 7 August 1796; baptized 2 October 1896
65.	Maria	born 15 February 1803; baptized 23 June 1803

30. **Catherine Cool,** daughter of William and Mary Cool, born 28 March 1773 and died 10 May 1860. She is buried in the Swayze Cemetery. The Swayze Cemetery or Swayze Burial Ground is located near Hope in the county of Warren in New Jersey. Catherine married William Swayze before 1796.

Catherine Kuhl and William Swayze had the following children:

66.	Barnabas	born 13 April 1794; baptized 3 August 1794
67.	Mary	born 3 July 1797; baptized 26 September 1797
68.	Phoebe	born 12 November 1799

69.	John	born 28 October 1802; baptized 23 June 1803
70.	Elizabeth	born 26 October 1805; baptized 25 November 1805

55. John Friese Cool was born 27 August 1815/16 in Knowlton Township, Sussex County, New Jersey. His parents were Paul Cool and Susannah Raub. John was the ninth of ten children. He married 6 December 1845, in Blairstown, Warren County, New Jersey, Sarah Ann Snover who was born 14 April 1826 in Blairstown. She was the daughter of Samuel Snover Sr. and Delilah Brugler.

John and Sarah (Snover) Cool and four of their children arrived in Albion, Michigan, around 1854. John and Sarah purchased two hundred and four acres of raw and unimproved land, with a partially built brick house. This was to become the home of the Cools. Once completed, it became one of the "finest residences in this part of the country."[2]

John and Sarah Cool had the following children:

71.	Samuel Snover Cool	born 10 November 1846
72.	Dewitt Wilson Cool	born 4 February 1848, Knowlton Township, Sussex County, New Jersey; died 14 October 1854 (age 6), Albion, Michigan; buried in Riverside Cemetery, Albion, Michigan
73.	Crittenden Irelius Cool	born 8 May 1849
74.	John Austin Cool	born 7 October 1852, Knowlton Township, Sussex County, New Jersey; died 17 October 1854 (age 2), Albion, Michigan; buried in Riverside Cemetery, Albion, Michigan
75.	Leonard Dyer	born 8 July 1855
76.	Warren Jay Cool	born 20 January 1857/58
77.	Sarah Levantia Cool	born 8 October 1861

Mrs. Sarah Cool Dead
Passed Away Saturday Night At Her Home East of Albion, Aged 79

Mrs. Sarah A. Cool died about 1:30 o'clock Saturday night aged 79 years after having suffered from heart trouble for some years. Funeral services

will be held from the home, one and one-half miles southeast of the city at
1:30 o'clock tomorrow. Rev. W.H.B. Urch will be in charge on account of
the absence from the city Rev. W.T. Jaquess, the deceased having been a
long life member of the Presbyterian Church.

Sarah Ann Snover was born in Blairstown, N. J. April 14, 1825.
She was married to John C.* [sic] Cool Seven children came to bless their
home of whom five are living, those being Samuel S. of Huron, S. Dakota,
and Crittenden I., Leonard D., Warren J., and Sarah Lavantia, all of
Albion. Mr. Cool died in April 1863. The deceased was one of the oldest
residences of the vicinity, having lived on the same farm near Albion for
nearly 49 years. *(Sarah was married to John F. Cool.)

62. **Jehiel Cool** born ca. 1842 and died 28 January 1913 in Marshall, Michigan. He was the son of Jacob and Mary Cool. Jehiel married 9 November 1869 Fanny J. Lacey.[14] Jehiel and Fanny had one daughter, Gertie Cool.

This was reported in a Michigan newspaper on 28 January 1913:

Jehiel Cool Fell Dead at Marshall
Homer Man Who Talked With Several Friends Here in Morning
Found Dead in Bank

Jehiel Cool, of Homer, age 71 years, was found dead in the toilet of the
First National bank in Marshall about 11:45 o'clock Monday morning
by G. E. Grant, assistant cashier. Mr. Cool went to Marshall with his
daughter Monday morning to transact some business at the bank where
he had opened an account. He went into the bank and talked a short time
with Cashier Billings who was just going to dinner. Miss Cool went out to
do some shopping and on her return asked for her father. Assistant Cashier
Grant said he thought Mr. Cool had gone but said he would see He found
him lying on the floor where he had fallen some forty-five minutes before.
Dr. Shurtliff, Justice Cortright and Sheriff Fonda were notified but an
inquest was not deemed necessary.

The remains were removed to the undertaking rooms and were taken
to Homer in the afternoon. Mr. Cool had resided alone with his daughter
since the death of his wife about two weeks ago. He talked with several
friends here, while waiting for his car to the county seat, Monday morning
and seemed in his usual health.

71. **Samuel Snover Cool,** son of John F. Cool and Sarah Ann Snover, was born 10 November 1846, Knowlton Township, Sussex County, New Jersey,

and died 11 August 1926.[12] Sam married about 1873 Mary Elizabeth "Aunt Libby" Miller, daughter of George Miller and Catherine Young. According to the 1900 Federal Census, Elizabeth was born in May 1853 in Michigan. Sam's occupation was that of a crockery salesman.

Sam and Elizabeth left Albion, Michigan, and moved to Davenport, Iowa, sometime before 1874, where their oldest daughter, Catherine Evelyn was born. In fact, all three of their children were born in Davenport. Sometime after January 1881, probably in the spring or summer, the Cool family moved to Huron, South Dakota. In 1876, Samuel Cool was listed in the Finger's city directory and was living at 520 Rock Island. The house in which they live is still being occupied as of 3 January 2008. The 1890 Beadle County tax records show Samuel S. Cool, residing in section 13, Theresa Township, South Dakota.

> *Cool, Sam S., father of John and Kate. Kate married a Baptist minister Rev. Malley. Mrs. Cool was a daughter of John Miller who was prominent in Huron. A newspaper item reads, "In 1879 John B. Miller, father of Ed Miller, came with horse and wagon from Mitchell and filed on land known as Miller's tree claim-later occupied by Harold Young. Sam Cool adopted Bill Miller, brother of Rev. Chas. Miller, I have heard.*[13]

Huron, South Dakota, was plotted in May 1880. The first city directory was printed in 1883 and shows no one by the name of Cool. The next directory was printed in 1905, and that one showed a Cool. However, the 1890 Beadle County tax records show a B. Cool residing in Huron. It also showed Samuel S. Cool, residing in section 13, Theresa Township, South Dakota.

The Hawley's city directory of Davenport, Iowa, shows the following:

> 1875—Cool, Samuel S., traveling agent, res. 215 Rock Island

The Finger's city directory of Davenport, Iowa, shows this information:

> 1876—Cool, Sam, traveling salesman, with J. Lorenzen, res 520 Rock Island

The street directories of Huron show the following addresses:

> 1905—Cool, John, conductor C & N.-W., r 474 Dak Ave. (Res. Dakota Ave.)

1905—Cool S. S. Trav. Salesman, r 1023 Kan. (Res. 1023 Kansas
   Ave)

Death of S. S. Cool Early This Morning

*S. S. COOL, age 79 years, one of the oldest residents of Heron, died at
his home, 719 Wisconsin avenue south west, at 7:45 o'clock this morning.
Mr. COOL had been ill for several months.*

   *He is survived by his wife, three children, John S. Cool, of Redfield,
George Cool of Grand Junction, Colorado and Mrs. Cornelius Malley of
Detroit, Michigan, and five grandchildren.[12]*

Samuel S. and Elizabeth (Miller) Cool had the following children; all born
in Davenport, Iowa.

78.	Catherine Elizabeth	born 18 September 1874; married Cornelius Malley
79.	John Friese Cool	born 21 January 1878; married 14 December 1900, Huron, Adah Mable Iverson (born 21 November 1880, Capron, Illinois; died 9 November 1948, Redfield, South Dakota); died 23 September 1936, Huron, South Dakota
80.	George Miller Cool	born 3 January 1881, Davenport, Iowa

Cemetery records for Beadle County, South Dakota, show a Riverside
Cemetery with four Cools as of 23 November 1999.

(Note: The numbers inside the parentheses mean the block-lot-grave #.)

   Cool, Samuel S (1-83-2) 11 August 1926, age 79
   Cool, Elizabeth E, (1-83-1) 17 August 1936, age 83 Cool, John F.
      (2) (29-12-3) 23 September 1935, age 57
   Cool, Ada Mabel (Mrs. John) (29-12-2) age 66

79. John Friese Cool son of Samuel S. Cool and Elizabeth Miller, was born
   21 January 1878. John was named after his uncle—Samuel S. Cool's
   brother.

The following was written in the *Evening Huronite*, Huron, South Dakota
Tuesday, 24 September 1935, page 2, column 5:

"Rites Tomorrow for John Cool"
C & N Railroad Conductor—Stricken While
on Run, To Be Buried Tomorrow

A veteran employee of the Chicago & North Western railway, John F. Cool, Sr., of Redfield, died at an early hour Monday morning at a hospital in Brookings.

Mr. Cool, who formally lived in Huron, left Redfield a week ago on his regular run to Brookings as freight conductor. Upon his arrival in Brookings he complained of feeling ill and a doctor was called, who had him removed to a hospital about midnight that evening, September 16. Death followed a week's illness of pneumonia and heart disease.

Born January 21, 1878, at Davenport, Iowa, Mr. Cool was the son of Mr. & Mrs. S. S. Cool. When he was three and a half years old, his family moved to Huron and he lived here until 1912 when he moved to Redfield. He started work with the Chicago and North Western railway in 1898 and was made a conductor in 1901. His marriage to Mrs. Mabel Iverson of this city took place December 14, 1900, here in Huron.

Surviving him are the widow Mrs. Mabel Cool of Redfield, two daughters and one son, Miss Katherine Cool of Redfield, Miss Helen Cool of Brookings, and John F. Cool, Jr., of Marshall, Minnesota, his mother Mrs. Elizabeth Cool, 535 Kansas avenue southwest, Huron, one brother George Cool of Ventura, California, and a sister Mrs. Katherine Malley of Detroit, Michigan.

Mr. Cool was a member of the Brookings lodge No. 24 A. F. & A.M. and for twenty-five years he was a member of the Order of Railway Conductors.

The funeral service will be held at 2:30 O'clock tomorrow afternoon at Kinyon's chapel, with the reverend Alfred Trenerry of the First Baptist church officiating. Burial will be made in Riverside Cemetery. (Huron, SD)

Helen Cool, mentioned above, married Harold Burton Rae, a physician and living in Lurk, Wyoming. Helen was born 13 October 1908, Huron, South Dakota. Harold Rae was born 12 February 1900 and died 15 September 1960, Lusk, Wyoming. In checking the Social Security Death Index (SSDI), I found that Helen Rae died in May 1984 in Goshen, Wyoming. Dr. Rae had a son by a previous marriage, Thomas W. Rae.

80.   **George M. Cool,** son of Samuel S. and Elizabeth (Miller) Cool, married 5 September 1924, Grand Junction, Colorado, Elizabeth Tays who was born 22 September 1903, Chrystal, Colorado; daughter of Havelock E. and Helen F. (Phillips) Tays. George died 14 June 1964, Eureka, California.

George and Elizabeth A. (Tays) Cool had two children:

Alma Kathryn Cool	born 1 December 1926, Santa Paula, California; married 26 October 1944, Robert J. Anderson
Tays Douglas. Cool	born 7 June 1929, Santa Paula, California

73. **Crittenden I. Cool**, son of John F. Cool and Sarah Ann Snover, was born 8 May 1849, Blairstown, Warren County, New Jersey. He died 22 January 1933, Albion, Michigan, and is buried in Riverside Cemetery. His occupation was that of a farmer. Crit, as he was known, married Lydia Elizabeth Ackley 25 February 1880, Albion, Michigan. Lydia was born 3 August 1856, Fort Ann, New York. She was the daughter of Robert O. Ackley and Lydia Osborn (see Ackley chapter).

Crittenden and Lydia (Ackley) Cool had one child:

80.   LaVanchie Margaret Cool born 11 May 1882, Albion, Michigan LaVanchie married Charles Robert Looney. (See Chapter One for narrative.)

Albion Recorder dated 23 January 1933 made this report:

Crittenden I. Cool

Crittenden I. Cool, age 83 years old and a resident of Albion and vicinity for 79 years, died at his home at 903 South Superior Street about two o'clock Sunday morning. He had been failing in health for about two years. About three weeks ago he fell and suffered a hip fracture. Mr. Cool was born in Columbia, N. J. May 8, 1849. He came here when he was four years of age. For many years he was a farmer in South Albion. He retired about twenty years ago and moved to Albion.

He is survived by his widow Mrs. Lydia E. Cool, one daughter, Mrs. Charles Wark of Valparaiso, Ind., a brother L. D. Cool of Albion and twelve grandchildren.

Funeral services will be held Tuesday afternoon at 2:30 at the family residence with F. S. Goodrich officiating. Burial will be at Riverside cemetery. Friends are asked to omit flowers.

Albion Recorder dated 14 September 1943 gave this accounting:

Mrs. Crittenden Cool

Mrs. Lydia E. Cool, 87, widow of the late Crittenden I. Cool, died Monday evening at her home 900 South Superior Street, after a brief illness. She had been in failing health for several years. She was born 12 August 1856.

She is survived by 12 grandchildren and eight great grandchildren. Her only child a daughter, Mrs. Charles Wark of Valparaiso, Ind., having passed away seven years ago. Mr. Cool was a prominent South Albion farmer some 39 years ago. He died in 1933.

Funeral services will be held Thursday at 2:30 at the Marsh funeral home. Dr. D. G. Goodrich officiating: burial Riverside cemetery.

75. Leonard Dyer Cool, son of John F. Cool and Sarah Ann Snover, was born 8 July 1855, Albion, Calhoun County, Michigan. He died 16 July 1936 and is buried in Riverside Cemetery. Leonard married Georgia Sabrina Canniff 2 December 1891, Albion, Michigan. Georgia was born 12 September 1864 and died 26 February 1955 in Albion. They were farmers.

Leonard and Georgia (Canniff) Cool had three children, all females:

81.	Adah Cool	born 30 December 1893; married 26 December 1917 John Henry Hughes
82.	Edith Cool	born 8 April 1895, Albion Michigan; married 17 July 1914 Frank Densmore Cummings; died 10 December 1957, Albion
83.	Charlotte Cool	born 20 March 1900, Albion; married 11 January 1921 John Lynn Houck

The following was reported in the 23 July 1936 issue the *Albion Recorder.*

Leonard D. Cool

Leonard D. Cool was born July 8, 1855 on the old Cool farm south of Albion, the son of John Cool and Sarah Snover. During the pastorate of Dr. Oldham, he united with the Methodist church and has been a loyal member.

On Dec. 2, 1891 he was united in marriage to Georgia S. Canniff. To this union, three daughters were born; Adah, now Mrs. J. H. Hughes of Detroit; Edith, Mrs. F. D. Cummings of Chicago; and Charlotte, Mrs. J. Lynn Houck, Ypsilanti.

Mr. Cool was held in the highest esteem by all his many friends and neighbors. He was a friend to all and a most kind and devoted husband and father. In recent years his greatest interest and concern were his grandchildren.

The many friends of Mr. Cool will remember him as a man of outstanding business integrity. His memory will always be a source of inspiration to those who knew him because of the example he set in up righteous living and honesty in all his business dealings

He is survived by the widow, three daughters and one sister, Mrs. LaVanchie Welch, 11 grandchildren, Leonard, Cathleen and Jane Cummings; Phyllis, Charlotte and Jack Hughes; Nancy, Bobby, Rachael, Billy and Dorothy Houck.

The following was reported in the *Recorder* the day of Georgia's death: (26 February 1955)

Mrs. Georgia S. Cool

Mrs. Georgia S. Cool, 90, widow of Leonard D. Cool died at 6:15 a. m. today at the Brenner rest home near Parma. Mr. and Mrs. Cool resided at 602 Michigan Avenue at the time Mr. Cool died in July 1936. The body was taken to the Marsh Funeral Home, Further information will be available in Mondays Recorder.

The following was reported the Monday, following Georgia's death:

Mrs. Georgia S. Cool 90, widow of Leonard D. Cool, died Saturday morning at the Brenner Hill Top home in Parma.

Mrs. Cool was born Sept. 12, 1864, in Cannifton, Ontario, the daughter of Jones Canniff and Lucinda Warren Canniff. She had lived in Albion since 1889, when she came here to live with her sister, the late Mrs. Harry Harton, mother of William C. Harton. On Dec. 2, 1891 she was married to Leonard D. Cool at the Harton home on South Superior Street by Dr. R. W. Vallschoick. The couple made their home on a farm in South Albion.

Mrs. Cool was a member of the First Methodist church for more than 60 years, its W.S.C.S. and the adult Bible class, the South Albion Women's Club, and the.

Surviving Mrs. Cool are three daughters, Mrs. Adah M. Hughes of Highland Park, Mrs. F. D. (Edith) Cummings of Chicago Heights, Ill., and Mrs. J. Lynn (Charlotte) Houck of Ypsilanti, 11 grandchildren; 31 great grandchildren; and several nieces and nephews. Mrs. Cool died 26 February 1955 at their home 602 Michigan Avenue.

Services will be held Tuesday at 2:30 at the Marsh funeral home, Dr. John W. Tennant officiating; with burial in the family plot at Riverside cemetery.

76. **Warren Jay Cool**, son of John F. Cool and Sarah Ann Snover, was born 20 January 1858, Albion, Calhoun County, Michigan. He died 12 March 1913, Albion, Michigan, and was buried at Riverside Cemetery. Like his brothers, he was also a farmer. Warren married Catharine "Kate" Warner 8 May 1889, Albion, Michigan.

Kate liked to travel and wrote the following letter that was reprinted in the Journal of Albion Saturday October 8, 1988—eighty years after the trip referred to in her letter. The caption reads "Different Florida 80 Years Ago" "It's a far different Florida today than existed 80 years ago. Attesting to that fact is a letter furnished by Helen Kreger and written by Kate Cool, her great aunt. The letter appears below"

Saint Petersburg Florida 1908.
My Dear Ben, Mart Kings and Fred Minars!
I am going to write a letter to all of you. I will send it to Ben and he will pass it around for all of you to read. In consequence I will expect an answer from every one of you. When we left home the 14th of January, I had a hard cold and we were driven to the depot in a sleigh. There were eight in our company. The first night took a sleeper. There was some mistake about our tickets so Jay and Mr. Godfry were up all night. The mistake was ratified about six o'clock in the morning when we were awoke and found ourselves in Kentucky, that day was the last snow we saw, but mornings there would be a heavy frost. Our first stop was at Ashville, N.C. There we commenced to notice what a line was drawn between the whites and colored. They had separate coaches for the colored to ride in. Also separate waiting rooms at the depot. I never in all my life saw as many colored people as I have seen since we have been in the south. Kentucky and Tennessee are very rough, hilly, rocky, and everything else. I heard a person saw they did not see what the Lord ever made such a place for.

Ashville, N. C. is a very nice place with twenty-five thousand inhabitants. There we visited George Vanderbilt's estate of several thousand acres. We hired a rig with a colored driver. We drove to Biltmore, about two miles from Ashville. Mr. V. owns the whole city, there we got a permit and paid seventy cents and drove in on the estate. Mr. V. sent twelve men around over the world to select the most healthy and pretty place for his estate. They finally settled on this one. The mansion cost three million and he expended four million on the grounds. You may judge by that what a beautiful place it is.

In the mansion are 18 pianos and one pipe organ. We rode about eighteen miles over the estate. The next day we all climbed Sun-set Mountain, and went to the tower which had eighty-four steps. So you may know we had a fine view of the valley and all wrote our names on the top of the tower.

Our next stop was at Jacksonville, Florida. There you will find more colored than whites. One afternoon we went to the pier, an oh my it was fairly black. Why in some of those Negro settlements it would not be safe for a white person to go through at night. Sunday afternoon we rode in the observation auto car, saw many beautiful places. I forgot to tell you Mr. Vanderbilt stays about two months out of a year on his estate, then he brings a lot of his friends with him and they have a big time.

We arrived at St. Petersburg last Monday evening about nine o'clock and put up at the Belmont Hotel where we found good accommodations. Then the next thing was to rent a house and go to light housekeeping, so here we are located. If you should happen in this city go four blocks south from the First National bank, then the third house west, you will find us, 426-4ᵗʰ Ave. South. We rented a whole house for forty dollars a month that divided among four of us does not make it very expensive for any of us. There are four rooms and a half below and four rooms and a half above. Mr. and Mrs. Godfry and Mrs. Mrs. Brown occupy the rooms below and Mr. and Mrs. Rogers and Jay and I the upstairs. We use the same kitchen and dining room. In our kitchen we have a little cook stove about three feet square, a little cupboard with some dishes and a little table to wash dishes on. Our dining table is about four feet long and two feet wide but we are going to have a larger one tomorrow. Yes and we have a white oil cloth on it. The water we use is forced upstairs. In our front room is some new matting on the floor, an iron bedstead painted blue, a dresser with the mirror cracked in four pieces and a commode wash bowl and pitcher, a little stand, two chairs and a rocker, and our trunk, a little stove two feet long and a foot wide but we have no use for a stove. The weather is warm as a summer day in dear old Michigan. Yesterday p.m. was eighty-five in the shade, ladies on the street with thin white dresses on and bare headed, saw some children bare footed.

As I sit here writing I can look out of the window and see orange trees and the grapefruit and several rose bushes in full bloom. We have orange trees in our back yard.

(Thursday morning) Yesterday p.m. Jay and Mr. Godfry walked a mile and a half out in the country and bought a cord of wood, paid 2.25 per cord, had oranges, grapefruit and tangerines enough given them to last us two weeks. Kerosene is twenty cents a gallon. I like the water here. We expected to fine it perfectly awful. They say the water is boiled, filtered so the sulphur [sic] is taken out. It beats the water in Dakota all to pieces.

I awoke in the night, heard two cats fighting under our window, by the sound, think the fur flew rather high, when then had subsided the fire bell rung. After that we heard the frogs singing, so you see we had plenty of music, and when we awoke this morning the robins were singing.

St. Petersburg is a pretty place of four thousand inhabits and in winter it goes up to fifteen thousand. Main Street is paved and street cars run to the bay. There are some fine homes here.

Jay's rheumatism hurt him last night in his hip. He is thinking of taking salt water baths here. All the stores here seem so clean. The city has good sewerage. What fine gardens they have a few miles out of the city. We saw acres of lettuce, cabbage, beets, peas, onions and everything. Jay and I are going up town in a little while.

Hope this will find you all well. All write soon, direst.

The letter was signed Mrs. Jay Cool—426-4th Ave., South—St. Petersburg, Florida.

ALBION NEWS NOTES (13 March 1913)

Warren J. Cool who had been ill for several months died this morning at 1 o'clock, at his home on East Erie street. Death was thought to be due to pernicious anemia but as the attending physicians are in some doubt as to the cause a post mortem examination will be held. Warren J. Cool was born on the old Cool farm, about a mile and a half of South Albion, January 20, 1857. His parents were John F. and Sarah Cool. His father died when he was five years old and his mother died in 1906. He received his early education at the district and later attended Albion high school. He also attended Albion college, but did not graduate. In 1899 he was married to Miss Kate Warner. Mr. Cool spent his life on the Cool farm south of the city until last summer, at which time he moved into the city and took up his residence on East Erie street.

He is survived by his wife, three brothers and one sister: Leonard Cool, of Albion, Samuel Cool of Heron, S. D., Mrs. Lavansha [sic] Welch of Albion, and Crittenden Cool of Albion.

Catherine "Kate" I. Warner was born 20 June 1860, Hudson, Michigan. She was the daughter of I. Warner and C. Jennings, both of New York. Kate married 8 May 1899 Warren Jay Cool. Warren died 12 March 1913, and Kate died 20 December 1920. Warren is in crypt F-7 and Kate is in crypt F-8 at Riverside Cemetery in Albion.

Albion, Michigan, December 29, 1920
Mrs. Cool Leaves Estate of $34,000

In the probate court yesterday, the will of Mrs. Catherine I. Cool, who at her home on East Erie street, Dec. 20, committed suicide, by turning on the gas, was filed and a petition to admit it to probate. It was made Jan. 1, 1917, and the estate consists of $16,000 real and $18,000 personal.

There were eight heirs. Ben F. Warner, a brother was named executor. He is bequeathed the Murray farm during his life then it is then to go to a niece Effie May King. Should he not keep it in good condition she is to take it. Miss King is given the home at 218 East Erie street. Fred D. Minor is given $500. Delta Louise King Osborn is given the Dodge sedan and $2,000 to apply on buying a home. Grace Leola King Court of Homer gets $2,000 and Effie May King $3,000 All of the rest of the estate goes to Ben Warner. The strong box in the Albion State bank is not to be opened until all the heirs are present.

The following story was printed December 21, 1920, one day following the death of Catherine "Kate" I. Cool. The name of the newspaper is unknown but believed to be that of the *Recorder* in Albion.

Mrs. C. I. Cool Kills Herself By Taking Gas
Wealthy Resident of East Erie Street, in Spell of Melancholia Suicides
Leaves Unique Instructions Regarding Her Funeral

Leaving a note which contained unique instructions regarding her funeral services, which included a list of seven people she wished to attend them, Mrs. Catherine I. Cool, 218 East Erie Street took her own life yesterday afternoon during a spell of melancholia by turning on the gas in her bedroom on the second floor of her residence, all openings of which she had previously stuffed with cloth. She was sixty years and six months old and was considered one of the wealthiest women in this community.

The fact that a tragedy had occurred first became known about five-thirty, when Elvin Finkbeiner, a college student rooming in Mrs. Cool's home, smelled gas. He took a flashlight and made an investigation. When he opened

*the door of the bed-room occupied by Mrs. Cool a terrific cloud of gas poured
out and he rushed to the telephone and called the city police department.*

*City manager E. J. Mallory and Chief of Police Clyde Stoddard hurried
to the scene and it was the former who first entered the room and discovered
the dead body of Mrs. Cool. A physician was called at once but he stated after
an examination that she had been dead for about two hours. She was dressed
in her best clothes and had planned her demise very painstakingly.*

*The note left by Mrs. reads as follows: "Have a private funeral—just
Ben Warner, Martin King, Fred Miner, George Court, Richard Osborn,
Mr. Helrigle and Elvin Finkbeiner. No minister but Mr. Helrigle." Rev.
William Helrigle, also a college student whom she desired to preside at
her services, roomed at her residence, in addition to Mr. Finkbeiner. Ben
Warner is a brother residing at Marshall.*

*Justice P. D. Wright was called but considered an inquest unnecessary,
as it was a plain case of suicide.*

*Mrs. Cool was born June 20, 1860, in Hudson Mich. She was the
widow of Jay Cool, a prominent farmer in the vicinity [sic], who died seven
years ago. She had considerable means, it is said, and had been accustomed
to spending her winters in Florida, but had not gone this winter, for some
reason. She had not been seen Monday prior to the discovery of her body
but friends who had seen her Sunday state that she was then in excellent
spirits. She was subject to occasional periods of depression, however, and
it was during one of these that she ended her life.*

The complete funeral arrangements have not been announced.

77. **Sarah Levantia Cool**, daughter of John F. Cool and Sarah Ann Snover,
was born 5 October 1861, Albion, Michigan, and died 31 October 1948,
Albion, Michigan. She was buried in Riverside Cemetery. She first married
(1) Hugh W. Duncan 12 November 1884.[15] Sarah remarried 30 July 1889
Charles R. Welch.[15]

Enquirer & News, Battle Creek, Michigan
Tuesday, 2 November 1948, page 10

Mrs. Levantia Welch
ALBION

*Mrs. Levantia Welch, 87, died Sunday night in her home at 311 North
Mingo, following an extended illness. She was born in October 1860, in
the South Albion community and had been a resident of this area all her
life. For 40 years she had lived in the home in which her death occurred.
Her parents were the late John and Sarah Cool.*

Also preceding her in death were a daughter, Mrs. Mildred Griffin, and four brothers, Leonard, Crittenden, Samuel, and Jay Cool—all of Albion. Funeral services will be held at 2 p.m. Wednesday from the Marsh chapel by the Rev. H. J. Bryce and burial will be in the Riverside cemetery abbey. Sarah Levantia and Charles R. Welch had one child:

81.   **Adah Cool** was born 30 December 1893. The following letter was written by Adah (Cool) Hughes:

After graduation from Albion High (class of 1912) I attended Albion College and graduated in June 1916. I accepted a position in Stambaugh High School to teach English and History.

It was here that I met John H. Hughes who was working in an office for the summer for an iron mining company. He had another year to finish his course in dentistry at Ann Arbor—the University of Michigan.

We were married December 26, 1917 and Dr. Hughes opened a practice in Iron River, Michigan. Here we had our four children. The first child, Wayne Charles died at the age of six months. Our other children are Phyllis (Mrs. John H. Bennett) of Southfield, Michigan, Constance Jean (Mrs. Arthur Wright) Detroit, Michigan, and Charlotte, (Mrs. Robert Henry Tiderington) of Saginaw, Michigan.

We continued to live in Detroit until 1926, for Dr. Hughes wanted a larger place. He died here in 1943.

I continued to live in Detroit and in time took a position with Sears Roebuck where I spent 18 years and then retired, since then have lived in Saginaw, Michigan.

I have seen my children graduate from high school and four graduate from college. Have three little great grandsons and one great granddaughter to enjoy.

(Signed) Adah Cool Hughes

83.   **Charlotte Cool,** born 20 March 1900 in Albion, married 11 January 1921, John Lynn Houck.

This is from the *Journal of Albion* dated Sunday, August 13, 1988:

Burial Here Wednesday for Charlotte (Cool) Houck, 88

Burial was in Riverside cemetery Wednesday afternoon for Charlotte (Cool) Houck, 88 following the funeral services in Ypsilanti.

She died Saturday in St. Joseph Mercy hospital in Ann Arbor following a short illness.

Born in Albion, March 20, 1900, she was the daughter of Leonard D. and Georgia (Caniff) Cool. She graduated from Albion High school in 1918 and attended Albion College, where she was a member of the Alpha Chi Omega sorority. Jan. 11, 1921 she married Lynn Houck a high school and college classmate. He died May 10, 1986. For 15 years the couple resided in Nappanee, IN. They resided in Ypsilanti and Ann Arbor until 1980 when they established residence in the Glacier Hills Retirement home near Ypsilanti.

She was active in the Ypsilanti First United Methodist Church, was second president of the United Methodist Women, and was a member of the official board. She was on the board of trustees of the United Church Women and took part in many volunteer services, including the Girl Scouts Council, blood donor programs, Visiting Nurses board, and did volunteer work at Glacier Hills.

She is survived by five children, Nancy Mills, Marion, OH; Robert J. Houck, Ann Arbor; Rachael McCormick, West Bloomfield; William J. Houck, Lyons, NB; and Dorothy Borgerson, Long Creek, OR; 19 grandchildren, 26 great grandchildren and many nieces and nephews. She was preceded in death by two sisters, Adah Hughes and Edith Cummings.

Following the obituary for Charlotte, her daughter, Rachael McCormick, 20 August 1988, wrote this letter to the local newspaper, the *Journal of Albion*:

Letter of Appreciation

The recent story here of the death of Charlotte (Cool) Houck brought a letter of appreciation from her daughter Rachael H. McCormick of west Bloomfield which will be of interest to all who knew Charlotte and her husband, the late Lynn Houck. The letter follows:

Dear Rae:

You will never know what a comfort it was to read your beautiful tribute to my folks—Charlotte and Lynn Houck—in the August 13 issue of the Journal of Albion.

I have been working on our family history for three years now—and have been receiving the Journal for two. I love reading about the history and local events that took place over 100 years ago.

My Michigan roots all go back to the Albion area. My parents, all grandparents, six great grandparents and eight great-great-great grandparents are buried in either Riverside or Fairview cemetery in Homer.

The story behind my parents was a true love story. They knew each other all their lives and had been childhood sweethearts. They celebrated their 65th wedding anniversary before my dad passed away. Our home was always filled with love and caring. They taught me what it meant to be part of a family. I always knew they were there to give me love and understanding. They were truly a uniquely special couple and wonderful parents.

Thank you for your kind words. They were such a big part of my life that I will always miss them.

Sincerely,
Rachael (Houck) McCormack

84.   Mildred Iona Welch was born in the year1894 Battle Creek, Michigan, and died 15 April 1936, San Francisco, California. She graduated with the class of 1908 Albion High School and is listed as a teacher in the book, *A History of the Albion Public School.*[17]

The *San Francisco Chronicle* 16 April 1936, page 4, had this to report:

Woman Found Dead in Park
Matron Expires at Hospital from Poisoning

Found in a semi-conscious condition in Julius Kahn Playground, the Presidio, Mrs. Mildred Griffin, 45, 1600 Vallejo Street, died yesterday at Park Emergency Hospital. It was announced that she had taken poison.

Mrs. Griffin was said by acquaintances at her apartment house to have been in ill health. She was found lying in the shrubbery at the playground by T. S. Crawford, 126 Alta Street.

At the hospital, Mrs. Griffin refused at first to answer all queries as to her identity, but later told the authorities her name and address.

Mildred Iona Welch married Murray Andrew Griffin who died 17 December 1999, they and had two children:

Andrew Murray Griffin born 16 February 1922; married 1 January 1942 Bernice Skillman.

Elizabeth (Betty) Griffin born 25 November 1926; married 14 August 1946 Thomas Allen Bankhead

Notes

1. John Kuhl of Pittstown, New Jersey, (who researched the records from (a) *Knowlton Frame Church Baptismal Records*, (b) *Cemetery inscriptions from Knowlton Frame, Mt. Herman Swayze Cemetery*, and (c) *obit* of Anna Raub, September 9, 1854, Warren Journal

2. *Biographical Review of Calhoun County, Michigan*, Hobart & Mather of Chicago, 1904, page 566.

3. Xerox copy of traced names, traced by Helen Kinney and found in the family Bible of Mable Grover

4. William A. Lane, M. D. *Homer and its Pioneers and Its Businessmen of Today*, printed 1888, in Homer, Michigan.

5. William MacKellar Kern, *Original Raub Genealogy* 1934 *http://raub-and-more.com/kern.html*

6. Calendar of WillsC1751-1760, New Jersey.

7. John W. Kuhl, genealogist, member of the Hunterdon County Historical Society and descendent of Crest Kuhl

8. Henry Race, M. D. *The Jerseyman* Vol. 2, No.1, Flemington, N.J. March 1803

9. *Hunterdon Historical Newsletter* Vol 12, No. 2, Spring 1976.

10. From a "Service of Reception and Installation", Sunday November 22, 1981.

11. Henry Z. Jones Jr., *More Palatine Families* Some Immigrants to the Middle Colonies 1717-1776 and their European Origins, Universal City, California 1991

12. Obituary, The Evening Huronite, Wednesday, August 11, 1926, p. 8, column 5.

13. Mildred McEwen Jones, *A Historical Account of Beadle County South Dakota* (no date)

14. Jack and Marianne Dibean, "list of Michigan Marriages."

15. Calhoun County, Michigan "Marriage Index."

16. Hunterdon will number 793J-(very poor condition).

17. Frank Passic, *A History of the Albion Public Schools* 1991, E. Weil Publishing
      Services, Albion, Michigan

FIVE

John Burbank

(See Appendix D)

———————◆◆◆———————

The Burbank name has been spelled several ways, some of which being: *Borebancke, Burbanck, Bourbank, Bowerbank, Bowbank, and Burbank.* To say that it is of English origin might be true, but it has also been suggested that it might be of German or the Netherlands origin. According to George Burbank Sedgley,[1] "The origin of the name 'Burbank' is not found after considerable research in England. A letter from the College of Arms, London, England, reads: In my opinion the surname Burbank is the same as that of Bowerbank. We have a pedigree of a family of Bowerbanks living in Cumberland. It shows John Bowerbank of Lamonby, who was born about 1670, and his descendants. The family is entitled to Arms and Crest. A member of this family married Captain Dartiquenave, an illegitimate son of Charles II." The (alleged) statement from the College of Arms regarding Bowerbank heraldry written prior to the book by George Burbank Sedgley[1] was contradicted in another alleged letter from the college to James W. Burbank stating that although the Bowerbank arms are mentioned in various books, "they do not appear in our records and so are not authentic." Another source says that they had written to the college and received a letter denying the first letter. This is the type of information that one must steer clear of, so rather than repeat what might be a deliberate attempt to corrupt an otherwise proven line of genealogy, I will change courses.

Our immigrant ancestor, John Burbank left little with which to trace our ancestry. We may never know from where he came or who his parents were. There are just a few things that we can say for certain about John (1). We are not sure when John arrived in America; but in December 1638, Rev. Ezekiel Rogers, with about twenty families, spent the winter in Salem, Massachusetts. Rogers and his party were looking for a place to settle and decided on land between Ipswich and Newbury. By the summer of 1639, forty more families had joined the first group, bringing the total families to fifty-nine. However, it is not known of which group John Burbank belonged. This land, which was to be their new home, was purchased at a price of £800. At first, the new settlement was known as Mr. Rogers's Plantation but later changed to Rowley, probably named after Rowley, Yorkshire, England.

John was made a freeman on 13 May 1640. In 1643, the land was surveyed and each freeman or family was granted one and a half acres of land on which to build their house. Those who could afford to contribute toward the original purchase price of £800 were rewarded with lots greater than one and one-half acres.

> *To John Burbanke one Lott containinge an Acree and an halfe bounded on the South side by Thomas Sumners house Lott: part of it lyinge on the West side, and part of it on the East side of the street.*[1]

This lot was to be John's "home lotte" and was located on Bradford Street, with the town brook running along the back of the east side portion. In the book *The Early Records of the Town of Rowley, Massachusetts, 1639-1672*, there are at least ten entries relating to land granted to John; some were used as pasture and the others for farming.[1]

John (1) Burbank, born 1611, married before 1640 in Rowley, Massachusetts, Ann (Jordan) who was born ca. 1619. Ann died ca. 1641/2. John (1) married (2) before 1644 in Rowley, Massachusetts, Jemima (last name unknown). Jemima died on 24 March 1692/3.

At the general town meeting held on 7 October 1661, John was elected as one of the overseers for the year 1661-1662. At the town meeting on 8 January 1663, John was again appointed as one of two overseers of the west end of town. In 1663, an ordinance pertaining to trees within "a mile and one halfe" of town either "fall or lop" and anyone charged with violating this ordinance was fined ten shillings. John Burbank, along with three other men, was appointed to execute this order. In 1671, John, again, was appointed as the overseer of the west end of town.

One of the main reasons John's ancestry cannot be traced is all of the church records were kept in Rogers's dwelling. And on the night of his third marriage, 16 July 1651, his house burned to the ground; and there goes some of our history.

John's will was written on 5 April 1681 and was proved on 10 April 1683.[1] His exact date of death is not known. John is buried in Rowley, Massachusetts.

The Will of John Burbank (1) of
Rowley, Essex County, New England

(Note: The will is as copied from pages eight and nine of ref [a] without any changes or corrections.)

I being att this day aged and Decriped in body thought having Mercy of Perfect Memory & understanding, Knowing how fraile my Life is and not Knowing the Day of my Desolutions, that my House may be so far sett in Order & trouble as much as in me lieth, prevented after my departure I therefore appoynt this to be my Last will. My soule I committ into the hands of him that gave it and my body to be interred by decent buriall in hope of a blessed Ressureection through the Lord Jesus Christ.

As to my outward estate I dispose of it in a Manner following:

To my beloved wife Gemima, I give half my dwelling house & half my Lands throughout to be at her dispose during her natural life. Also I give her all my household stuff bedding utensils & necessary things in the house for her natural life and what of them she hath not occasion to Dispose of for her comfortable Maintenance & livelyhood after her decease to my son Caleb, also I give her one cow and the keeping of her Winter & Summer, also convenient fire wood shall yearly be provided for her during her Naturall Life by my Executor. Also, I give her the third part of the fruit of the orchard yearly, also I give her the keeping of a pig or swine yearly during her life.

To my son John Burbank I give the sum of forty shillings in Cattle to be paid within one year after my Decease if he come and Receive it in Rowley the reason I now give him no more is because I have given him what I thought was sufficient according to my ability in Cattle and Household stuff & Village Land, all I judge to be worth about three score pounds which when I gave it him it was accepted by him as his full portion and that in presence of Capt. Brocklebank and his wife before whom he gave it under his hand that he would Desire no more of what I have Left. To his son Timothy my grandchild who lieth with Capt. Saltonstall after he cometh to the age of twenty-one years I give a beast of about three pounds price.

To my Daughter Lydia having given her Merrimack Land or my Land at Bradford and other necessaries I hereby Confirm it to her Husband and her and their Children Also I give her ten pounds to be paid in Rowley within one year after my Wife he decease) in cattle.

To my son Caleb I give the half of my Dwelling and Barn and the other half of all my Lands & Meadows that is to say Lands Divided or not Divided, or Layd out within the bounds of Rowley and the other half given to his Mother for Life to be to him & his Heirs after her Decease and all my Moveables not given to my Wife.

My will is that my son Caleb Burbank be my sole Executor and that he pay all Debts and Legacys given in my Will as an Explanation of what I have given my wife. My will is that my Executor provide all comfortable necessaries for my beloved wife During her Natural Life both for Health and sickness according as my overseers shall think and Judge convenient.

If my son or those that survive him provide not according to her need and expectation my will is, and that which I desire that my loving friends Daniel Wycombe & Nehemiah Jewett be my overseers to see that my will be performed and especially that my wife be well provided for. For as she may need and he thus providing according to her need then the Lands given her to be free to my son Caleb as the other Lands given him.

Signed Sealed and Declared to be his Last Will and Testament the fifth Day of April Anno Domini: 1681

In Presence of Witness: *his mark*
Nehemiah Jewett   *John   X   Burbank*
Danl. Wickam
Att Court at Ipswich 10th of April 1683
Attest Daniel Appleton Reg.

John (1) and Ann Burbank had two children:

1.	John (2) Burbank	born about 1640
2.	Timothy Burbank	born 18 March 1641; buried 14 July 1660

John (1) and Gemima/Jemima Burbank had three children:

3.	Lydia Burbank	born 7 February 1644; married Abraham Foster (she was his second wife); died 3 March 1697/8
4.	Caleb Burbank	born 17 March 1646
5.	Mary Burbank	born 16 March 1655; buried 12 July 1660

In several instances, when reviewing the official records, it was impossible to tell the difference between John (1) and John (2); but most of the court records of which there were many, belonged to John (2). It appeared that of the two, only John (2) could write his name, while John (1) signed with an *X*, as he did in his will, that is on file in Rowley, Massachusetts.

In John's (1) will, Timothy, son of John (2), is mentioned as living in the home of Captain Saltonstall which might indicate that John (2) may not have been as prosperous in the earlier years as he was in later years. It, of course, could also mean that Timothy was living with Captain Saltonstall as an apprentice, which was a custom for that period. An apprenticeship allowed the child to learn a trade. The child usually lived with the family and received an education in the chosen field. He was also schooled in the art of reading, writing, and arithmetic. In exchange for this, the child was expected to perform chores around the house. Around the age of twenty-one, he would be finished with his apprenticeship and given a new suit and sent on his way. At the start of this apprenticeship, an agreement was customary—where the conditions would be spelled out.

On 12 October 1670, John Pynchon of Springfield was granted permission by the General Court of Massachusetts Bay Colony to settle Stoney Brooke Plantation on land purchased by Pynchon from the Indians. At that time, this land was a part of the Massachusetts Bay Colony. The grant stipulated that a minimum of twenty families be settled within a period of five years and that these families would be able to support a minister and his family.[7] In January the following year, John Pynchon and several other members of his party put together basic guidelines for the establishment of this new town. They diagramed how the town would be laid out with the main artery being High Street, which, by the way, is still the main road today. They selected a place for the meetinghouse to be built, and they granted land to the original settlers to build their homes. Remember, these settlers came from England and accustomed to a more structured way of life. There was a "class structure" that they were accustomed to, "people of quality" and the "common man." The title "gentleman" was a term used with much distinction and identified a person whose lifestyle was not that of a manual-labor type of lifestyle. The "gentleman" was a step above that of a "goodman" or a "yeoman," referring to the lower-class shopkeeper and the farmer. It was this thinking that established the amount of land each family received. The highest classes were the petitioners, followed by the men of estates, "those who were able to layout considerable sums to the advantage of ye place." The third class was the good, honest planters, though of lesser estates.[4] There was a constant struggle just to survive. The unfriendly Indians had to be dealt with, and there were wild animals to be on the lookout for. Then to add to their problems, there were the bitter cold winter months.

The leaders of the settlement set rigid regulations that settlers had to abide by. Prices were set for goods in order that those without money had something with which to barter. Rye, wheat, peas, corn, and other food items were given a set price per bushel; and these items were to be accepted as money to pay for a service or for items needed by the family. Fencing around the home lot had to be built to certain specifications in order to achieve its purpose, which was not decorative in nature but rather to keep wild animals away from the house. Other type of fencing was mandatory and had to adhere to strict specifications in order that the livestock would be kept from roaming into town.

Houses had to be built, but keep in mind that the families were from a fairly sophisticated environment; thus they were accustomed to houses being built from wood planks and not logs as one might imagine. These houses were made from planks and clapboard, some of which still stand today.

By the end of 1674, thirty-seven families were living in Suffield; but in 1675, they were forced to flee to Springfield during King Philip's War. Houses and mills were burned to the ground. The settlers returned in 1676 and resumed building their town. Suffield remained a Massachusetts town until 1749 when it became a part of Connecticut. Suffield was, for most of its history, primarily a small agriculturally based town. Tobacco put Suffield on the map economically. As in so many Connecticut valley towns, tobacco was an important crop almost right from the beginning. It was the primary crop in the 1800s and through much of the 1900s. The first cigar factory in the United States was built here in 1810.

1. **John (2)**, born in 1640 in Rowley, Massachusetts, married on (1) 15 October 1663 in Newbury, Massachusetts, Susannah who was the daughter of Nathaniel and Susannah (Jordan) Merrill. John and Susannah lived in Newbury, Rowley, and Haverhill, Massachusetts, but in 1680, moved to Suffield.

Their sons John (3) and Ebenezer were afterward prominent men in the Suffield town affairs. John (2) appears several times in the Suffield records prior to 1680,[a] but he did not live there for any length of time until 1680. On 17 July 1674, he was allotted fifty acres of land in Suffield. It appears from all records that John was an energetic, well-to-do prominent citizen and large landholder. Susannah (Merrill) Burbank died on 10 October 1690 at Suffield.

John (2) and Susannah Burbank had the following children:

6.	Mary Burbank	born 24 June 1666
7.	Timothy Burbank	born 30 May 1668 at Haverhill, Massachusetts

8. John (3) Burbank   born August 1670
9. Ebenezer Burbank   born 4 March 1673/4

6. **Mary Burbank,** born on 24 June 1666 in Haverhill, Massachusetts, married on (1) 2 December 1685 in Springfield, Massachusetts, Lazarus Miller (1655-1697).

Lazarus and Mary (Burbank) Miller had the following children:

6a. **Obadiah Miller** born 1 March 1687, Springfield, Massachusetts; she died 14 July 1697, Springfield.[16]

6b. **John Miller** born 18 October 1688, Springfield.[16]

6c. **Noah Miller** born 2 December 1691; he died 27 July 1697, Springfield.[16]

6d. **Nathaniel Miller** born 6 December 1693; he married Rebecca Prichard.[16]

6e. **Martha Miller** born 11 March 1695, Springfield; she died before 16 June 1697.[16]

6f. **Martha Miller** (twin) born 16 June 1697, Springfield.[16]

6g. **Mary Miller** (twin) born 16 June 1697, Springfield.[16]

6. **Mary (Burbank) Miller** married (2) in 1702, William Mackeranney (McCranney); they did not have children. Mary (Burbank) (Miller) Mackeranney (McCranney) married (3) in 1734 James Sexton who was born in 1667 [15] He died 12 December 1741, Westfield, Massachusetts. He was the son of George and Katherine Sexton. There are no records of children of this marriage.[16]

7. **Timothy Burbank,** born 30 May 1668, Haverhill, Massachusetts; married 3 July 1695, Salem, Massachusetts, Rebecca Darling. They later lived in Boston.[15]

8. **John (3) Burbank,** born August 1670, Haverhill; died in 1729. He was the son of John Burbank (2) and Susannah Merrill. He married 21 December 1699, Suffield, Connecticut, Mary Granger who was the daughter of Launcelot Granger and Joanna Adams. Mary Granger, born in Newbury, Massachusetts, died in Suffield, Connecticut. John (3) and Mary lived in Suffield until his death 25 March 1729 at the age of fifty-eight. While living in Suffield, John was town treasurer, selectman, and several other important offices of the township. John Burbank (3) and Launcelot Granger were among the names of voters of the town of Suffield and were allowed to vote on all town affairs (20 March 1681-82). Not all men were allowed to vote. Mary (Granger) (Burbank) married John Austin,

her second husband 3 July 1734. John Austin was born 22 October 1672 and was the son of Captain Anthony Austin. John died 18 May 1737.[15]

John (3) and Mary (Granger) Burbank had the following children:

11.	John (4) Burbank	born 18 February 1701; died 12 March 1793
12.	Abraham Burbank	born 8 September 1703, Suffield, Connecticut
13.	Joanna Burbank	born 19 August 1705
14.	Mary Burbank	born 26 May 1707
15.	Timothy Burbank	born 1 August 1709
16.	Caleb Burbank	born 21 December 1712; died 16 August 1716
17.	Lois Burbank	born 15 January 1714/15; married 24 March 1734 to Richard (born 31 March 1708, Windsor, Connecticut, son of Atherton and Mary Mather)

9. **Ebenezer Burbank**, born 14 March 1673/74, Haverhill, Massachusetts, married 9 October 1699, Suffield, Connecticut, Rebecca (Taylor) Prichard (widow of William Prichard).

John (2) (continued) following the death of Susannah, John (2) married Sarah (Hunt) who was the widow of John Scone of Westfield whom she married in 1675. John (2) and Sarah were married 15 July 1692 in Springfield, Massachusetts. Sarah was the daughter of Elisha Hunt. She died 19 August 1692. They had no children. [15]

John (2) married for the third time, 9 January 1693, Springfield, Massachusetts, Mehitable (Barlett) Sanders who was the widow of George Sanders (Saunders of Windsor). Mehitable died 24 February 1727/8. During the last year or two of John's (2) life, he began to lose his mind, which was the same sickness of his half brother Caleb, only at a younger age. John (2) Burbank died 1 June 1709 and is buried in Suffield, Connecticut.

John (2) and Mehitable (Barlett) (Sanders) Burbank had one child:

10.	Susanna Burbank	born 23 November 1695

10. **Susanna Burbank** was born on 23 November 1695 in Suffield. She married in 1726 Ebenezer Philips, son of Isaac and grandson of George Philips. She died on 19 December 1752 in Westfield, Massachusetts.

11. **John (4) Burbank** son of John (3) and Mary (Granger) Burbank was born 18 February 1701 and died 12 March 1793 in Suffield, Connecticut.[17] He was married to Rachael Austin.

13. **Joanna Burbank,** daughter of John (3) and Mary (Granger) Burbank, was born 19 August 1705, Suffield; married (1) John Rowe. Following Joanna's death, John married (2) Lydia Hanchett who was born 14 September 1714, Suffield. This was Lydia's second marriage, her first being to Isaac Remington.

12. **Abraham Burbank,** son of John (3) and Mary (Granger) Burbank, was born 8 September 1703, Suffield. Abraham married 31 January 1728 Mehitable (2), daughter of Nathaniel and Mehitable (1) (Partridge) Dwight. Mehitable (2) (Dwight) Burbank was born 5 November 1705, Northampton, Massachusetts. According to a book by George Burbank Sedgley, both Mehitable and Abraham died on 20 November 1767;[1] however, only Abraham's death was recorded in Vital Records of Suffield and Hartford. This joint death was first reported in the late 1800's in volume 1 of the New England Historical and Genealogical Register (NEHGR), and it looks as though George Burbank Sedgley relied on this information for his book.[1] In 2001, I received a letter from the assistant town clerk of Suffield. It stated that after a thorough review of the old records, neither the date of Mehitable's death. Abraham and Mehitable had several children (see below) one of which was Anne who was born 20 August 1744. I mention this because in the book by George Sedgley Burbank, Anne married 20 November 1767 the same day her mother and father died. In the letter mentioned above, her marriage record could not be found. In the probate records of Captain Abraham Burbank, there is mention of Mehitable being a widow and if that is the case, then the information in Sedgley book is incorrect. Where the information originally came from will probably remain a mystery.

In October 2000, while searching the Burbank file during a visit to the library at Suffield, I found and copied a six-page typed report on some of the history of the Phelps-Hatheway House, which was built for Abraham and Mehitable Burbank.

(Note: Corrections in spelling and spacing have not been made to this report.)

In the year 1742, Captain Abraham Burbank, tanner by trade, moved into his new house. He had bought his home lot in 1735 and so the house may have been seven years abuilding. It was a fine house and probably the earliest (with the exception of the Josiah King House) open today of the old houses now standing on Suffield's High (or Main) Street. No diaries or accounts exist that might give us a clue to the builder of the house, although it might have been

Captain Asaph Leavitt, "house carpenter." At any rate the builder was a man of more than ordinary ability, as it is shown by the fine paneling, moldings and pilasters with their carved roses. Here Burbank lived until his death. We can picture him from his inventory a stately gentleman wearing a white wig, black velvet waistcoat and "inelasting" breeches and blue coat. Perhaps he often wore his silver hilted sword. In the house, among other things, were tables, cases of drawers, sway-back chairs, much pewter, silver teaspoons, a punch bowl, decanters and wine glasses, brass candlesticks, and a surveyor's compass.

In 1764, Abraham sold to his son, Shem, a lot south of Abraham's home-lot, which is now the south garden of the Hatheway House. Here had stood a very ancient house and two shops, one of which was a blacksmith shop. The old house was probably replaced by 1764, by a smaller new one, perhaps built by Dr. Pelatiah Bliss about 1747. In reviewing the probate records of Abraham, the index indicates that a will was included, however, the will could not be found. Shem, being the oldest son, would have and did inherit the house. It was either Shem, or Oliver Phelps who later moved and attached the smaller house (or part of it) onto his the newer house, forming the present south ell. It is different in construction from the main house, but is definitely old and shows some signs of interior change.

The report goes on to say this:

We know very little of Shem Burbank, except that he was a graduate of Yale, captain of the Trainband, as his father had been before him, and he had a large family. In 1788, he sold his house, the now large farm to Oliver Phelps of Granville, Massachusetts He and his family moved up into the hills and occupied the house Phelps had vacated.

The rest of the report talks about the various changes that took place on and in the house. The six-page report was typed on an old typewriter and was neither dated nor signed.

Abraham owned several pieces of property in Suffield and was considered a very large landholder. One such partial of land was used to build his home, which still stands today. For its time, this home was a fine colonial two-story, gabled-roof structure. There are several accountings as to when Abraham began building his home. Some say 1735 while other say 1736. One such accounting says he moved into his new home in 1742, indicating that it took six to seven years to build. If we are to accept 1742 as the time he and Mehitable (2) moved into their new home, Anne would have been the only child born in the new house. However, all of the children were too young to be on their own, so the house had to be large enough to accommodate all seven children.

When Abraham died, his estate was inventoried[8] and consisted of about 1,058 acres in Massachusetts and about 282 acres in Connecticut. He had an inventory of cattle—some for reproducing and others for the dining room table. He also was one-fourth owner of a grist mill in Massachusetts. Abraham's net estate was valued at about £3,970 and was considered a large estate for that period and for one living in a colonial town. Included in Abraham's estate were many "accounts payable" and many "accounts receivable" both to and from those living in Suffield and surrounding towns. Shem, Abraham's son, was appointed executor of his estate and inherited the house where he, Ann, and their children lived until 1788. The house was sold to Oliver Phelps. Shem and his family moved to Granville, Massachusetts, and lived in a house once owned by Phelps.

Due to bad investments in land speculations, in 1806, Oliver Phelps was forced into foreclosure by the State of Connecticut, which held the mortgage at that time. Shortly after the foreclosure, Asahel Hatheway Sr., a Suffield resident and a successful merchant in New York, purchased the house from the state; and again, the house was the center of good living. Between Asahel Hatheway Sr. and his son, Asahel Hatheway Jr., several additions were made; but still, the original house was kept intact. For a while, a portion of the house was used as a law office by Henry, son of Asahel Hatheway Jr.

Ms. Louise, as she was known, the daughter of Asahel Hatheway Jr., was mistress of this place; and her stately dignity and gracious but firm refusal to open her home to any but a few intimate friends during her life left an air of mystery to the old mansion. Ms. Louise died in 1910, and many of the treasures and heirlooms are now cherished in the Wadsworth Athenaeum in Hartford.

The final owners of the house were Sumner F. Fuller and his family. Upon Sumner's death, the house was inherited by his three nieces: Mrs. Elizabeth Fuller Carter of Suffield, Mrs. Laurene Fuller Vinette of White Plains, New York, and Mrs. Claudine Fuller Ackroyd of Park Ridge, New Jersey.

According to a 7 May 1962 article published in a local newspaper (possibly the *Times*), "The Burbank, Phelps, Hatheway house is to become the property of the Antiquarian and Landmarks Society, Inc. of Connecticut." The article goes on to say that "the Society has announced that the structure thus will be preserved posterity as a memorial to its former owner, the late Sumner F. Fuller in accordance with the wishes of his three nieces."

In addition to Abraham being a tanner by trade, he was also a captain and the commanding officer in the militia, or what was known as the Trainband of Suffield. The following is from a copy of the orders, issued upon the death of Captain Burbank—directing the acting commanding officer to hold elections, appointing a new commanding officer.

(Note: Neither corrections nor spelling has been made.)

To Daniel Austin, Lieutenant and present commanding officer of the first Company of Trainband in the town of Suffield, in the first Regiment in the Colony of Connecticut.

GreetingsB

The above said military company being now destitute of a Captain occasioned by the Removal of their late Captain Abraham Burbank, by Death.

You are therefore hereby ordered and directed having first notified the soldiers and all other persons within the limits of said company who have right by law to vote in the choice of commission officers to meet for that purpose at such time and place as you shall appoint to lead the said company to the choice of a captain in the room and head of him the said Captain Burbank deceased and likewise to the choice of such of officer or officers, as may be then formed requested for said company and to make return of your doings in performance of the Warrant to the General Assembly of the Colony at this in Hartford on the second Thursday of May next.

Dated at Hartford this 25th Day of April in the 8th year of the Reign of his Majesty George the 3 King of Great Brittan Anno Dom: 1768

(Signed) George Wyllys [sic] Colonel

In 1760, George III became the King of England upon the death of his grandfather, George II.

Abraham and Mehitable (Dwight) Burbank had the following children:

18.	Mehitable Burbank	born 28 July 1729; married 11 June 1752, Suffield, Ebenezer Ripley.[18]
19.	Abiah Burbank	born 5 January 1731/2, Suffield
20.	Eleanor Burbank	born 4 April 1734
21.	Shem Burbank	born 21 May 1736; married Anne Fitch of Lebanon, Connecticut, 29 December 1761
22.	Abraham (2) Burbank	born 24 February 1738/9
23.	Ruth Burbank	born 26 August 1741
24.	Anne Burbank	born 20 August 1744; died 27 December 1767; married a "Mr. Burbank" 20 November 1767.

Both Shem and Abraham (2) attended Yale College,[5] Shem in 1758-1762 and Abraham (2) who received his BA in 1759.

22. **Abraham Burbank (2),**[5,6] younger son of Captain Abraham and Mehitable
     (Dwight) Burbank of Suffield, was born in that town 24 February 1738/39.
     He spent his life in West Springfield, Massachusetts. and received a
     commission of justice of the peace in June 1772.

He died in West Springfield on 8 August 1808 in his seventieth year, leaving
an estate valued at $16,275.

He married in 1764 Bethiah, third daughter of the Hon. John and Mary
(Cotton) Cushing of Scituate, Massachusetts. Bethiah died 24 December 1768
at the age of twenty-nine

Abraham (2) second marriage was 26 December 1770, to Sarah, youngest
daughter of Colonel Seth and Mary (Hunt) Pomeroy of Northampton,
Massachusetts. Sarah died in December 1808 at the age of sixty-five. Two sons
and two daughters survived him.

21. **Shem Burbank,** elder son of Captain Abraham and Mehitable (Dwight)
     Burbank and even though he is listed as both Shem or Thomas in several
     records, he was mostly known as Shem. Like his father, Shem was a
     merchant in Suffield. He attended Yale College and received his B A
     in 1758 and his M A in 1762. The following is from the Biographical
     Sketches of the Graduates of Yale College. [7]

> *Shem Burbank, fourth child and elder son of Captain Abraham Burbank,*
> *a wealthy resident of Suffield, then in Massachusetts and grandson of*
> *John and Mary (Granger) Burbank, was born on May 21, 1736. His*
> *mother was Mehitable, daughter of Nathaniel and Mehitable (Partridge)*
> *Dwight, of Northampton, Massachusetts. He was thus a first cousin of*
> *Major Timothy Dwight (Y. C. 1744). A brother was graduated here*
> *in 1759.*
>
> *He became a merchant, like his father, in his native town, which had*
> *been transferred to Connecticut in 1749; and was also locally distinguished*
> *for the pains he took in cultivating fine varieties of fruits. He was appointed*
> *a Lieutenant in the Militia in May 1771, and Captain in October 1774,*
> *but does not appear to have served in the Revolutionary struggle.*
>
> *He removed at a later date to Granville, in Massachusetts, a little*
> *distance northwest from Suffield, where he died, suddenly, during the*
> *night of January 31, 1800, in his 64th year. The notice of his death in*
> *the papers of the day appended the significant couplet.*
>
> *Go, stranger, and in distant climate tell,*
> *The noble mind, the friend of man, has fell.*

Shem married 29 December 1761[10] in Lebanon, Connecticut, Anna Fitch who survived him. Anna was the daughter of Joseph Fitch of Lebanon. Their children were six sons and three daughters. His estate was inventoried at $2,000 but proved to be insolvent.

From the *Public Records of the Colony of Connecticut, 1636-1776*, vol. 13, May 1771, page 430 is this information:

> [12] *This Assembly do establish Shem Burbanks to be Lieutenant of the first company trainband in the town of Suffield.*

This is from vol. 14, October 1772, page 58:

> *Upon the memorial of Gideon Granger, of Suffield in the county of Hartford, shewing* [sic] *to this Assembly that he has lately had his dwelling-house destroyed by fire in which were consumed large numbers of notes and executions he had of other persons to collect, all his own notes, books of account and other papers, whereby he conceives the whole of said notes, debts and other papers &c. may be wholly lost, unless some relief be devised &c.; praying that a committee may be appointed with authority and power to convene before them such person or persons as the memorialist* [sic] *shall request, who were indebted to the memorialist* [sic] *by any way or means, or had any dealings with him, or that were indebted on any of the notes &c. he had in his hands to collect, and being so convened to enquire and examine into the matters which shall then be laid before them relative to any of the notes and book-debts &c. mentioned in said memorial, by such way and manner as this Assembly shall direct, as per memorial on file: Resolved by this Assembly, that Messrs, Aaron Hitchcock, Shem Burbank and David Todd, all of Suffield, in the county of Hartford, be appointed, and they are hereby appointed, a committee, with full power and authority to convene before them, at such time and place as they shall appoint, such person or persons as the said Gideon Granger shall request, who were indebted to him by notes, bonds, book or otherwise, or with whom he had any dealings, and also any person or persons that were indebted on any note or execution &c. he had of other persons in his hands to collect, and being so convened to proceed to enquire and examine into the matters which may then be laid before them relating to any of the notes, bonds, executions &c. aforesaid, by the oaths of the parties or by any other evidence, ways or means they shall think fit whereby truth may be had, and to ascertain as far as may be what may be due and owing from any person or persons to the said Gideon on notes or otherwise, on what*

was due and owing on any notes &c. he had in his hands to collect, and report thereof make to the General Assembly to be held at Hartford in May next or some future Assembly.

Vol. 14, October 1774, page 332 provides this information:

This Assembly do establish Shem Burbank to be Captain of the first company or trainband in the town of Suffield.

And vol. 14, October 1774, page 374 gives this information:

Upon the memorial of Daniel Austin, of Suffield in the county of Hartford, shewing [sic] to this Assembly that on the evening of the ninth of May, A. D. 1774, he had his dwelling-house consumed by fire and therein a large number of receipts books of account and a number of deeds of several pieces of land, all unrecorded, were likewise consumed, and that thereby he conceives himself in danger of paying over again large sums of money, of losing the monies due to him by book, and that his title to the aforesaid lands are thereby also rendered very preearious [sic] and uncertain, having lost his receipts, books and deeds as aforesaid, his only vouchers in the several respects forementioned [sic] &c.; praying for a committee, as per memorial on file: Resolved by the Assembly, that Messrs, Alexander King, Esq. Shem Burbanks and Benjamin Banevroft, all of said Suffield, be a committee, and they are hereby appointed a committee, with full power and authority to convene before them all and every person or persons interested or who are any wise concerned in any of the matters and facts alledged [sic] in the memorial above referred to, at such time and place as said committee shall appoint, said committee first giving three weeks' notice in the public papers of the time of such meeting and to enquire into the matters and facts aforesaid by the oaths of the parties or other evidence, and by such ways and means as they shall judge proper, so that truth and equity may be had and done in the premises; and, of the facts they shall find therein, with their opinion thereon, report to make to this Assembly in May next, or to some future Assembly.

In 1771, Shem held office of a selectman for Suffield.[4] Shem was considered among the trusted and respected leaders of the community.

On a recent trip (October 2000), while searching through the Kent Library in Suffield, I found a handwritten note in the Burbank file, which has been referred to the Reverend Samuel Peters's List. At the top of the list was handwritten "Suffield Loyalist." The list contained four names: Alexander

King, Esq., Captain Shem Burbank, Seth Austin, and Isaac Pomeroy. This list was said to be a list of those who were loyal to the King of England and therefore could not be counted on to defend the colonies during the Revolution. So far, this list has been the only reference linking Shem to the Revolutionary War. In the book about the history of Suffield, he is alleged to be a Tory, but the reference is Peters's list. There are a couple of newspaper articles dated in the 1960s, addressing the history of the house Shem grew up in and later sold to Phelps; and in doing so, reference is made about Shem being a Tory, but no citation is given. Everything that I have read so far refers back to Peters's list.

In the book *Celebration of the Two Hundred and Fiftieth Anniversary of the Settlement of Suffield, Connecticut,* published by authority of the General Executive Committee, 1921. page 166, it is mentioned that Shem was one of four men who were Tories and living in Suffield. However, Rev. Samuel Peters's list was given as a reference. Further research discovered that Rev. Samuel Peters was not a reliable person and was somewhat of a troublemaker. He was known as a person who did not always tell the truth.

Further research produced the following events that occurred during the period leading up to the war. Alexander King served as a selectman for the years 1768, 1770-74, and 1777-1802. He was also the town clerk from 1775 to 1801. Alexander King and Isaac Pomeroy were deputy and representative to the Connecticut General Assembly from Suffield (Isaac, 1777, 1780, and 1785; Alexander for the years 1768-9, 1771-80, and 1784). Isaac fought for the colonies during the Revolutionary War.[4] So far, of the four names on the list of "Loyalist," two of the men proved the reverend wrong in his accusations.

In December 1775, an act was established—addressing the punishment that would be imposed for various acts against the United Colonies. "An Act for restraining and punishing Persons who are inimical to the Liberties of this and the Rest of the United Colonies, and for directing Proceedings therein." This would include loss of home, property, and the right to own property. It also included fines and imprisonment and the inability to hold or serve in any office civil or military.[11]

Shem was a captain in the Suffield Trainband, and he would have been stripped of his rank if he had been guilty of any wrongdoings. Shem entered into a contract to sell a piece of property, "an acre and a half, more or less." At the bottom of the contract it reads, "Personally Appeared, Captain Shem Burbank, signer and sealer of the foregoing instrument, and acknowledged the same to be his free act and deed before me." His signature was witnessed by Alex King, justice of the peace, and dated 15 September 1787. Again, had Shem been guilty of any act against the United Colonies, he would not have had land to sell as it would have been confiscated; and the lifetime privilege to the use of the title captain would have been taken away.

There were those who supported the Colonies (Patriots), and there were those who supported the British. Those who supported England were called Loyalist or the more derogatory name of Tory. Then there were those that just wanted to stay out of the war altogether and live their lives without conflict or confrontation. I am reminded of the movie *The Patriot*, with Mel Gibson. You may recall that he refused to fight for the Colonies and just wanted to remain free of the war; that was until the fighting affected him personally.

Depending on the town or village, the treatment for those who did not defend the Colonies varied. Parts of Connecticut and Massachusetts were more forgiving than, say, Boston or New York State. From what we have learned about Shem, I am sure it was a hard decision for him to make. It appears that he fought neither for America nor England. Had he chosen to engage in the war, he would have been fighting against his brothers, brothers-in-laws, cousins, and friends, no matter which side he favored. Shem must have been well liked and trusted as his property was not confiscated, and he was allowed to continue to live in his house on High Street.

Because of the war, Shem could no longer ship to England and therefore must have suffered financially. Or it might be that because he chose not to engage himself for the cause, he was shunned by the townspeople and therefore suffered a loss of income. Whichever the case, Shem sold his house[4] to a very large land speculator, Oliver Phelps. Perhaps Shem and Phelps did a little "horse trading" because it appears that as part of the deal, Shem and his family became residents of the house that Phelps once owned in Granville, Massachusetts.

Shem and his family moved to Granville in 1788. Shem died—"found dead in bed on 31 January 1800." His grave has not yet been discovered. He was survived by his wife, Anna (Fitch), and their children, the youngest being Ann, seventeen years of age at that time. Since Ann was still considered a minor, a guardian had to be appointed. Her brother, Henry, was appointed guardian in addition to being the appointed administrator for Shem's estate. This appointment was made and recorded in the Probate Court at Springfield, Hampshire County, Massachusetts, on 17 October 1800.

The following documents were found among the probate records:

(Letter from Thomas Burbank, Justice of Peace)

To the Honorable Samuel Henshaw, Esquire, Judge of the Probate of Wills for the County of Hampshire. This may certify that Anne Burbank, a

*minor above the age of fourteen years, Daughter of Capt. Shem Burbank
late of Granville in the County aforesaid Living more than ten miles
distance from your Honors Dwelling house, this day came before me the
subscriber, one of the Justice of the Peace, within and for the said County
of Hampshire, and made of Henry Burbank of said Granville, to be her
Guardian, given under my hand this twelfth day of October 1800*

Another letter found in the probate records of Shem was written by Ann
Burbank, widow of Shem Burbank, and signed "Anny" Burbank.

*To the Honourable Samuel Henshaw, Esquire, Judge of Probate of Wills
for the County of Hampshire.*

> *This may certify to your Honour, that I, the subscriber Widow of late
Capt. Shem Burbank am left wholly destitute of household furniture, of any
description or any means whereby I am enabled to procure any necessities
for housekeeping and also destitute of any convenient way to get around,
In my advanced and quite infirm state in life, being destitute of a horse,
and as there is but one low prized Beast of that description belonging to the
Estate, and as the appraising of my right of Dower, have not considered
me in any of the above described necessaries.*

> *Consider your Honour in your Wisdom, will apportion to me such
of those necessaries as shall be sufficient for the intended purpose /viz/ for
my private benefit and.*

The above letter to Judge Samuel Henshaw was not dated, but also found
in the probate records was the following note:

*At a Court of Probate held at Springfield Febr 2nd, 1802 I hereby allow
to Anna Burbank widow of Shem Burbank late of Granville deceased
the sum of one hundred & fifty dollars out of the personal Estate of wid
deceased.*

(Signed) Samuel Henshaw Jus. Prob

Following the death of Shem, Anne, in her letter requesting funds from
the estate, said that she was in an advanced and quite infirm state in life and,
because of this, she probably lived with her son Henry as he was appointed
guardian of her youngest daughter Ann. Henry died, "sudden," on 9 July 1834
at the age of sixty-two.

Anne Fitch was born in Lebanon, Connecticut, 12 July 1737. She was
the daughter of Joseph Fitch and Ann Whiting. Anne and Shem married in
Lebanon 29 December 1761.[10] On 6 September 1807, Ann[1] applied to transfer

her membership from the Congregational Church of Suffield to the "Church of Xt" in East Granville. However, certain conditions were not met, and the transfer never took place; and it was not until 1810 that Ann finally had her church membership transferred from the Congregational Church in Suffield. [14] This time the transfer was to the Church of Christ in Granville, New York: "1810—Ann Burbank to ye Chh of Chs in Granville, New York State." Why Ann decided to move to Granville in 1810 may be another mystery that will remain unsolved, but as you will or may have already discovered, she did have a reason to move, but why 1810? (see Ackley chapter).

Anne died 4 February 1813 and is buried in the Otis Cemetery in Fort Ann, Washington County, New York. Anne's headstone reads:

Sacred
To The Memory of
Ann Burbank
Relict of Shem
Burbank Who Died
Feb. 4, 1813 in the
76 Year of Her
Age.

Shem and Anne (Fitch) Burbank had the following children:[13]

25.	Thomas Burbank	baptized 3 October 1762
26.	William Burbank	baptized 20 November 1763
27.	Anna (1) Burbank	baptized 15 December 1764; died before December 1782
28.	Lucy (1) Burbank	baptized 11 June 1766; died 13 January 1769
29.	Abraham Burbank	baptized 30 December 1767; died December 1808
30.	Samuel Fitch (1) Burbank	baptized November 1769; died 1 January 1770
31.	Lucy (2) Burbank	baptized 10 January 1771
32.	Henry Burbank	baptized 20 November 1772; died 31 July 1834
33.	Samuel (2) Burbank	baptized 20 December 1774
34.	George Burbank	baptized 11 May 1777
35.	Robert Burbank	baptized 1 August 1779
36.	Ann (2) Burbank	baptized 15 December 1782; died 29 March 1872

36.   Ann (2) married Joseph Ackley (see Ackley chapter).

As was customary, when a younger child died, that child's name would usually be used again. For example, Lucy (1) died on 13 June 1769. The next daughter born was named Lucy, meaning that Anna (1) was probably still living. With this thought in mind, Anna (1) would have died after 10 January 1771 but before December 1782, when Ann (2) was born. In the case of Samuel Fitch (1) who died on 1 January 1770, another son was born who was named Henry. On 20 December 1774, another son was born and the name Samuel was again used, implying that Samuel (2) had probably died.

Notes

1. George Burbank Sedgley, *Genealogy of The Burbank Family and The Families of Bray, Wellcome, Sedgley (Sedgeley) and Welch* Knowlton and McLeary Company 1928.

2. John R. Burbank, Various correspondences (1/10/2000).

3. Benjamin P. Mighill and George B. Blodgette, *The Early Records of the Town of Rowley, Massachusetts 1639-1672*, Volume one of the printed records of the town; printed Rowley, Mass. 1894.

4. Robert Hayden Alcorn, *The Biography of a Town, Suffield—Connecticut 1670-1970*, pages 317-323, Three Hundredth Anniversary Committee of The Town of Suffield.

5. *Biographical Sketched of the Graduates of Yale College with Annals of the College History*

6. Dean, *History of Scituate*, page 256. *Hist. and General Register*, xix, 40: Conn. Puritan Settlers

7. A Brief History of The First Church of Christ, Congregational

8. Captain Abraham Burbank "Probate Records" dated 1768, Hartford, Connecticut, file number 925.

9. Franklin Bowditch Dexter, M.A., *Biographical Sketches of the Graduates of Yale College with Annals of the College History*, Volume II, pp 517-518 New York, Henry Holt & Co. 1896.

10. Frederick W. Bailey, Editor *Early Connecticut Marriages As Found On Ancient Church Records Prior to 1800*, pg 47, Bureau of American Ancestry.

11. Public records of the Colony of Connecticut 1636-1776.

12. *Vital Records of Granville, Massachusetts to the year 1850*, pg. 185, published by New England Historical Genealogical Society, Boston 1914.

13. "Church Baptismal records from the First Church of Christ, Congregational United Church of Christ," photo copied by Richard C. Witters.

14. *Records of the Congregational Church in Suffield Connecticut 1710-1836,* pp. 33, Hartford, Connecticut Historical Society 1941.

15. Clarence Almon Torrey, *New England Marriages Prior to 1700,* Prepared for publication by Elizabeth P. Bentley, Genealogical Publishing Co. Baltimore 1985.

16. Suffield Historical Society

17. "Headstone Inscriptions," Suffield, Hartford County, Connecticut 1660-1937

18. Barbour Collection *Connecticut Vital Records, 1674-1850* Connecticut State

SIX

Rev. James Fitch

1622-1638/9-1702
(See Appendix E)

It wasn't until the twelfth century that surnames came into focus. Surnames were used to distinguish people from one another. Surnames were derived from occupation such as Joseph the blacksmith became Joseph Smith or Henry the wheelwright became Henry Wright. Surnames also came from the location of the person: Peter who lived by the river became known as Peter River, which led to Rivers, or John who lived near the woods became known as John Woods, or James who lived on a hill became known as James Hill. Later the children became known as Samuel de Smith, Thomas de Hill, or Robert de Bruce, meaning child of. Normally the name would refer to the male ancestor, but there were names that related to the female; however, it was not common practice—usually it was used for an unwedded mother. Another characteristic would be that of description of the person—names like Pepin the Short, Eric the Red (red hair), and William the Conqueror.

Stanstead Mountfitchet is a village and civil parish in the county of Essex and is about thirty miles north of London. Stanstead was a Saxon settlement (the name means stony place in Saxon) and predates the Norman invasion of England. It wasn't until the invasion that the name Mountfitchet was founded and done so by the Norman baron who settled there. The only remains left standing from the original castle is a huge stone.[17]

Montfitchet is the surname of a person, and Mountfitchet is the name of a town in Essex, England.[18]

William de Gernon assumed the name of Montfitchet from the Castle of Stanstead, Essex County, England, from the raised mount (Mons Fixus) constructed by his father Robert de Gernon where the castle stood; however, nearby stood a castle known as Mountfiquet.

William de Gernon, now known as de Montfitchet, married Margaret, daughter of Gilbert, Second Lord of Clare. Margaret gave birth to a son and named him Gilbert de Montfitchet, who in turn had a son, Richard de Montfitchet.

The following is a publication—*Colonial Families of the United States of America*—edited by George Norbury Mackenzie LLB who at that time was a member of the Society of Genealogist of London, England; National Genealogical Society; Old Northwest Genealogical Society; and Maryland Historical Society. This was dated MCMXIV (1914).

> *Robert De Gernon came to England with William the Conqueror and was of the House of Boulongue and a kinsman of William's. For Robert's service, he was granted large estates, forty-one Lordships, principality in County Essex, and one of his seats being in Stanstead. He was Baron of Stanstead Montfitchet so called from the village of Montfiquet, near Bayeaux his home in Normandy, France. He was living in 1086 and is mentioned quite often in the Doomsday Book.*

Robert De Gernon's descendents are as follows:

1. **Robert**
2. **William de Gernon** inherited from his father the barony of Stanstead Montfitchet and became the second baron thereof. It was at this time William dropped the "de Gernon" and became William de Montfitchet. He married Margaret, daughter of Gilbert (Second Lord of Clare), and had one son.
3. **Gilbert de Montfitchet** was the son and heir of the Second Baron of Stanstead and had one son.
4. **Richard de Montfitchet**, son of Third Baron of Stanstead, was keeper of the Kings House in Havering and keeper of the Kings Forest in Essex. He later became sheriff of Essex and Hertfordshire. Richard married Millicent and had one son and three daughters. He died in 1202.
5. **Richard de Montfitchet**, son of the Fourth Baron of Stanstead, was underage at his father's death in 1202. He was one of the barons at Runneymede in 1225 who rested Magna Charta from King John (1166-1216) (John Lackland) and was one of the twenty-five appointed to rule the realm. In 1266, Richard de Montfitchet was appointed Justice of the Royal Forest in Essex and, in 1242, High Sheriff of Essex and Hertifordshire and governor of Hertford Castle. He had three sons and one daughter.

6.   **Roger de Montfitchet** of Wraybury, son of Richard de Montfitchet, became the sixth baron. He married and had one son.

7.   **John de Montfitchet** dropped the prefix "de Mont" and final *t* from his surname and thus became Fitche. He became the Seventh Baron of Stanstead Montfitchet, was granted armorial bearings in 1263, and was living at Fitche Castle in the Parish of Widdington in Northwestern Essex during the reign of Henry III (1216-1272) and Edward I (1272-1307). John had one son (William) and one daughter (Joan).

8.   **William Fitche** was born at Fitche Castle and was living there in 1331. He had two sons: William and Thomas.

9.   **Thomas Fitche** was born at Fitche Castle in 1370. He married in 1390, Cora, daughter of Abram Worth of Essex and had sons: William and Thomas.

10. **Thomas Fitche**, born at Fitche Castle in 1400, was living in the reign of Henry V (1413-1422). He had three sons: Richard, Thomas, and William.

11. **William Fitche**, born at Fitche Castle in 1422, lived there during the reign of Henry VI (1422-1461 and 1470-1471).

(Note: Henry VI was born at Windsor Castle 6 December 1421 and was the son of Henry V and Catherine of France. He succeeded to the thrones of England and France when he was less than a year old. His rule in France was soon undermined by Joan of Arc, and within a generation, all of his father's conquests were lost. Being of such a young age, Henry VI was appointed a protector, Richard, Duke of York. Because of Henry VI's failure to comprehend more than once, he had to submit the kingdom to his protector. This led to civil war, and his throne was taken away from him by the protector's son, Edward IV—in 1461-1470 and 1471-1483—but was given back to him in 1470 and again taken away in 1471. A few weeks later, on 27 May 1471, Henry was murdered in the Tower just days after his first son was killed in battle.)

12. **Thomas Fitche** was born at Fitche Castle in 1447 and served under the Earl of Oxford. He married Joan Marston, daughter of William Marston of Salon. They had one son.

13. **Thomas Fitche** was born in 1472 at Fitche Castle and was proprietor of Lyndersill in Essex. He was living at Fitche Castle in 1500 and married Agnes Alger, daughter of Sir Robert Alger of Brazen Head, in Essex. Brazen Head was so-called from large Wolf's Head, made of brass and affixed to the top of an outer gate. Thomas and Agnes had four sons: William, Richard, Thomas, and Roger.

14. **Thomas Fitch**, heir to Brazen Head, married Lady Margaret Meade and had two sons, Thomas and Robert, and one daughter.

15. **Thomas Fitche**, eldest son and heir to Brazen Head and proprietor of Margature, was born in 1522. He married Lady Ann Bently and had a daughter and two sons: Thomas and Robert.

16. **Thomas Fitche**, born in 1562, was living at Brazen Head in 1612. He married Mary Munck, daughter of Sir John Munck of Sapford, and had two sons and three daughters: Thomas, Richard, Joanne, Mary, and Jane.

17. **Thomas Fitche**, born in 1590 at Brazed Head near Bocking, married 6 August 1611, Anna Reve. He died in January 1632. In his will, he names seven sons and three daughters (see copy of will below).

18. **Thomas Fitche**, an emigrant, was born 24 October 1612, Bocking, England (see narrative below).

Dr. Asa Fitch (24 February 1809-8 April 1879), state entomologist of New York, was of the opinion that the English Fitches were not of Norman but rather of Saxon origin. Dr. Fitch's genealogy works on the Fitch family was never published, but his manuscript was given to the New York Genealogical and Biographical Society and can be viewed at the society's building in New York City.

Before the capital letter came into being, the normal way of spelling was to use two lowercase letters in the spelling, such as ffytche for Fytche and ffitch for Fitch.

According to Roscoe Conkling Fitch,[1] the Fitches are of one of the old Anglo-Saxon families of England coming from Saxony. It was thought that at that time, the country was under the control of Hengist and Horsa—brothers that led the invasion of Britton and founded the Kingdom of Kent. Horsa died in AD 455. According to some, the names may be mythical; however, the war and invasion did occur.

Prior to what we know as our modern-day census, in England, it began as "Visitation" of a certain part of England. We are referring to "The Herald's Visitations of Essex" where the Fitch family has been traced back from sons to father, step-by-step to William, second son of John Fitch who was living in Fitch Castle in 1294. It has been established that John Fitch of Fitch Castle in the North is the direct ancestor of the Fitch brothers who settled in Connecticut. John Fitch was living in 1294, and his name appears as of that date in the ancient records of the British Museum in London.[1]

Thomas Fitch of Bocking, Essex, England, was the father of the four Fitch brothers who settled in Connecticut. He was born in 1590 and christened in 1598. He was the eldest son and heir of George of Braintree, Essex, England, and his wife Joan (Thurgood) Fitch. He was the grandson of Roger and Margery Fitch of Panfield and Bocking, Essex, England. He was the great-grandson of

Thomas of Brazen Head, Lindsell, Essex, England, and his wife Agnes (Alger) Fitch.[1]

Thomas Fitch of Bocking married Anne Reeve 8 August 1611 at St. Mary's Church in Bocking. Thomas died in January 1633. His will was dated 11 December 1632.[1] He was a large landowner and cloth manufacturer. His will mentions seven sons and three daughters. Following the death of Thomas, Anne and four of her sons were early settlers in Connecticut. Anne (Reeve) was living with her son, Joseph Fitch I, in 1669.[1]

Following is the will of Thomas Fitch:

I, Thomas Fitch, in the full possession of my mental faculties make this my last will and testament, Dec. 11, 1632.

To the poor of Bocking three pounds.

To my eldest son, Thomas that chief Messuage wherein I now dwell in Bocking and the messuage adjoining, now in the occupation of the said Thomas and all the lands, tenements &c. which I purchased of William Collyn in Bocking and the land and tenements in Bocking which I lately purchased of Edward Pepper, gent, and his wife and John Amptill and his wife and the barn in Bocking by Panfield Lane, which I lately purchased of Thomas trotter, upon condition that he pay my sister, Stracey, twenty shillings yearly, during her natural life.

To my son John and his heirs forever, the messuage in Bocking late of Richard Usher, deceased, and which I lately purchased of Paul Usher and Peter Kirby and Ursula Bond, widow, and the little garden or orchard in Bocking, now in the occupation of Richard Skinner or his assigns and the tenement in the occupation of Thomas Laye, in Bocking, by Panfield Lane and the great orchard adjoining which I purchased of Mr. Thomas Trotter to enter upon the same at his age of one and twenty years.

To my son John, two hundred pounds at one and twenty

Item, I give to my son James, one hundred pounds, to be paid him when he shall be a bachelor of Arts of two years standing at the University of Cambridge, for I desire that he should be bredde [sic] a scholler. [sic] And I also give him, and my minde [sic] is that he shall have thirty pounds a year paid him by my Executrix out of my lands and tenements, from the time of his admission to be a scholler at Cambridge until he be or shall have tyme [sic] to be a master of Arts.

To my sons, Nathaniel and Jeremy, to either of them a moiety and half part of the farm, messuage, lands and tenements, both free and copy, lying and being in Birch or elsewhere in Essex, which I lately purchased of William Brock, gent., to be equally divided them and they to enter upon the same at their several ages of one and twenty.

My Executrix shall lay out six hundred and fifty pounds within one year after my decease and shall purchase with the same as much lands and tenements within the County of Essex as the same will buy in a frugal and good manner, to be assured to the use of my two younger sons, Samuel and Joseph. And my wife Anne shall have the land and tenements in Birch, which I have given to Nathaniel and Jeremy and the land &c. to be purchased for Samuel and Joseph until these four sons shall severally accomplish their ages of sixteen years, &c.

To my three daughters, Mary, Anna and Sara, three hundred pounds apiece, where of two hundred pounds apiece are to be paid at their several ages of eighteen and the other hundred at one and twenty.

To my loving friends, Mr. Hooker, Mr. Nathaniel Rogers, Mr. Daniel Rogers and Mr. Collins, twenty schillings apiece as a token of my love.

To my son Thomas my great oil cistern of land, so as he give and deliver to my son John the little cistern of land for oil which I late bought and gave to Thomas.

To my brother, John Malden and my sister, his wife, twenty shillings apiece; To Henry Stracey, my kinsman, five pounds. To my brothers, John Reeve and William Stracey, forty shillings apiece, and to my brother Jeremy Reeve twenty shillings as a token of my love. The residue to my wife whom I make sole executor, she to enter upon a bond of two thousand pounds to my said brothers, Reeve and William Stracy With condition to prove this will within two months after my decease, and to pay all the legacies and perform all things contained therein. My said brothers to be supervisors

Wm. Lyngwood, one of the witnesses. Proven and probated on the 12th day of Dec. 1633–Annoque Dom.[4]

Based upon the above, Thomas and Anna (Reeve) Fitch had the following children:[1]

1.	Thomas Fitch	born 14 October 1612
2.	John Fitch	died 1676, Windsor, Connecticut
3.	Rev. Mr. James Fitch	born 24 December 1622
4.	Nathaniel Fitch	born 26 December 1623; died 1649
5.	Jeremy Fitch	born 5 August 1625
6.	Samuel Fitch	born 9 November 1626
7.	Joseph Fitch	
8.	Mary Fitch	born March 1629
9.	Anne Fitch	born 6 August 1630
10	Sara Fitch	born 24 July 1631

1.   **Thomas Fitch I** was born 14 October 1612. He married 1 November 1632 in Bocking, England, Anne Stacie of Bocking, Essex, England, who was the daughter of William Stacie. He served in the Parliamentary wars in England; and in 1650, he and his brother Joseph (7) were two of the leading founders of Norwalk, Connecticut.[1] Thomas became a freeman in 1657 and continued to live in Norwalk until his death in 1704.[1,5] He also became clerk of the trainband in 1655; recorder of laws, 26 February 1659; a selectman in 1650; king's commissioner from 1669 to 1694; deputy of the General Court, 1673, 1676, 1680-1686, 1691-1692, and 1694; and deputy governor of Connecticut. Thomas died in 1704, leaving three daughters.[21]

2.   **Captain John Fitch** (?-1676), According to Roscoe Conkling Fitch[1] and John T. Fitch,[19] John Fitch, son of Thomas and Anne Reeve, never came to America. He is suspected to have participated in the Civil War (1642-1651), thus the rank of captain. The Great Plague of 1665 claimed lives of fifty or more per week. John was appointed as one of the "overseers" and therefore one of those who looked after the poor in Braintree during the plague. John probably died in 1666 and, according to the *Essex Review*, vol. 36, page 22, was mentioned "John gallant Capt. John Fitch of Braintree, clothier, the leading overseer" who died in the plague.[19]

There was another John Fitch who settled in Windsor, Connecticut, in 1643. He was mortally wounded 19 December 1675, the Great Swamp Fight at the Narragansett Fort (King Philip's War) and was buried 10 May 1676. He married 9 December 1656, Windsor, Connecticut, Ann Hillier (?-1673).[1,5] I have been unable to tie this John to the Fitches of this chapter.

3.   **Rev. Mr. James Fitch** came to Connecticut either in 1638 or 1639 (see below for history).

4.   **Nathaniel Fitch** was born 26 December 1623. His will is on record in England and is dated 15 August 1648 and proved 8 May 1649. The reference says that he was of Brittlewell, Essex County, England; but it was probably Prittlewell.[1]

5.   **Jeremy Fitch** was born 5 August 1625. The only information that I can find for Jeremy is, he did not come to America.

6.   **Samuel Fitch**, born 9 November 1626, came to America and, in 1650, was engaged to keep the school at Hartford. He was made a freeman 15 May 1651. Samuel married in 1651 in Hartford Susanna (Whiting) who was the widow of William Whiting of Hartford.[20]

Samuel was elected Deputies of the General Court at Hartford for the years 1654 and 1655.[1] In 1640, as a form of self-governing, the General Court at Hartford consisted of a governor, a deputy governor, six magistrates, and four deputies (representatives) nominated by the towns

(Windsor, Wethersfield, and Hartford). The deputies were sent to the legislative body of the General Court to represent their towns. This would appear to be the beginning of what we know as Congress today and that form of government lasted for more than three hundred years.

Samuel died in 1659. He and Susanna had two children. Susanna married for the third time, 27 June 1662, Milford, Connecticut Alexander Bryan.[5]

7. **Joseph Fitch** was born in 1655. It is not certain when he came to America; but he and his brother, Thomas, are listed as "lead founders" of Norwalk, Connecticut, in 1650 where he first settled. Joseph stayed in Norwalk for about three years. He sold all of his land and housing to Mark St. John and moved to Northampton, Massachusetts. He then moved to Hartford, ending up in Podunk, located in the southern part of Windsor, Connecticut, in 1672. He was named as beneficiary in the will of his brother Nathaniel in 1648 then living in England.[1, 20]

Joseph was living in Hartford in 1660 and was made a freeman in 1662. Joseph engaged Samuel Wyllys as his attorney and directed Mr. Wyllys, while in England, to sell all of his land in great Birch, Essex, England, land left to him in the will of his brother Nathan.[20]

Joseph married before December 1657,[7] probably in Hartford, Mary Stone, daughter of Rev. Samuel and Elizabeth (Allen) Stone of Hartford. Joseph died ca. 1727.[5]

8. **Mary Fitch**, born in March 1629, married (1) Thomas Sherwood (1586-1655) and (2) John Banks.[5]

(3) Rev. Mr. James Fitch

Our progenitor, James Fitch, son of Thomas and Anne (Reeve) Fitch, came to America at the age of sixteen, according to his headstone. He was born 24 December 1622, Bocking, Essex, England, meaning he arrived in America either in 1638 but more likely 1639. James died 18 November 1702. He is buried in the Old Cemetery now known as Trumbull Cemetery in Lebanon, Connecticut. Below is the translated inscription (from Latin to English) that appears on his headstone.

> *In this grave are deposited the remains of that truly reverend man, Mr. James Fitch. He was born in Bocking, in the County of Essex, in England, the 24th day of December, in the year of our Lord 1622; who after he had been most excellently taught the learned languages came into New England at the age of sixteen, and then spent seven years under the instructions of those very famous men, Mr. Hooker and Mr. Stone. Afterwards he discharged the pastoral office fourteen years at Saybrook.*

Thence he removed with the major part of his Church to Norwich, where he spent the other years of his life in the work of the gospel. In his old age indeed he was obliged to cease from his public labors by reason of bodily indisposition and at length retired to his children at Lebanon, where after spending nearly half a year, he slept in Jesus in the year 1702, on the 18th day of November, in the 80th year of his age. He was a man as to the smartness of his genius, the solidity of his judgment, his charity, holy labors, and every kind of purity of life, and also as to his skill and energy of preaching, inferior to none.

Upon arrival in America, James Fitch located in Hartford, Connecticut, where he studied and completed his theological studies under the tutelage of Rev. Thomas Hooker (mentioned in James's father Thomas Fitch's will) and Rev. Samuel Stone, whose daughter Mary Stone married James's brother Joseph Fitch I. In 1646, at Saybrook, Connecticut, a church was organized; and James Fitch was ordained as its minister. "As a pastor, he was zealous and indefatigable. He trained several young men for the ministry while at Saybrook and continued doing so after he moved to Norwich. One such man was Rev. Samuel Whiting" (see Whiting chapter).[13, 14]

On 13 September 2002, I received the following e-mail from David A. Oat, historian of the First Congregational Church of Norwich, stating that they have very little historical material and that most of their information comes from local town historical records and local history books. David did however state that James was the first minister of Norwich and led the original group of Puritans (thirty-five families) from Old Saybrook, Connecticut, to what is now Norwich in 1659.

The town of Norwich was purchased from Uncas and his two sons, Oneco and Altawanhood, sachems of the Mohegan tribe, for the price of £70. The township consisted of nine square miles of land and is outlined in the deed by the General Assembly of the colony in 1671. Norwich was settled in the spring of 1660. The purchase of the town was made in the month of June 1659 by thirty-five men who became the first settlers of Norwich. Most of those thirty-five were from Saybrook with the remainder from the settles of New London, Groton, and Plymouth and Marshfield (Massachusetts).[8]

In 1660, Rev. James Fitch, the pastor of the church in Saybrook, with most of his flock, moved from Saybrook to Norwich. James Fitch continued as pastor of the church in Norwich until he was forced to resign in 1696 due to his age and infirmity. Fitch and his father-in-law, Major John Mason, had property adjoining one another, facing the Green, with the Yantic River at the rear. The road to the river (New London Turnpike) ran between the two homesteads. Fitch's house is no longer standing, but in its place stands a real estate office, 86 Town Street.

Rev. James Fitch, upon surrendering the pulpit, was replaced by his son, Rev. Jabez Fitch, who had just completed his studies at Harvard.[10] In 1702, Fitch left his hometown of Norwich and moved to Lebanon where the Indian had given him five square miles of land. Joshua Uncas, an Indian chief, had also willed Fitch five thousand acres in Windham, Connecticut.[8]

Rev. James Fitch was chaplain of the Connecticut forces during the King Philip's War under Major Robert Treat in 1675 and Major John Talcott in 1676. He preached the election sermon in 1674 and ran the Missionary to the Mohegan Indians preaching in their own tongue.[8]

Rev. James Fitch married in (1) October 1648 in Saybrook, Connecticut, Abigail Whitfield who was born on 1 September 1622 in Ockley, Surrey, England. She was the daughter of Rev. Henry and Dorothy (Sheaffe) Whitfield of Guilford, New Haven County, Connecticut. Abigail died on 9 September 1659 in Saybrook, Connecticut.[10]

Rev. James and Abigail (Whitfield) Fitch had the following children:[9]

3a.	James Fitch	born 2 August 1649
3b.	Abigail Fitch	born 5 August 1650
3c.	Elizabeth Fitch	born 2 January 1652; died 1689
3d.	Hannah Fitch	born 17 September 1653
3e.	Samuel Fitch	born March 1655
3f.	Dorothy Fitch	born April 1658; married Nathaniel Bissell

Rev. James Fitch married (2) October 1664 in Norwich, Connecticut, Priscilla Mason who was born in October 1641,[24] in Windsor, Connecticut. She was the daughter of Major John Mason (see Mason chapter) and Anne (Peck) who was the daughter of Rev. Robert Peck (see Peck chapter).

Rev. James and Pricilla (Mason) Peck had the following children:

3g.	Captain Daniel Fitch	born August 1665; died 3 June 1711
3h.	Captain John Fitch	born January 1667; died 24 May 1743
3i.	Captain Jeremiah Fitch	born September 1670
3j.	Rev. Jabez Fitch	born April 1672; died 22 November 1740
3k.	Ann Fitch	born April 1675
3L.	Captain Nathaniel Fitch	born October 1679
3m.	Joseph Fitch	born November 1681; died 9 May 1741
3n.	Eleazer Fitch	born 14 May 1683; married Martha Brown

3a.   **(Major) James Fitch** was born 2 August 1649, Saybrook, Connecticut. He died 10 November 1727. He married (1) in January 1670, Norwich, Elizabeth Mason (1654-1684). James married (2) 8 May 1787, Norwich, Connecticut,

Alice (Bradford) Adams, daughter of Deputy Governor William Bradford, widow of Rev. William Adams and granddaughter of William Bradford.[9]

Major Fitch did quite well for himself during his lifetime. He stood out as one of the most successful and versatile man of his time. He was a "land surveyor, land registrar, land speculator, and land owner. He served as a military man, magistrate, founder and statesman. He was considered champion of the people's rights and of the Connecticut charter. He has the reputation of being "Father of Windom County, Conn.'"[9]

3b. **Abigail Fitch,** born 5 August 1650, married in 1670 in Norwich, Connecticut, Captain John Mason (1646/48-1676).[9]

3c. **Elizabeth Fitch** was born 2 January 1652 and died in 1689. She married 5 September 1674 (some say November) in Westfield, Connecticut, Rev. Edward Taylor (1642-1729) of Westfield. Following the death of Elizabeth, Taylor married 2 June 1692 in Hartford Ruth Wyllys, granddaughter of Governor Haynes.[5, 9]

3d. **Hannah Fitch** was born 17 September 1653 and married 30 June 1677, Norwich, Thomas Mix (Meeks).[5, 9]

3e. **Samuel Fitch,** born in March 1655, married Mary Ann Brewster, granddaughter of Elder Brewster.[5, 9] Elder Brewster was of Plymouth and came over on the *Mayflower*. He was the same Brewster that took William Bradford of the *Mayflower* under his guidance at Scooby Manor in England.[16]

3f. **Dorothy Fitch** was born in April 1658 and married 4 July 1683 Nathaniel Bissell (1640-1714). Dorothy was Nathaniel's second wife, his first being Mindwell Moore (1643-1682), on 25 September 1662, Windsor, Connecticut.[5, 8]

3g. **(Captain) Daniel Fitch** was born in August 1655 and died 3 June 1711. He married 4 March 1698, Preston, Connecticut, Mary Sherwood. Following the death of Daniel, Mary married (2) ca. 1716 James Bradford.[5, 8]

3h. **(Captain) John Fitch** was born in January 1667 (some say 1668) and died 24 May 1743. He married 10 July 1695, Windham, Connecticut, Elizabeth Waterman (1675-1751).[5, 11] John was a distinguished citizen of Windham and served as town clerk from 1704 until his death in 1743. John also represented the town in the legislature from 1712-1742.[15]

Their son, John Fitch, born in January 1706, died of smallpox 10 February 1760 at the age of fifty-four years and one month.[11]

3i. **(Captain) Jeremiah Fitch** was born in September 1670 and died 22 May 1736. He married before 1699 in Lebanon, Connecticut, Ruth Gifford, who was born in 1676.

3j. **Rev. Jabez Fitch** was born in April 1672 and died 22 November 1740. He graduated from Harvard College in 1694. He married Elizabeth Appleton, daughter of Colonel John Appleton.[9]

3k. **Ann Fitch** was born in April 1675 in Lebanon, Connecticut, and died 17 October 1715. She married 5 October 1698 in Norwich, Connecticut, Joseph Bradford (1674-1747) who died at the age of seventy-three.[5] He was the grandson of Governor Bradford (see Bradford chapter).

3l. **(Captain) Nathaniel Fitch** was born in October 1679, died 14 May 1759 at the age of seventy-nine, and was buried in Old Cemetery, Lebanon, Connecticut. He was captain of the trainband in Lebanon (1719-1726). He married (1) 10 December 1701 Anna Abell, who was born 2 April 1681. She died 3 July 1728 and was buried in the Old Cemetery in Lebanon, Connecticut. [12] She was the daughter of Joshua Abell. Nathaniel married (2) Mindwell (Highley) Tisdale who died 1 September 1769 at the age of seventy-seven years and four months and was buried in Old Cemetery, Lebanon, Connecticut. She was the daughter of Colonel John Higley, aunt of Governor Trumbull, and widow of James Tisdale.[9]

   Nathan, son of Captain Nathaniel and Anna (Abel) Fitch was born 20 March 1705, and died 12 June 1751 at the age of forty-six. He was buried in the Old Cemetery, Lebanon, Connecticut.[12]

   Jabez son of Nathaniel and Mindwell (Highley) Fitch was born ca. 1730. He died at the age of six on 14 November 1736 and was buried in the Old Cemetery in Lebanon, Connecticut. [12]

3m. **Joseph Fitch** was born in November 1681 and died 9 May 1741. He married (1) 2 November 1703, Sarah Mason who was born about 1687 and died in February 1720 in Lebanon, Connecticut. She was the daughter of Major Samuel and Judith (Smith) Mason and granddaughter of Major John and Anne (Peck) Mason. Fitch married (2) 29 December 1721 in Windham, Connecticut, Ann Whiting who was born 2 January 1698 in Windham and died 18 September 1788 in Windham. She was the daughter of Rev. Samuel and Elizabeth (Adams) Whiting of Windham (see Whiting chapter).[15]

   Joseph and Sarah (Mason) Fitch had the following children:

3m1. Judith Fitch	born
3m2. Sarah Fitch	born 1705
3m3. Mason Fitch	born 1708; died 1734
3m4. Captain Joseph Fitch Jr.	born 1711; married 1738 Zerviah Hyde, born 1721 and daughter of Captain Daniel and Abigail (Wattles) Hyde

Joseph and Ann (Whiting) Fitch had the following children:[15, 22]

3m5. **Samuel Fitch,** born 15 January 1723/4, graduated from Yale College in 1742. He died in 1784 in England. He married in March 1753 Elizabeth

Lloyd who was born in 1722 and died in 1800 in Lloyd's Neck (Queen's Village), Long Island, New York. She was the daughter of Henry and Rebecca (Nelson) Lloyd.

3m6. Colonel Eleazer Fitch, born 30 August 1726, graduated from Yale in 1743. He died 17 June 1796 in Chambly, Canada. He married 4 April 1746 Amy Bowen of Providence, Long Island, who was born about 1728 and died 25 August 1790 in Castleton, Vermont. They had twelve children.[15]

3m7. Captain Azel Fitch, born 7 November 1728, married (1) 1 January 1752 in Lebanon, Connecticut, Silence Howe who was born 28 February 1732 in Pomfret, Connecticut and died 5 August 1756 in Lebanon. She was the daughter of David and Silence (Humphrey) Howe. Captain Azel Fitch married (2) about 1767 in Litchfield, Connecticut, Rhoda (Collins) Hyde—Hopkins who was born 3 May 1771. She was the daughter of Rev. Timothy and Elizabeth (Hyde) Collins and widow of Joshua Hyde who died in 1758 and widow of Asa Hopkins who died on 18 September 1766. Azel and Silence (Howe) Fitch had eight children. Azel and Rhoda had one child. Captain Azel died about 1769 in Albany, New York.[15]

3m8. Ichabod Fitch, born 17 May 1734, married (1) 8 May 1758 in Norwich, Connecticut, Lucy Lothrop who was born September 1735 in Norwich, Connecticut, and died 19 August 1774 in Lebanon, Connecticut. She was the daughter of Simon and Martha (Lothrop) Lothrop of Norwich. Ichabod and Lucy Fitch had five children. Ichabod Fitch married (2) widow Mary Hyde. Ichabod died 24 April 1794 in Lebanon, Connecticut.[15]

3m9. Ann Fitch was born in 1737 and married 29 December 1761, Lebanon, Connecticut,[23] Shem Burbank (see Burbank chapter). As per a letter dated 29 June 2001 from Danelle Moon of Yale College, "Unfortunately women were not admitted to Yale as undergraduates until 1969," Ann did not graduate from Yale as indicated in another source.

3m10. Thomas Fitch was born in 1739 and died in 1746/7.

3n. Eleazer Fitch was born 14 May 1683 and married (first cousin) Martha Brown who was born 20 November 1681 in Swansea, Massachusetts. She was the daughter of Captain John and Anne (Mason) Brown and granddaughter of Major John Mason. There were no children of this marriage.[9]

Notes

1. Roscoe Conkling Fitch, *History of the Fitch Family A. D. 1400-1930, A record of the Fitches in England and America Including "Pedigree of Fitch" Certified by the College of Arms, London, England.* Volume 1 Published privately by the Fitch Family Record Publishing Company Haverhill, Massachusetts, 1930

2. Morant's *History of Essex*

3. Plantagenet Somerset Fry, *The Kings and Queens of England and Scotland*, Grove Press, New York

4. New England Historical and Genealogical Register, Vol. 46, pg 323, 1892.

5. Clarence Almon Torrey, *New England Marriages Prior to 1700*, prepared for Publication by Elizabeth P. Bentley, Genealogical Publishing Company, Baltimore, Maryland 1985.

6. Norwalk Historical Society

7. Melinde Lutz Sanborn, Third *Supplement to Torrey's New England Marriages Prior to 1700*, Genealogical Publishing Company 2003.

8. New England Historical and Genealogical Register, Vol I

9. George Norbury Mackensie, Editor *Colonial Families of the United States of America*, Vol. IV. page 148, Seaforth Press Genelogical Publishers Baltimore 1914

10. John T. Fitch, *Descendants of The Reverend James Fitch 1622-1702, Vol. 1, The First Five Generations with the assistance of Patricia M. Geisler, Printon Press Camden, Maine* 1997

11. Headstone, Trumbull Cemetery Lebanon, Connecticut.

12. Old Cemetery Records in Lebanon, Connecticut.

13. Marian K. O'Keefe and Caterine Smith Doroshevic *Norwich Historic Homes and Families*, Published in Cooperation with The Society of the Founders of Norwich, Pequot Press, Stonington, Connecticut.

14. Nathaniel Goodwin, *Genealogical Notes or Contributions to the Family History of some of the First Settlers of Connecticut and Massachusetts*, original printing 1856; Reprint Genealogical Publishing Company, Baltimore 1995

15. John T. Fitch, *Puritan in the Wilderness*, a biography of the Reverend James Fitch 1622-1702, Picton Press, Camden, Maine 2nd printing 1995

16. Bradford Smith, *William Bradford, Pilgrim Boy*,

17. Wikipedia Dictionary

18. Frederick Lewis Weis, with additions and corrections by Walter Lee Sheppard, Jr., assisted by David Faris, *Ancestral Roots of Certain American Colonist who Came to America before 1700.*, 7th Edition, Genealogical Publishing Company, Baltimore

19. John T. Fitch, *A Fitch Family History, English Ancestors of the Fitches of Colonial Connecticut, Picton Press, Camden, Maine 1990.*

20. Mary K. Talcott, Edited by J. Hammond Trumbull 1886, *the Original Proprietors of Hartford, from Memorial History of Hartford County* first published 1886; Tuttle Antiquarian Books, Rutland, Vermont

21. Burke's *American Families with British Ancestry*, page 2667 Genealogical Publishing Co., Inc 1975

22. Mary E. Perkins *Old Houses of The Antient [sic] Town of Norwich 1660-1800*, Norwich, Connecticut 1895.

23. Frederick W. Baily. *Early Connecticut Marriages as Found on Ancient Church Records Prior to 1800.*

24. Vital Records of Norwich 1659-1848, Hartford Society of Colonial Wars.

SEVEN

William Whiting

(See Appendix G)

During the years 1085 and 1630, there have been at least sixteen different variations of the spelling of the Whiting name; but no matter how it was spelled, it retained virtually the same pronunciation. The following names were carefully copied from English records: Whiten, Whitene, Whiting, Whitingh, Whyten, Whiting, Whytying, Whytyng, Whytynge, Witeing, Witen, Witeng, Witon, Witting, Wystyng, Wyten.[1a]

William Whiting and his wife Susannah emigrated from England to America and were among the early settlers of Hartford, Connecticut. William is listed on the Founders Monument located in the old burial ground behind the First Church of Christ in Hartford.

William is mentioned in the history of America as early as 1632.[1] "He was one of the most respectable of the settlers in 1636; one of the civil and religious fathers of Connecticut" and a man of wealth and education styled in the records, "William Whiting, Gentleman."[2] William was made a freeman in 1640.

William retained his interest in Piscataqua, New Hampshire, until his death. The Piscataqua River separates Portsmouth, New Hampshire, and Kittery, Maine, and was used as a port of entry for ships from Europe (mainly England). He was one of the most efficient promoters of trade and commerce in Hartford. He also engaged in a patent for land at Swampscott, Massachusetts, with Lords Say and Brook. Lords Say and Brook lived in Bristol, England, and were often referred to as "the Bristol men." Lords Say and Brook never immigrated [*sic*] to America but rather conducted their business through agents.

William Whiting was one of the committee, which, for the first time, sat with the Court of Magistrates in 1637 and was the treasurer of the Colony from 1641 to 1647. He was chosen the magistrate in 1642 and continued in that office until his death.[1] In 1638, William was allowed to trade with the Indians and, in 1642, was appointed with Major John Mason (see Mason chapter) and others to erect fortification. In the same year, he was appointed with Major Mason to collect tribute of the Indians on Long Island and the mainland. He was a merchant of wealth and had dealings with Virginia and Piscataqua. He had a trading house at the Delaware River in Westfield.

William began writing his will on 20 March 1643 by stating that he intends "a voyage unto sea." His last entry was made on 24 July 1647.[2] During the four years it took to write his will, William made several additions to it and made an additional voyage or two "unto sea." William earned the title of major in 1647 and died the same year (July). In the addition to his will, dated 24 April 1649, William left "to his father twenty pounds, five pounds to his sister Wiggen, and three pounds apeece [sic] to her children." There have been some genealogist that have assumed that since William left five pounds to his sister Wiggen, they insinuated that she was the sister of William's wife, Susannah, and therefore Susannah's last name would be Wiggen. In those days, like today, one might consider a sister-in-law or a stepsister or a half sister as just a sister. Since no one has come up with proof positive facts indicating that Wiggen was the last name of Susannah, I choose to leave it as unknown.

These were the children of William and Susannah Whiting:

I.	William Whiting, Jr.,	born ca 1699
II.	John Whiting	born 1635; died Hartford, Connecticut, 1689
III.	Samuel Whiting	no information
IV.	Sarah Whiting	born about 1637; died 1704
V.	Mary Whiting	died 28 October 1709
VI.	Joseph Whiting	born 2 October 1645; died 1717

Following the death of William, "Susannah Whiting married Mr. Samuel Fitch of Hartford and by him, had two sons. Samuel Fitch died in 1659. Susannah's third marriage was to Alexander Bryan of Milford, Connecticut. Susannah died at the house of her daughter, Mrs. Collins, and was buried there 8 July 1673."[2]

I.   William Whiting Jr., the son of William and Susannah, was probably born in England and came over with his parents. When he became of age, he returned to London, where he was a merchant. In 1686, the Assembly of

Connecticut appointed him their "agent to present their petitions (in ref. to the Charter) to the King" (King James II).[2] William Jr. died in 1699. His son, John, was appointed the administrator of William's estate.

IV. **Sarah Whiting,** born about 1637 in Hartford, Connecticut, married (1) 27 November 1654 in Hartford, Connecticut, Jacob Mygate who was born in 1633 and died before 1683. In 1683 Sarah married (2) John King who died in 1703.[13]

II. **John Whiting,** the son of William and Susannah, was born in 1635. John, a Harvard College graduate in 1653, preached for several years in Salem, Massachusetts. On 8 March 1659, the selectmen, together with the deacons of the church in which John was serving as minister, met with Mr. Whiting and questioned his intentions as to whether or not he intended to remain their minister. Following this confrontation, John Whiting and his family moved to Hartford, Connecticut. John was ordained in 1660 at the First Church of Christ in Hartford.

John may have been born in England shortly before his parents came to America.[3] In the book *Biographical Sketches of Graduates of Harvard University,* volume 1, 1642-1658, under the title "Class of 1653," reference is made to the book written by Nathaniel Goodwin, *Genealogical Notes or Contributions to the Family History of Some of the First Settlers of Connecticut and Massachusetts* (one of the sources used for this chapter) and presumes that John's date of birth was 1635. He married Sybil Collins before 1655. She was the daughter of Deacon Edward Collins of Cambridge, Massachusetts. Sybil died in early 1673.[4]

In 1673, John married (2) Phebe Gregson, who was born in 1643. She was the daughter of Thomas Gregson of New Haven, Connecticut. Thomas was lost at sea in 1646 while on board the ship *Phantom.* Following John's death in 1689, Phebe married (2) Rev. John Russell of Hadley.[2] Phebe died 19 September 1730 in New Haven, Connecticut.

Rev. Thomas Hooker was the first minister of the First Church of Christ in Hartford (now known as Central Church). Behind this church, you will find the old burial ground and the Founders Monument. Hooker's tenure was from 1633 until his death 7 July 1647.

Rev. Samuel Stone was one of the ministers and served from 1633 until 1663. Rev. John Whiting was also one of the ministers of the First Church of Christ in Hartford and served from 1660 to 1670. Another minister that was involved in the history outlined on the following pages is Rev. Joseph Haynes who served from 1664 to 1679.

During the time that Hooker led his flock, things ran pretty smooth. There were no major problems, in fact, "the church flourished in harmony and in peace under the able and judicious ministry of Rev. Hooker."[4]

Following Rev. Thomas Hooker's death, a controversy arose and continued to cause problems, which became a contention that soon separated the church into two parties. The contention became quite complicated, so much so that it was like a contagious disease within the church and finally ended up before the councils, the synod, and the courts. For many years, the majority of the church members, along with Stone, formed one of the parties. The other party comprised of a "strong and respectable minority, striving in vain for a peaceable dismission [*sic*] from the church, which they conceived themselves to be unjustly treated and subjected to certain novelties of church order and discipline which seemed to them subversive of good old Congregational policy in which the church was founded."[4] The trouble between the two parties involved those who received baptism but did not receive Communion, which were the new qualifications for baptism and church membership. Over time, it became a question as to whether or not the old Congregationalism was being too strict with its test for membership, so much so that it was becoming intolerable for many good men and women in the colonial communities. They did not wish to endure the harsh terms of church membership, nor did they wish for their families to be outside or away from the religious societies, which was quite a powerful influence over their social life and for whose support they were obliged to give of their substance. Something had to be done to correct this uncomfortable situation; and finally, after approval of the courts and powers to be, permission was granted to the smaller party, to separate them from the First Church and build their own.

"The long looked-for way was now clearly opened to the minority in the Hartford Church, to organize into a new and distinct church."[4] In October 1669, the petition to form a distinct church was presented to Rev. Mr. John Whiting; and in October, the General Court approved said petition and directed the Hartford Church "to take some effectual course that Mr. Whiting &c., may practice the Congregational way without disturbance either from preaching or practice diversely to their just offence, or else to grant their loving consent to these brethren to walk distinct according to such, their Congregational principals."

On 22 February 1670, Rev. John Whiting and thirty-one members of the Hartford Church, with their families, formed themselves into a distinct church, the Second Church of Christ in Hartford.

The following are the founders of the Second Church of Christ in Hartford founded in 1670:

Brothers in Full communion:
John Whiting, James Richards, Thomas Bull, Robert Webster, George Graves, George Stocking, James Ensing, Thomas Bounce, Thomas Watts, James Steele, Joseph Nash, John Cole, Andrew Benton, Benjamin Harbert, John Biddall.

Sisters in Full communion:

Frances Stebbling, Sibilla Whiting, Susannah Bull, Sarah Bounce, Agnes Stocking, Margaret Watson, Margaret Nash Sanford, Bethiah Steel, Hanna Benton, Sarah Biddall, Susannah Arnold, Christian Harper Whapples, Anne Cole.

(Note: If you wish to learn the complete history of the Second Church of Christ in Hartford, then I suggest that you obtain a copy of the book *History of the Second Church of Christ in Hartford* by Edwin Pond Parker, published in 1892. It took me several months to locate the book, and then it was in very poor condition but still worth having. You may be able to find a copy online under "out-of-date books.")

Cotton Mather said this of John Whiting, "He will never be forgotten till Connecticut Colony do forget itself and all religion. [*sic*]"

Sybil (Collins) Whiting died in early 1673; and following her death, John married Phebe Gregson (1643-1730), daughter of Thomas Gregson of New Haven, who was lost at sea on the *Phantom* ship. Rev. John Whiting died 8 September 1689 in Hartford, Connecticut. Phebe then married Rev. John Russell (1626-1692) of Hadley (his third wife), and after his death, she returned to New Haven where she died 19 September 1670.

These were the children of John and Sybil (Collins) Whiting:

7.	Sybil Whiting	born 1655; married Alexander Bryan of Milford (son of Richard Bryan and grandson of Hon. Alexander who was one of the first settlers of Milford)
8.	John Whiting	born 1657; died at a young age
9.	William Whiting	born 1659
10.	Martha Whiting	born 1662; married at Hartford, 25 December 1683, to Samuel Bryan of Milford who was the son of Richard Bryan of Milford (Colonel Allyn performed the ceremony)[2]
11.	Sarah Whiting	born 1664; married 19 March 1685 to Jonathan Bull of Hartford who was the son of Captain Thomas Bull, a Pequot officer and grandson of Thomas Bull, one of the first settlers in Hartford (Major Jonathan was a merchant in Hartford and died in 17 August 1702 at the age of 53)[2]

| 12. | Abigail Whiting | born 1666; died 7 May 1735; age 67[2] |
| 13. | Samuel Whiting | born 24 April 1670 (see below) |

Rev. John Whiting and his second wife, Phebe (Gregson) Whiting, had the following children:

14.	Thomas Whiting	born 1674; died in infancy
15.	Mary Whiting	born 1676; died 30 September 1689
16.	Elizabeth Whiting	born 1678; married Nathaniel Pitkin
17.	Joseph Whiting	born 1680 (see below)
18.	Nathaniel Whiting	born 1683; died young
19.	Thomas Whiting	born 1686; died young
20.	John Whiting	born 1688; died 1715; unmarried

VI. **Joseph Whiting**, the son of William and Susannah, was born in 1645. In 1678, Joseph was appointed treasurer of Connecticut, which office he maintained for thirty-nine years until his death 19 October 1717. His son, Colonel John Whiting, succeeded him in 1717 and held the office for thirty-two years. Colonel Whiting's ledger, in which the first entry bears the date March 1716, passed to the youngest surviving son of each generation in direct line of descent until it came into the hands of Andrew Fuller Whiting, who was born 17 February 1844 at Avon, Connecticut, was one of the victims of the Park Central Hotel explosion in Hartford in 1899.He married (1) 5 October 1669 Mary Pynchon, daughter of the Honorable John Pynchon and Amy Wyllys. In 1676, Joseph married (2) Anna Allyn, daughter of Colonel John Allyn and Hannah Smith. Anna was born 18 August 1654 and died 3 March 1735. Both Joseph and Anna were buried in the old burial ground at the rear of the First Church of Christ, Hartford, now known as the Center Church.

> *Here lieth ye Body of Mrs. Anna, ye widow*
> *of Capt. Joseph Whiting, who died March ye 3d*
> *AD 1734/5 in ye 82d year of her age.*

> *Here Lyes*
> *Ye Body Of*
> *Mr. Joseph*
> *Whiting Treus'r*
> *Who Died October*
> *Ye 19, 1717, Aged*
> *73 Years.*

Joseph and Mary (Pynchon) Whiting had the following children:

21.	Mary Whiting	born 19 August 1672; married (1) Joseph Sheldon of Suffield; married (2) John Ashley, his second marriage
22.	Joseph Whiting Jr.	born 5 October 1674; died young
23.	Anna Whiting	born 28 August 1677; died 16 April 1684
24.	John Whiting	born 13 November 1679
25.	Susanna Whiting	born 18 June 1682; married (1) Samuel Thornton; married (2) Thomas Warren
26.	William Whiting	born 14 March 1683; died 6 September 1702
27.	Anna Whiting	born 18 August 1687; married Nathaniel Stanley
28.	Margaret Whiting	born 5 January 1690; married Jonathan Marsh
29.	John Whiting	born 5 December 1693; married Jerusha Lord

9. **William Whiting**, in 1693, went as the captain of a company of one hundred Englishmen and fifty Indians to assist in the defense of the Eastern settlements in the Providence of Maine and Massachusetts. In 1703, he held the rank of major and, in 1709, as a colonel and led a body of horse (cavalry unit) and infantrymen into the county of Hampshire, Massachusetts, to repel the French and Indians. In 1710, he was in command of troops at Fort Royal and, in 1711, the expedition against Canada. Colonel Whiting represented Hartford in the General Court from 1710 to 1715 and was speaker in 1714. Whiting was sheriff of Hartford County. He moved to Newport, Rhode Island, which is where he probably died. He married (1) 6 October 1686 Mary Allyn, daughter of Colonel John Allyn and great-granddaughter of Hon. William Pynchon. Mary was born 3 April 1657 and died 14 December 1724.[2]

12. **Abigail Whiting** daughter of John and Sybil (Collins) Whiting; married (1) in 1685, Deerfield, Massachusetts, Rev. Samuel Russell. They moved to Branford, Connecticut, where Samuel became the second minister of Branford. Samuel (1650-1731) was the son of Rev. John Russell, second minister of Wethersfield, Connecticut, and then first minister of Hadley, Massachusetts. Rev. Samuel Russell died 24 June 1731 at Branford at seventy-one years of age and in his thirty-fourth year of his ministry. Abigail died 7 May 1733.[2]

13. **Samuel Whiting**, the son of John and Sybil (Collins) Whiting, was born 24 April 1670. He received his early education from his father, who died

when Samuel was nineteen years of age. Samuel then looked to Rev. James Fitch of Norwich, Connecticut, for his continuing education in the ministry (see Fitch chapter).[1]

On 12 May 1692, the people of the settlement received a grant from the Court to establish the Town of Windham and to relieve them of any taxes for the four following years. They were informed that they should immediately find and maintain an able and faithful ministry.[11] The first town meeting was held 11 June 1692 with the following men assigned to various positions: Jeremiah Ripley, town clerk; Jonathan Crane and Jonathan Hough, townsmen; Thomas Huntington and John Royce, surveyors; Joseph Huntington, Jonathan Hough, Samuel Hide, and John Fitch, to lay out the highways. It was also decided that John Fitch would have the responsibility of recommending a minister, and therefore a vote was taken to allow Thomas Huntington to go to Milford (Connecticut) and apply to Mr. Samuel Whiting for his services. It was agreed to use the home of John Fitch as their meetinghouse until one could be built. After repeated requests, Mr. Whiting agreed to come to Windham.

Rev. Samuel Whiting was ordained 4 December 1700 and became the first minister of Windham First Church, known today as the First Congregational Church of Windham, Connecticut. At the time this chapter was written, the minister was Rev. James P. Beesley Jr., who was kind enough to send copies of two sermons (see sources 8 and 9 at the end of this chapter).

On page 1 of the book *Records of the Congregational Church in Windham, Conn. (Except Church Votes) 1700-1851*, it reads (spelling changed to present-day English), "The Rev. Samuel Whiting was ordained the Pastor of the first Church then to be gathered in Windham, 4 December 1700. The Church was gathered 10 December 1700. Mr. Whiting was gathered with it as the Pastor. The number of males was 15. Mr. Whiting's records were so worn and decayed as renders it impossible to collect all the names of those Persons."

According to A Sermon, Preached at Windham, AD 1721, on Thanksgiving Day, by Rev. Samuel Whiting, pastor of the First Church in Windham, printed by John Byrne, 1801 (spelling changed to present-day English), "Tradition says, and from the records it appears it may say correctly, that the first sermon Mr. Whiting preached at Windham was on the first day of the week and the first day of the year, from the first chapter of the Bible, and the first verse."

"At the time Mr. Whiting pursued his studies, there was no college in Connecticut; yet, with his father and the excellently learned Mr. Fitch, he had every advantage for improvement to qualify himself for an able and useful ministry. After the fist town-meeting in Windham, 11 June 1692, it was voted to apply to Mr. Samuel Whiting, for the purpose of carrying on the work of the ministry."[9]

When Samuel was just twenty-three years of age, in May 1693, as an inducement to stay with them for four years, they offered him £50-a-year allotment and to build him a house two-stories high and eighteen feet square. The land was laid out to him; and for the first year, instead of the house, they added £10 to his salary. In 1696, they built him a house, in1697 they gave him a call to ordination in 1699. It was repeated, and eighty loads of wood added to his salary. On 4 December 1700, he was ordained. On 10 December 1700, the church was gathered, and he was gathered with it as pastor. His salary was afterward raised to £100 plus his wood.[9]

In 1725, while on a visit to his friends at Enfield and at the home of Rev. Mr. John Collins, he was suddenly seized with pleurisy. He died a few days later, 27 September 1725, in the fifty-sixth year of his age and in the thirty-third after he began preaching.[9]

Under Mr. Whiting's administration, "eighty persons were added to his church in one half year, A. D. 1721, without extraordinary apparent occasion, but through the secret operation of the Spirit of God upon their hearts. In grateful acknowledgment of the goodness of God, a day of thanksgiving was set aside. Mr. Whiting's sermon on that occasion was from 1 Thessalonians Chapter 3 Verse 8, and was printed at New London, with a preface by the pious Mr. Adams. This sermon illustrates his piety, zeal and abilities, as a preacher in the truth, as it is in Jesus; and by this, though dead, he still spoke the necessity of regeneration and standing fast in the Lord. Among the people of his charge, he walked a shining light, and was esteemed by his friends of religion, and honored as a useful minister. He was much devoted to prayer, and in its efficacy had strong faith. In his last sickness, after his life was despaired of, it is said that he made two special prayers, one for his own family and one for the prosperity and continuance of his Church."[9]

"He was a man of stature tall, and well proportioned. His abilities were highly useful in the civil transactions of the town of Windham; and he assisted in gathering many of the churches in this county. But how soon those are forgotten whose labors, hardships and dangers have procured extensive blessings! In 100 years after he came to this town, his name was almost unknown. The facts above stated, were obtained after much enquiry of many persons and at different places. The only remaining printed copy of the sermon now republishing, was found in the family of Mrs. Tracy, of East-Haddam, a woman above 80 years of age, remarkable for her memory of ancient and curious facts, relative to persons and families."[9] Windham, December, AD 1800

Samuel married 14 September 1696 Ms. Elizabeth Adams, daughter of Rev. William and Alice (Bradford) Adams of Dedham and sister of the Rev. Eliphalet Adams of New London, by whom he had thirteen children: eight sons and five daughters. Alice (Bradford) Adams was the daughter of Deputy Governor

William Bradford Jr. and the granddaughter of William and Alice (Carpenter) (Southworth) Bradford. Following Samuel's death in 1725, Elizabeth Whiting married 22 December 1737 in Windham, Connecticut, Rev. Samuel Niles of Braintree, Massachusetts. Niles was born 1 May 1674, New Shoreham, Rhode Island. He died 1 May 1762, at which time, Elizabeth moved to New Haven to live with her son, Colonel Nathaniel Whiting, where she died 21 December 1766 at the age of eighty-five. The marriage ceremony of Elizabeth and Niles was performed by Elizabeth's son-in-law, Rev. Thomas Clap.[10]

Rev. Samuel and Elizabeth (Adams) Whiting had the following children:

30.	Anne Whiting	born 2 or 5 January 1698
31.	Samuel Whiting	born 20 February 1700; lost at sea
32.	Elizabeth Whiting	born 11 February 1702; died September 1730; unmarried
33.	William Whiting	born on 22 January 1704; lived in Norwich, Connecticut
34.	Joseph Whiting	born 17 February 1705; unmarried
35.	John Whiting	born 20 February 1706; lived in Windham
36.	Sybil Whiting	born 6 May 1708
37.	Martha Whiting	born 12 March 1710; died 29 June 1719
38.	Mary Whiting	born 24 November 1712; married Rev. Thomas Clapp
39.	Eliphalet Whiting	born 8 April 1715; died 9 August 1736; unmarried
40.	Elisha Whiting	born 17 January 1717
41.	Samuel Whiting	born 15 May 1720; lived in Stratford, Connecticut
42.	Nathan Whiting	born 4 May 1724; died 9 April 1771 (Colonel Whiting graduated from Yale College and married Mary, daughter of Roswell and Mary Saltonstall.)[10]

30. **Anne Whiting**, eldest daughter of Rev. Samuel Whiting, married 29 December 1721 Joseph Fitch (his second marriage). Joseph, born in 1681, was the son of Rev. James and Priscilla (Mason) Fitch. Joseph died at Lebanon, Connecticut, 7 May 1741. Anne died in Lebanon, Connecticut, 23 September 1778 (see Fitch chapter) (see Mason chapter).

38. **Mary Whiting** married Rev. Thomas Clap (also spelled Clapp) 23 November 1727. Thomas was born 26 June 1703 in Scituate, Massachusetts. He graduated from Harvard in July 1722 and, in 1725, moved to Windham where he was ordained 3 August 1723. Clap became the minister of the

First Church of Windham following the death of Rev. Samuel Whiting. Clap was dismissed from the church 10 December 1739, at which time he was inducted into the office as president of Yale College.[6] His interests were mathematics, astronomy, and philosophy, which led him to construct the first orrery (planetarium) in America.[12] Clap became the rector at Yale College (1740-1745) and became the first president of Yale University (1745-1766).[12] Mary (Whiting) Clap died 9 August 1736 and was interred at the burying grounds in Windham. Clap died in New Haven, Connecticut, 7 January 1767. You can read more about Rev. Thomas Clap's accomplishments on the Internet.

Rev. Thomas and Mary Clapp had two children:

42.	Mary Clapp	born 25 April 1729; married David Wooster, who later became major general in the Revolutionary army
44.	Temperance Clapp	born April 1732; married Rev. Timothy Pitkin, son of Governor William Pitkin of Connecticut

17.   **Joseph,** the son of Rev. John and Phebe (Gregson) Whiting, was born in 1680 and settled in New Haven, Connecticut. He was elected to the General Court in 1716, 1722, and 1724. He was also the clerk of the House. He was elected to the Upper House in 1725 where he continued for twenty-one years. He married 30 January 1709/10 Hannah Trowbridge, daughter of Thomas Trowbridge of New Haven. Hon. Joseph Whiting died 4 April 1784. Hannah (Trowbridge) Whiting died 9 August 1784.

Notes

1. William Whiting, former president of the New England Historical Genealogical Society and author of War Powers Under the Constitution of the United States. *Memoir of Rev. Samuel Whiting, D. D. and of his wife, Elizabeth St. John; with reference to some of their English Ancestors and American Descendants.* 250 copies printed (not published)

2. Mary K. Talcott *The Original Proprietors of Hartford*, Cfrom *Memorial History of Hartford, Connecticut. First publishe 1886; Tuttle Antiquian Books Rutland Vermont*

3. John Langdon Sibley, M. A. *Biological Sketches of Graduates of Harvard University*, Volume I, 1642B1658, Cambridge Charles William Sever, University Bookstore, printed 1873.

4. Edwin Pond Parker *History of The Second Church of Christ in Hartford*, Belknap & Warfield, Hartford, Connecticut 1892.

5. Lucius Barns Barbour, *Families of Early Hartford, Connecticut*, Genealogical Publishing Co., Inc 1982

6. Records of the Congregational Church in Windham, Conn., 1700-1851, by Hartford, Connecticut Historical Society and The Society of Mayflower Descendants in the State of Connecticut, 1943

7. John T. Fitch, with the assistance of Patricia M. Geisler, *Descendants of the Reverend James Fitch, 1622-1702*, the first Five Generations Volume I, Picton Press Camden, Maine 1997.

8. John Byrne, (printer) *A Century Sermon Preached Before the First Church in Windham, December 10 A. D. 1800*, printed 1801.

9. John Byrne, *A Sermon Preached at Windham, A. D. 1721 on Thanksgiving Day, by Rev. Samuel Whiting, Pastor of The First Church in Windham*, printed, 1801.

10. Jane Devlin, (transcriber) Extracted from *Inscriptions of Tombstones in New Haven, Erected prior to 1800*, From the papers of the N. H. Colony Hist. Soc., Vol. III, 1882.

11. Ruth Swift, *A History of the Village and The First Congregational Church of Windham, Connecticut*, 275th Anniversary, December 10, 1975.

12. Wikipedia the free Encyclopedia.

13. Clarence Almon Torrey with Third Supplement by Melinde Lutz Sanborn, *New England Marriages Prior to 1700*, Genealogical Publishing Company, Baltimore, Maryland 1985

EIGHT

William Bradford

(See Appendix H)

———————•◆•———————

(Editor's note: As you read through this chapter, you will notice a lot of marriages to members of the same family. Perhaps many of the marriages were "convenience marriages," meaning that the husband who was widowed with several children married a widow also with several children. This then would allow for someone to be at home to take care of the youngsters and, at the same time, allow for someone to support both families.)

There have been many books written about our ancestor, William Bradford. I merely wish to point out a few events that I feel might be interesting and of importance to our family history with hopes that you will be inspired to learn more about this incredible man. Please do not take his accomplishments lightly as he began the writings that all stories of the Pilgrims landing in America are based. It is his diary that forms whatever is or was written about the Pilgrims, the *Mayflower*, and Plymouth. Should you have an interest in learning about your ancestor, there are a few books that are a must. The titles of these books are at the end of this chapter and, for the most part, are what I used as some of the sources for this chapter.

William Bradford of the *Mayflower* was baptized on 19 March 1589/90 in Austerfield, York, England, and was the son of William and Alice (Hanson) Bradford. His father died before William's second birthday. At age four, when William's mother remarried, William went to live with his grandfather. A few years later, before he was seven years old, his grandfather and his mother died. William was then sent to live with his two uncles. William's only sibling was Alice, who lived with another family.

Robert and Thomas Bradford were both sheep farmers and earned a good living. For years and years, sheep farming had been the way of life for the Bradford family. They enjoyed a good reputation from their friends and neighbors. But William did not take to sheep herding. This kind of life was lonely. He had to go out and watch the sheep all day long with no one to talk to. William loved to read, but there were never enough books for him.

While living in Austerfield, William attended an Anglican church, which to him was very boring and dull. Every Sunday was the same—they would attend church and sit in the same pew, listening to the same ideas. When William was twelve years old, things became a little more exciting. One Sunday morning, William decided to join a friend and attend a Puritan church service. William had to sneak out of the house while his uncles and their families were still sleeping. Both William and his friend walked eight miles through the thick forest to Babworth. When William returned home, his uncles asked him where he had been and reminded him that his place was with the other members of the Bradford family in their pew. His uncles were very angry as they did not agree with the Puritan way of worship.

William did not listen to his uncles, instead, he listened to his heart. The Puritan way of thinking was exciting to William, and the people that he met were much friendlier. William decided that he would walk to Babworth every Sunday just to listen to the Puritan preacher, even though it angered his uncles.

Four more years went by, and one Sunday, William attended a secret church service at a member's house. William had to ensure that he was not seen by anyone outside the group attending this meeting. If someone from town had noticed him going inside the house, all would have been arrested. Finally when William was sure it was safe, he quickly went to the front door and knocked. The door was opened by his friend, Mr. Brewster, and William went in.

This Sunday (the year was 1606), the small group had decided to separate themselves from the Puritans and the Church of England. To make this feat official, they made up a membership agreement of which William Bradford was one of the signers. They would become known as the Separatist of Scrooby (manor).

The Puritans had hoped James I, King of England, would be open to new ideas. But that was not to be. King James put into law, stating that the Puritans could not meet by themselves and wanted them to behave as other member of the Church of England. He even stated, "I will put down this Puritan devil even if it cost me my crown." King James did his best to destroy the Puritans. There were many suggestions as how to change the Church of England, and those who spoke out were either imprisoned or killed. Mr. Brewster was one of those imprisoned. William Bradford wrote that Mr. Brewster was a kind, gentle man who was always cheerful, sociable, and pleasant among his friends. He would loan William books and let him live in his large forty-room house.

Mr. Brewster did not agree with the way King James wanted the people of England to worship, rather he wanted to worship God the way he thought the Bible instructed. This new way of worship allowed those who had questions ask them. The Church of England did not allow this form of worshiping.

At first William's uncle did not say anything about the Separatist meetings, that is, until King James made another new law. It stated that every man in England had to go to the Church of England, or he would be put in jail. William's uncles again warned him about this new religion, but that did not sway William. They even threatened to kick him out of the house.

As the word spread about the new religion, so did the hatred from the English people that were faithful to the king and the Church of England. The king's men confiscated land and farm animals from the Separatists, and many people were arrested. It became unsafe anywhere in England. One of those arrested was Mr. Brewster. He confessed about the meeting at Scrooby and was fined a very large sum. He was warned to discontinue the meeting and then was released from custody. It was then that the Separatist group decided to move to a different country, which turned out to be Holland.

Arrangements were made for the group to sail to Holland, and once on board with their belongings, did they then discover that the captain had been a part of a plot to turn them over to the king. The captain never planned to take them to Holland. The Separatists were then separated, with the men in one boat and the women in another. Then they were searched thoroughly, looking for gold, silver, money, books, and other valuable things. Then the entire group was thrown into jail. The year was 1607. While William was in jail, he had plenty to think about. Was going to Holland the right move? True, Holland did not have a king to tell them what to do or what church to attend. But what about finding work or learning a new language? Did he really want to leave the Bradford family forever? On the positive side, the Separatist could enjoy the religious freedom they were seeking; and this meant more to them than money, their country, their trades, or even their family ties. Many were willing to die for this freedom. Even at the age of eighteen, William truly believed that he was right. He had already spent time in jail for what he believed and now believed more than ever that his decision to remain with the Separatist group was the right decision and that he would get to Holland no matter what. Sometime later, all but seven members (of which one was Mr. Brewster) of the group were released from jail; but in a way, being out of jail was no better. They had lost all of their money and their homes. They were in a foreign port city, and to add to their problems, their leader was still in jail.

In August 1608, William finally was headed toward Holland. As he stood on deck of the ship, he could see his new home off on the horizon. The town of Middleburg was to be where he would be able to enjoy the freedom to worship as he pleased. The other Separatists were there waiting for him. Instead of all sailing on the same ship, they sailed individually on small ships of which William was one of the last groups.

William found work at a loom, making silk, and shared a small house in Amsterdam with the Brewster family. He wondered if he would ever get used to the big city, which was a lot like London and not like the small country farm life he was use to. Although the group from Scooby made friends quickly, they were still unhappy with Amsterdam. At this time, there were about twenty members of the small group from Scrooby. They had little money, and there were days that they went without food. There were also many disagreements between the Separatists and other members of the community, so they decided to move to the coast of Leyden, which was fine with William. When word got out that the Scrooby friends were moving, about eighty other English Separatists from another church wanted to journey with them.

William was okay with the move to Leyden as there was nothing special about Amsterdam that would sadden him, that is, with the exception of Dorothy. Dorothy was a very pretty young girl, but her youth was the problem—she was too young to marry. Besides Dorothy being young, William did not have a house, a good job, or any other means to support a wife.

Good things began to happen to William once he arrived in Leyden. He received some of the Bradford money from England. With the money from England and what he was earning from his job as a weaver, William bought a house. Now, he had enough money to marry Dorothy who was now sixteen years of age.

Even though—on a personal note—things were going well for William and Dorothy, as for the Separatists, the future looked bleak. Holland was going to war with Spain. And if Holland lost the war, then a king or queen would rule Holland and the Separatist would no longer be free to worship as they pleased. It was again time to move on.

The 22 July 1620 was the date that the Pilgrims set out from Leyden toward the New World. The Pilgrims boarded the ship *Speedwell*. The ship could not take all of the Separatists, nor could many afford the tariff, so some had to stay behind—but not before promising that they would again meet, but next time in America. They sailed to Southampton, England, where they were to join up with those that was sponsoring the voyage. The group was not Separatist, but rather a group of mixed religion. They were just anxious to leave England and perhaps find a much freer life in the New World.

The passengers, now numbering 102, boarded the *Speedwell* and the larger ship, the *Mayflower*, and thus their voyage began. Troubles began almost immediately as the *Speedwell* began to sprout leaks throughout the ship. The captain communicated with the captain of the *Mayflower*, and it was agreed that they would head for the port of Dartmouth where they would repair the damaged ship. Once it was felt that the *Speedwell* was safe to sail, the journey was again underway. When the ships were about one hundred leagues (about three hundred miles) from Land's End, England, the captain of the *Speedwell* again felt uncomfortable about making the journey with his ship. After talking it over with the captain of the *Mayflower*, they both agreed to head back to England and the port of Plymouth.

Much time was lost, going back and forth for repairs; but finally on 6 September 1620, the overcrowded *Mayflower* last saw the shores of England as it began its voyage to America. Not all of the 102 passengers were Separatists, or sometimes referred to as Saints. There were about forty Separatists with the remainder being labeled as Strangers. The Strangers just wanted to leave England and find a new place to live. They were not at all concerned about religious freedom. On 11 November 1620,[1] after sixty-six days on the high seas, the *Mayflower* finally touched land, but not where they had intended. They were a few hundred miles north of their intended destination. After much discussion, the captain headed the *Mayflower* in a southward direction. After a few hours, they encountered dangerous shores and roaring breakers and very rough winds. So much so that they decided to turn around and head back toward Cape Cod.

They dropped anchor off the shores of Provincetown at the tip of Cape Cod. Although anchored, no one was allowed off the ship until after certain business was settled, like how they would live and according to what rules. Being on the new land, there were no "old laws" to abide by, so new ones had to be stated and agreed upon. Some stated that they did not want any rules while others felt that they should follow God's rules. The decision was eventually made to vote for a leader and to have "just and equal laws." The men came up with new ideas that were quite different from those of England. Once these ideas were written down, all of the men signed their names. The document thus became known as the *Mayflower Compact*. Once that was completed, John Carver was voted to become the first governor of Plymouth Colony.

THE MAYFLOWER COMPACT

In the name of God Amen We, whose names are underwritten, the Loyal Subjects of our dread Sovereign Lord, King James, by the Grace of God, of England, France and Ireland, King, Defender of the Faith, &.Having undertaken for the Glory of God, and Advancement of the Christian Faith, and the Honour [sic] of our King and Country, a voyage to plant the first colony in the northern parts of Virginia; do by these presents, solemnly and mutually in the Presence of God and one of another, covenant and combine ourselves together into a civil Body Politick, [sic] for our better Ordering and Preservation, and Furtherance of the Ends aforesaid; And by Virtue hereof to enact, constitute, and frame, such just and equal Laws, Ordinances, Acts, Constitutions and Offices, from time to time, as shall be thought most meet and convenient for the General good of the Colony; unto which we promise all due submission and obedience. In Witness whereof we have hereunto subscribed our names at Cape Cod the eleventh of November, in the Reign of our Sovereign Lord, King James of England, France and Ireland, the eighteenth, and of Scotland the fifty-fourth. Anno Domini, 1620.

Once agreed, the document received the signatures of 41 of the 102 passengers, 37 of whom were members of the Separatists who were fleeing religious persecution in Europe. This compact established the first basis in the New World for written laws. Half the colony failed to survive the first winter, but the remainder lived on and prospered.

Once the business end was out of the way, a search party went ashore to look for a fitting place to call home. They were also looking to see what dangers await the entire party once ashore. The search party consisted of sixteen well-armed men and was led by Captain Myles Standish, a seasoned military man. There were times that they saw a small party of Indians, but the Indians did not confront them at first. Rather, they ran in the opposite direction. The party discovered several brooks with clean clear water. They discovered cleared fields where the Indians had planted corn and where they also buried their dead. It was getting dark, so the search party returned to their boat and went back to the *Mayflower*, taking with them fresh water for the rest of the passengers.

The searches continued almost on a daily basis. The weather was bitter cold, and the ground was covered with a thick blanket of snow. Finally on December 15, they pulled up anchor and sailed across the bay to a spot where they could drop anchor. This new spot for the *Mayflower* was still pretty far from shore, so the passengers and supplies had to be tendered to the shore of their new home. The distance from the *Mayflower* to the shore was about six miles. On 25 December 1620, they began to erect their first house, which was the common house and which was used as a hospital for those who took sick from the very wet and cold winter. Christmas was not celebrated as we celebrate today. There were no gifts or special meals prepared. They did, however, recognize the birth of Christ as written in the New Testament.

William was among those that became sick and had to spend time in the common house. A few months later, the settlers had homes, some of which were left empty due to death. About fifty Pilgrims died that first winter, and it was thought that because there were so few left to defend the settlement, the Indians would attack them and kill the remaining few.

During a meeting of the men, while making plans as to how to defend their small settlement and much to their surprise, a Native American had walked into the middle of the settlement. The Pilgrims were startled, and before they could grab their weapons and fight, the Indian said, "Welcome." His name was Samoset, and he was one of those that were sold as a slave and sent to England several years earlier. This is where he learned to speak English. Samoset spent the night in the settlement, and over the next few days, there were other visitors. Two very important visitors were Squanto and the Indian chief, Massasoit. Squanto was also one of the ones who had been captured earlier and sent to England. He, like Samoset, knew the English language and was very helpful in communicating with the chief and other Native Americans.

As mentioned earlier, John Carver was selected by the passengers of the *Mayflower* to be the first governor of Plymouth Colony. He died on 5 April 1621 and was replaced by William Bradford. He was reelected thirty times and continued to serve as governor up until the date of his death, except for five years that he chose not to serve William Bradford who died on 9 May 1657. His ashes are buried in Burial Hill in Plymouth, Massachusetts.

William and Dorothy May were married on 10 December 1613 in Amsterdam, Holland. Because of the dangerous voyage, they left their son John behind with friends. He later came to America and married twice. John did not father any children. He died on 21 September 1676 while living in Norwich, Connecticut.

On 7 December 1620, while William, with the advance party, was on shore, Dorothy Bradford fell overboard. There was no one there to save her, and she drowned.

William Bradford was still corresponding with friends back in England and Holland. One such letter he received stated that Alice (Carpenter) Southworth's husband had passed away. William sent a letter to Alice, asking her to come to Plymouth.

In July 1623, the ships *Anne* and *James* arrived in Plymouth. The ships were mainly being used to transport supplies from England to the New World; however, there were a few passengers. Among the *Anne* passengers was Alice (Carpenter) Southworth. Alice was born in Somerset, Wrington County, England, on 3 August 1590 and was the daughter of Alexander Carpenter. She married Edward Southworth on 28 May 1613 in Leyden, Holland. They were both members of the same church as William Bradford. Edward died in Leyden about 1621. Alice and Edward had two sons: Constant, born in 1614 or 1615, and Thomas, born in 1616. It is not clear if Constant and Thomas arrived with their mother or if they were left behind in Leyden or England. The passenger list for the *Anne* indicates that Alice traveled alone. Other passengers with children were listed.

Constant Southworth was admitted a freeman in 1637 and, in 1640, was the receiver of a grant of fifty acres at North River. He lived in Duxbury, Massachusetts, and held the position of deputy. He married Elizabeth Collier 2 November 1637, and lived in Duxbury, Massachusetts, where Constant died 11 May 1679.

Thomas Southworth, later referred to as Captain, died 8 December 1669 in Plymouth, Massachusetts. He married 1 September 1641 Elizabeth Reynor and had one child who was also named Elizabeth.

On 14 August 1623, Alice (Carpenter) Southworth became the wife of William Bradford. William now had a family, but in addition to Alice and her two sons, they also took in orphans.

Alice died in Plymouth, Massachusetts, March 26/27, 1670.

William and Alice Bradford had the following children:

1   William Bradford Jr.   born 17 June 1624
2.   Mercy Bradford   born before May 1627
3.   Joseph Bradford   born ca. 1630

The Last Will and Testament of
Alice (Carpenter) (Southworth) Bradford

The Last Will and Testament of mistris Allice Bradford senir of Plymouth Deceased ; exhibited to the Court held att Plymouth in new England the 7th Day of June Anno Dom 1670 on the oathes of Nathaniel: Morton and Leift: Ephraim Morton; as followeth;

I Allis Bradford senir of the Towne of Plymouth in the Jurisdiction of New Plymouth widdow : being weake in body but of Disposing mind and prfect memory blessed be God; not knowing how soone the Lord may please to take mee out of this world unto himselfe : Doe make and ordaine this to be my last Will and Testament; in manor and forme as followeth; Impr I bequeath my soule to god that gave it and my body to the Dust in hope of a Joyfull resurrection unto glory; Desiring that my body may be Intered as neare unto my Deceased husband; Mr. William Bradford: as Conveniently may be; and as for my worldly estate I Dispose of it as followeth; Imprs I give and bequeath unto my Deare sister Mary Carpenter; the bed I now lye on with the furniture: thereunto belonging and a paire of sheets and a good Cow and a yearling heiffer and a younge mare Item I give and bequeath unto my son Mr. Constant Southworth my Land att Paomett: viz all my Purchase land there: with all my rights privilidges and appurtenances thereunto belonging; To him and his heires and assignes for ever; Item I give and bequeath unto

my said son Constant Southworth and unto my son Mr. Joseph Bradford:
the one halfe of my sheep; to be equally Devided betwixt them; and the other
halfe to my son Captaine William Bradford Item I give unto my said son
Joseph Bradford my paire of working oxen and a white heiffer; Item I give
unto my honored frend Mr. Thomas Prence one of the bookes that were my
Deare husbands Library; which of them hee shall Choose; Item I give unto
my Deare Grandchild Elizabeth Howland; the Daughter of my Deare son
Captaine Thomas Southworth Deceased; the sume of seaven pounds; for
the use and benifitt of her son James Howland Item I give unto my servant
maide Mary Smith a Cow Calfe to be Delivered her the next springe if I
Decease this winter; and if I Doe not Decease this winter; my will is that
she have one Delivered to her out of my estate in some short time after my
Decease; all the rest of my estate not Disposed of already by this my last Will
and Testament; as above said; I give and bequeath unto my sonnes Mr.
Constant Southworth Captaine William Bradford and Mr. Joseph Bradford
to be equally Devided amongst them in equall and alike proportions;

In Witnes that this is my Last Will and Testament I the said Allice
Bradford have heerunto sett my hand and seale; this twenty ninth day of
December anno Dom one Thousand six hundred sixty nine.

1. **William Bradford Jr.**, born 17 June 1624, Plymouth, married (1) ca. 1650 Alice Richards.[7] Alice was born in England in 1627 and was baptized in 1629. Alice was the daughter of Thomas and Welthean (Loring) Richards. The will of Welthean Richards (widow) who died in Boston, Massachusetts, names Thomas, Alice, Hannah, Mercy, William Jr., John, Samuel, Melatiah, Mary, and Sarah Bradford "children of William Bradford of Plymouth Colony & my daughter Alice deceased."

William Bradford Jr. was a high-ranking military man of the Colony. He served next to Miles Standish. He was commander in chief of the Plymouth forces during the King Philip's War. While fighting at the Narragansett Fort, he received a musket ball in his flesh, which was never removed. He held the rank of major and was appointed assistant treasurer and deputy governor of Plymouth from 1682 to 1686 and again from 1689 to 1691. Following the previous appointments, he was a member of the Council of Massachusetts.

William Jr. and Alice (Richards) Bradford had the following children:

1.	John Bradford	born 20 February 1652/3
2.	William Bradford	born 11 March 1654/5

3.	Thomas Bradford	born ca. 1658
4.	Alice Bradford	born 1659; married (Rev.) William Adams
5.	Mercy Bradford	baptized 2 September 1660
6.	Hannah Bradford	born 9 May 1662
7.	Melatiah Bradford	born 1 November 1664
8.	Samuel Bradford	born ca. 1667
9.	Mary Bradford	born ca. 1668
10.	Sarah Bradford	born 1671

Alice (Richards) Bradford died 12 December 1671 at the age of forty-four.[8] William Jr. married (2) in ca. 1673 Sarah (maiden name unknown) widow of Francis Griswold. Sarah died prior to ca 1676.

William Jr., and Sarah had one child:

| 11. | Joseph Bradford | born 18 April 1675 |

11. Joseph Bradford, born 18 April 1675, married 15 October 1698, Lebanon, Connecticut, Anna Fitch, daughter of Rev. James and Priscilla (Mason) Fitch of Norwich, Connecticut. Anna was born 6 April 1675, Norwich, Connecticut, and died 7 October 1715, Lebanon, Connecticut. Joseph married (2) Mary (Sherwood) Fitch who was born in 1674 and died 16 September 1752, Montville, Connecticut. Mary was Joseph's first cousin once removed. Mary was the daughter of Matthew and Mary (Fitch) Sherwood. Mary (Fitch) Sherwood was the daughter of Thomas, the brother of Rev. James Fitch. Mary (Sherwood) married (1) Daniel Fitch in Prescott, Connecticut, 7 March 1698. Daniel was the son of Rev. James and Priscilla (Mason) Fitch.

William Bradford Jr. married (3) ca. 1676 in Plymouth, Massachusetts, the widow Mary (Wood) Holmes, widow of John Holmes and daughter of John and Mary (Masterson) Wood (or Atwood). Mary (Wood) married (1) 11 December 1661 in Plymouth, Massachusetts, John Holmes and had three children: Joseph Holmes, Mary Holmes, and Isaac Holmes.[6]

William Bradford Jr. and Mary (Wood) (Holmes) Bradford had the following children:

12.	Israel Bradford	born ca. 1677
13.	Ephraim Bradford	born 1685
14.	David Bradford	born about 1687 or so
15.	Hezekiah Bradford	born about 1687 or so

The will of William Bradford Jr., who at the time of his death was living in Plymouth, Massachusetts, His will was dated 29 June 1703, and proved 10 March 1704.

William's will include the following:

> *Wife Mary and sons, David, Ephraim, Hezekiah, eldest son John who was to have "my father's manuscript viz.: a Narrative of the beginning of New Plimoth [sic]."*
>
> *Grandson, William, son of son William deceased and son Thomas to have lands in Norwich, Ct., which were the lands of my brother John Bradford.*
>
> *Sons Samuel and Joseph, the latter to have "a portion of lands near Norwich, part of which was his mother's;"*
>
> *Son, Israel; grandsons John Bradford and William Bradford, sons of son John; daughters, Mercy Steel, Hannah Ripley, Melatiah Steel, Mary Hunt, Alice Fitch, and Sarah Baker; Hannah wife of son Samuel; sons, John, Samuel and Israel executors.*

On March 17, 1704/5, Israel, Ephraim, David, and Hezekiah Bradford divided the land given them by their father, Major William Bradford.[2]

4. **Alice Bradford**, daughter of William Bradford Jr. and Alice (Richard), was born in 1659. She married on 29 January 1680 (some references say 29 March 1680) Rev. William Adams Jr. who was the son of William Adams Sr. Adams was born on 27 May 1650 in Ipswich; this was William's second marriage. William was a graduate of Harvard College in 1671 and was ordained second minister of Dedham, Massachusetts, on 3 December 1673. He died on 17 June 1685, shortly before his fourth child was born.[2]

These were the children of William and Alice (Bradford) Adams:

16.	Elizabeth Adams	born 21 February 1680/81; married Rev. Samuel Whiting of Lebanon, Connecticut (see Whiting chapter)
17.	Alice Adams	born 3 April 1682
18.	William Adams	born 17 December 1683
19.	Abigail Adams	born 15 December 1685

Following the death of Rev. William Adams, Alice (Bradford) Adams married Major James Fitch 8 May 1687, Norwich, Connecticut. Major Fitch was born in Saybrook, Connecticut, 2 August 1649. He died 10 November 1727, Canterbury, Connecticut. He was the son of Rev. James and Abigail (Whitfield) Fitch (see Fitch chapter). Major Fitch first married Elizabeth Mason at Norwich, Connecticut, in January 1676/7. Elizabeth was the daughter of Major John Mason (see Mason chapter) and Ann (Peck) Mason (see Peck chapter) and the sister of Priscilla Mason and wife of Rev. James Fitch, father of Major James Fitch.

James and Alice (Bradford) (Adams) Fitch had the following children:

21.	James Fitch	born January 1677; died one week later[4]
22.	James Fitch	born 7 June 1679; and died early in life[4]
23.	Jedediah Fitch	born 17 April 1681[4]
24.	Samuel Fitch	born 12 July 1683[4]

16. Elizabeth Adams, daughter of Alice Bradford and Rev. William Adams, was born in Dedham, Massachusetts, 23 February 1680. She married (1) Rev. Samuel Whiting (see Whiting chapter) in Windham, Connecticut, 4 September 1696. Rev. Whiting was baptized in Hartford, Connecticut, 24 April 1670 and was the son of Rev. John and Sybil (Collins) Whiting. Samuel Whiting died in Enfield, Connecticut, before 27 September 1725.[1]

Elizabeth (Adams) Whiting married (2) Rev. Samuel Niles in Windham, Connecticut, on 22 December 1737.

Elizabeth and Rev. Samuel Whiting had the following children:

25.	Anne Whiting	born 2 January 1698
26.	Samuel Whiting	born 20 February 1700; died 1718 at sea, age 18
27.	Elizabeth Whiting	born 11 February 1702
28.	William Whiting	born 11 January 1704
29.	Joseph Whiting	born 17 February 1705; died 1 March 1722; unmarried
30.	John Whiting	born 20 February 1705/6
31.	Sybil Whiting	born 6 May 1708
32.	Martha Whiting	born 12 March 1710; died 29 June 1719
33.	Mary Whiting	born 24 November 1712; died 9 August 1736; married Rev. Thomas Clap,

minister of the Congregational Church in Windham, Connecticut, formally known as Windham First Church [d]

34.	Eliphalet Whiting	born 8 April 1715; died 9 August 1736
35.	Elisha Whiting	born 17 January 1717
36.	Samuel Whiting	born 15 May 1720
37.	Joseph Whiting	No information
38.	Nathan Whiting	born 4 May 1724

Elizabeth (Adams) (Whiting) Niles died in New Haven, Connecticut, 21 December 1766 at the age of eighty-six.

Notes

1. William Bradford, Introduction by Samuel Eliot Morison *Of Plymouth Plantation 1620-1647*, Sometimes Governor Thereof. The complete Text and Notes and Introduction by, published by Alfred A. Knoff, Inc. Twenty-third printing 2004.

2. Robert S. Wakefield, F. A. S. G. and Lee D. Van Antwerp, M. D. Former C. G. *Mayflower Families in Progress; William Bradford of the Mayflower and His Descendants for Four Generations*, Second Edition General Society of Mayflower Descendants 1988.

3. Roscoe Conkling Fitch, *History of the Fitch Family A. D. 1400-1930, A record of the Fitches in England and America Including "Pedigree of Fitch" Certified by the College of Arms, London, England.* Volume 1and 2 Published privately by the Fitch Family Record Publishing Company Haverhill, Massachusetts, 1930

4. John T. Fitch with the assistance of Patricia M. Geisler, *Descendants of Reverend James Fitch 1622-1702, The First Five Generations*, Volume 1Picton Press, Camden, Maine 1997

5. *Records of the Congregational Church in Windham, Connecticut 1700B1851*; Hartford Historical Society and the Society of Mayflower Descendants in the state of Connecticut, published 1943.

6. Clarence Almon Torrey, *New England Marriages Prior to 1700;* prepared for publication by Elizabeth P. Bently, Genealogical Publishing Company, Baltimore, Maryland 1985.

7. Melinde Lutz Sanborn, Third Supplement to Torrey's New England marriages Prior to 1700 Genealogical Publishing Company, Baltimore, Maryland 2003.

Other books that may be of interest:

William Bradford, Pilgrim Boy by Bradford Smith

James Daugherty *The Landing of the Pilgrims, (Landmark Books)*

Marianne Hering. Arthur. M. Schlesinger Jr., Senior Consulting Editor, Colonial LeadersCWilliam

Bradford, Governor of Plymouth Colony, Chelsea House Publishers.

The Pilgrims:A Brief History, by L. D. Geller, New England Historical Series, Cape Cod Publishers, Plymouth, Massachusetts.

Bradford History of Plimoth Plantation From the Original Manuscript, printed under the direction of the Secretary of the Commonwealth, by order of the General Court, Boston: Wright & Potter Printing Co., State Printers 1899.

NINE

Rev. Robert Peck

(See Appendix I)

During the fifteenth century and into the sixteenth century, many of the Peck families in England added an *e*, thus changing the spelling to Pecke. But over the years, the *e* has since been dropped, and now Peck is the common spelling. Since ancient time, the Peck name has had various way of being spelled, i.e., Pek, Peck, Pecke, Peke, or Peake. These spellings have been found in different works on heraldry.

The genealogy of this line dates back to John Peck, Esq., and the twenty-first generation. This pedigree, up to Rev. Robert Peck and his brother Joseph, can be found in the British Museum in London, England. The records of the family of Rev. Robert Peck can be found in Hingham, England.

The Peck name is of great antiquity—they are found seated in England, in Belton, Yorkshire, at a very early date. One such branch of the Peck family settled in Hesden and Wakefield in Yorkshire, whose descendants later moved to Beccles, Suffolk County.

Robert Peck Sr. was from Beccles, England, and was born in 1546. He died in 1593 at the age of forty-seven. In England, his position in society was that of a Gentleman of Gentry, which entitled him to coat armor, which at the time was before the title of baronet, which was instituted by James I in 1611.[6]

Robert and Helen (Babbs) Peck had the following children:

1. Richard Peck   born 1574; died 1615; without issue

2.	Nicholas Peck	born 1576; who married Rachael, daughter of William Young
3.	Robert Peck	born 1580, rector at Hingham, England
4.	Joseph Peck	baptized 30 April 1580
5.	Margaret Peck	
6.	Martha Peck	
7.	Samuel Peck	died 1619

In 1638, two brothers (Robert and Joseph) and members of their families, along with member of Saint Andrew's Church in Hingham, England, sailed across the ocean on the ship *Diligent* (out of Ipswich, England) and set foot on the shores of Massachusetts. Further in this chapter, you will read about Rev. Robert Peck, his parishioners, and their trip to America.

4.   **Joseph Peck** was baptized 30 April 1587 and was the son of Robert and Helen (Babbs) Peck. Joseph came to America on the same ship as his brother, Rev. Robert Peck. Traveling with Joseph was his second wife (Deliverance?); three sons (Joseph Jr., John, and Nicholas); one daughter (Rebecca) and five servants, two male and three female.[2]

Joseph married twice, his first wife being Rebecca Clark whom he married 21 May 1617 in Hingham, England. Rebecca died 24 October 1637, Hingham, England. Joseph married his second wife, Deliverance (date unknown) before leaving England. Upon arriving in America, they lived in Hingham, Massachusetts, until 1645, and then moved to Seekonk and then to Rehoboth, Massachusetts.[7] Joseph became a freeman 31 March 1639.

Joseph's will starts out, "Known all men by these presents that I Joseph Peck Sen[r] of Rehoboth."

Family members mentioned in his will are: sons Joseph, John, Nicholas, Samuell [*sic*], Nathaniel and Israel, daughter Hubbert [*sic*] Joseph's will was recorded "upon the old Plymouth Colony Records of Wills, 2d part, Vol. 2d, Folio 12." The will was witnessed by Joseph, John, Nicholas, Samuell [*sic*], Nathaniell [*sic*], and Israell [*sic*] Pecke. [*sic*]

Nowhere can I find a date as to when the will was written or when it was recorded. There is, however, a statement by the sons mentioned in the will and referred to as "a further amplification of our father's will upon his death bed." The statement was signed by Joseph's six sons. His daughter, Rebecca, was the only one who did not sign the statement.

Joseph and Rebecca (Clark) Peck's children were born in Hingham, England, with the exception of Samuel, Nathaniel, and Israel. The following was taken from the book *Genealogical History of The Descendants of Joseph Peck* by Ira B. Peck. Joseph died in 1663 while living in Rehoboth, Massachusetts.[6]

8.	Anna Peck	baptized 12 March 1617; died Hingham, England, 27 July 1636
9.	Rebecca Peck	baptized 25 May 1620; married Rev. Peter Hobart
10	Joseph Peck Jr.	baptized 23 August 1623
11	John Peck	baptized about 1626; died 1713
12	Nicholas Peck	baptized 9 April 1630; died 27 May 1710
13	Samuel Peck	baptized 3 February1638/9, Hingham, Massachusetts
14	Nathaniel Peck	baptized 31 October 1641, Hingham, Massachusetts
15	Israel Peck	baptized 4 March 1644, Hingham, Massachusetts

9. **Rebecca** came to America with her father and stepmother, Deliverance, in 1638. She was referred as "daughter Hubbert" in her father's will. After much research and with the help of several genealogists on a Massachusetts mailing list, I learned that Hubbart was an older version of Hobart.

Peter Hobart (1604-1679) married (1) 12 October 1628 Elizabeth Ibrook in England. Their marriage was recorded at a church in the town of Covehithe, just south of St. Andrew's, where Rev. Robert Peck was the rector. Elizabeth was born in 1608 and came to America with her husband and two children. She died in 1645. Peter married (2) Rebecca Peck in 1646 in Hingham, Massachusetts. Rebecca was born in 1620 and died in 1693.[7] Peter Hobart was among the founders of Hingham, Massachusetts, and became their first minister. Rev. Hobart arrived in America in 1635. He immediately began church services in a structure called the meetinghouse. Town meetings and other gatherings were held in the meetinghouse and continued until 1681 when the new church was completed. The Old Ship Church is the oldest building in continuous ecclesiastical use in the United States. The church was registered as a national landmark in 1962.[8]

Rev. Hobart received his education in Cambridge, England. He was originally enrolled at Queens College, but at the suggestion of his mentor, Rev. Robert Peck, transferred to Magdalene College where he graduated and was ordained in 1629.

10 **Joseph Peck Jr.** born in the year 1623 and was about fifteen years of age when he came to America in 1638 with his parents and siblings. As an adult, he built his house near his father's home. In 1655, Joseph was one of a committee to impose a tax or mandatory contribution in order to support a minister. Over time, Joseph made several purchases of land, which he passed on to his sons at his death. There is no mention of a wife in Joseph's will therefore we must assume that she died prior to Joseph's death.

These were the children of Joseph Peck Jr.:

16. Rebecca Peck	born 6 November 1650
17. Hannah Peck	born 25 March 1653; married Daniel Reed
18. Elizabeth Peck	born 26 November 1657; married Captain Samuel Mason, later Major Mason.
19. Jathniel Peck	born 24 July 1660; died 1742; married Sarah Smith 28 January 1688, Rehoboth, Massachusetts[7]
20. Mary Peck	born 17 November 1662; married Benjamin Hunt
21. Ichabod Peck	born 13 September 1666
22. Patience Peck	born 11 October 1669; married Richard Bowen
23. Samuel Peck	born 1 October 1672

11. **John Peck** came to America with his father and was about eleven years of age at that time. He was baptized in the year 1626. He settled in the town of Seekonk and became a freeman in 1658. In 1680, he was one of the townsmen and represented the General Court of Massachusetts in 1670. He died in 1713 with his will being recorder in the records of Taunton, Massachusetts, B.3, page 163.[6] In John's will, he had made provisions for his wife, Rebecca. New England Historical Genealogical Society (NSHGS) shows the following:

> 1667 Peck, Elizabeth, wife of John buried 9 December 1667
> 1668 Preston, Elizabeth & John Peck, married 30 December 1668
> 1687 Peck, Elizabeth, wife of John, buried 26 May 1687

John Peck's first marriage was to Elizabeth (Hunting) who died in 1667. John's second marriage was to Elizabeth Preston 30 December 1668; Elizabeth (Preston) Peck was buried 26 May 1687. Sometime in the year 1687, John took for his third wife, Rebecca (last name unknown). John died in 1713.[7, 9]

John and Elizabeth (Hunting) Peck had the following children:

Elizabeth Peck	born 27 November 1657; buried 18 December 1657

Esther Peck	born 7 January 1658; married 29 December 1680 Jonathan Willmouth
Anne Peck	born 6 October 1661; buried 26 February 1662
John Peck	born 7 October 1664; buried 18 December 1666

John and Elizabeth (Preston) Peck had the following children:

Elizabeth Peck	born 13 November 1669; buried 29 July 1687
Dorothy Peck	born 28 June 1671; married Edward Glover 8 April 1707
Rebecca Peck	born 8 April 1674
Anne Peck	born 17 July 1677
Nathan Peck	born 6 July 1680
Abigail Peck	born 16 March 1682/3

12. **Nicholas Peck** was baptized 9 April 1630 and came to America with his father in 1638, at about eight years of age. [6] His first wife was Mary Winchester was baptized in 1637 and died in 1657. Their only child was born in 1650. They lived in Rehoboth, Massachusetts. Nicholas married (2) Rebecca Bosworth, born in 1641 and died in 1704. They also lived in Rehoboth, Massachusetts.[6] Nicholas and his family settled in the southeastern part of Seekonk, Massachusetts; and like others in his family, he took an active role in public affairs. He was one of the selectmen of the town, often taking on the role as assessors, referred to at the time as rater. In 1669, he was elected deputy of the Court at Plymouth. He was also elected deputy for the years 1677 through 1690; however, for the years 1687 and 1688, the town did not elect deputies. From 1677 to 1684, Nicholas held the rank of ensign. He worked his way through the ranks and finally was promoted to the rank of captain. Nicholas died 27 May 1710 at the age of eighty.[6]

Nicholas and Mary (Winchester) Peck had one child:

| Joseph Peck | born 27 October 1650 |

Nicholas and Rebecca (Bosworth) Peck had the following children:

| John Peck | born 8 August 1660; died 16 August 1660 |

Hezekiah Peck	born 1 April 1662; died 1723; married Deborah Cooper
Mary Peck	born 15 September 1664; died 1755; married Ensign Joshua Smith
Jonathan Peck	born 5 November 1666
Nicholas Peck	born 6 June 1669; died January 1690/1
Elisha Peck	born 11 April 1673

(Note: In the will of Nicholas Peck, he makes mention of a daughter named Martha: "I give to my daughter Martha wife of [unknown] feather bed in the bed room." I was unable to find her listed in the book *Descendants of Joseph Peck*.)

13. **Samuel Peck** was born at Hingham, Massachusetts, and baptized 3 February 1638/9. He served as a deacon in his church and held various offices for his town. He was elected deputy for the General Court at Plymouth for the years 1689 to 1692. He was the first representative from the town after the Colony of Plymouth and Massachusetts were united, meaning that Plymouth Colony was annexed to Massachusetts by the charter of William and Mary in 1692.[6]

Samuel married (1) 1 June 1666, Rehoboth, Massachusetts, Sarah Hunt. She was buried 27 October 1673. Samuel married (2) 21 November 1677, Rehoboth, Massachusetts, Rebecca (Paine) Hunt, widow of Peter Hunt and daughter of Stephen Paine. Rebecca, born 1666and died 12 June 1699,
In Samuel's will, he states that he only had one son (Noah), but mentions a daughter, Sarah Sabin. Sarah was born 2 February 1669. She married John Sabin 3 September 1689. Samuel's will was written 11 June 1704/5. He died in 1708 with his will being proved 2 June 1708.[6] Sarah died in 1738/7.
Samuel and Sarah (Hunt) Peck had the following children:

Ann Peck	born 22 December 1667; died 1703; married 16 December 1685 Samuel Paine
Sarah Peck	born 2 February 1669; died 1738; married John Sabin
Judith Peck	born 26 July 1671; died 1681

Samuel and Rebecca Peck had the following children:

| Noah Peck | born 21 August 1678; married Hannah Winter |
| Janet Peck | born 14 June 1680; buried 6 July 1680 |

Rebecca Peck   born 22 October 1681; buried 2 November
                                         1682

14. **Nathaniel Peck** was born at Hingham, Massachusetts, and baptized 31 October 1641. Nathaniel married Deliverance Bosworth prior to 1670. Deliverance was born in 1650 and died in 1675, possibly in childbirth. Nathaniel died a year later (1676). It appears that Nathaniel died intestate as the records indicate that on 1 November 1676, the court appointed Jonothan [*sic*] Bosworth and Samuel Peck to administer the estate of Nathaniel Peck as he was survived by minor children, "a son and a daughter." Nathaniel and Deliverance (Bosworth) Peck had three children:

Nathaniel Peck   born 26 July 1670
Daughter
Elisha Peck   born 19 April 1675; died 30 April 1675

15. **Israel Peck** was born in Hingham, Massachusetts, and was baptized on 4 March 1644. He settled in what is now known as Barrington, Massachusetts, on land left to him by his father and next to the lot of Ellis Peck, Esq.[6] Israel married Bethiah, daughter of Jonathan Bosworth on 15 July 1670. Israel Peck died on 2 September 1723 in the eightieth year of his life. Bethiah died on 4 April 1718 at the age of seventy-five.

Israel and Bethiah (Bosworth) Peck had the following children:

Mehitable Peck   born 6 August 1671; died 1718; married
                                         John Whitaker
Israel Peck   born 18 December 1673; drowned 23
                                         June 1686
Nathaniel Peck   born 27 September 1677
Deliverance Peck   born 21 June 1680
Israel Peck   born 3 September 1686
Mary Peck

3. **Robert Peck**; Perhaps a little history will help us to know and appreciate just how important Rev. Robert Peck really was. To do this, we will have to return to the year 1517, sixty-three years before the birth of our Robert Peck; and when we do, we find the German theologian, Martin Luther.

Luther published ninety-five arguments, which attracted the corruption that was taking place in the Roman Catholic Church. He became well-known throughout Europe and attracted many followers, who became what is known as Protestants. This rebellion was the beginning of a religious warfare that was to last for more than one hundred years.

During this rebellion, King Henry VIII defended the Catholic Church, that is, until Pope Leo X refused to grant Henry a divorce from his first of six wives, Catherine of Aragon. Their marriage took place in 1509, and they had eight children. All of their children, except Mary, died during infancy. Mary later became Mary I, Queen of England. Since Catherine could not provide Henry with a male heir and since Henry had his eyes on his soon to be second wife, Anne Boleyn, Henry had his marriage annulled in 1533. How did he accomplish this? 1

Because Henry was defending the Catholic Church and because Henry had published a pamphlet known as the Golden Book, which refuted all of Luther's ideas, Pope Leo X, in 1521, presented Henry with the title Defender of the Faith. This title has been held by all of the English monarchs ever since.

After Henry was refused a divorce by the pope, Henry broke away from the Church of Rome and established himself as Supreme Head of the English Church, while still retaining the doctrines of the Roman Church. In 1539, the Act of the Six Articles reasserted the doctrine, and breaches of this act were made punishable by burning at the stake. In the same year, a Bible was written in English and was licensed by Henry. It was ordered that a copy of this Bible be placed in every parish church.

Henry VIII died in 1547 and was succeeded by his son, Edward VI, born of Henry's third marriage (Jane Seymour). Edward was only nine years old when he became King, so the government was managed by two protectors throughout Edward's reign, which lasted for only six years, due to his death from tuberculosis in 1553. Edward, or rather Edward's protectors, supported Henry's Protestant's belief; and in 1549, an Act of Uniformity was passed so the use of the Catholic Mass was prohibited. Clergy were ordered to remove statues of saints and icons from the churches. Wall paintings were painted over; all of which led to a revolt, thus causing the use of German mercenary troops to end this revolt with much severity.

Upon the death of Edward, his protector, John Dudley, wanting to maintain the Protestant structure, appointed Lady Jane Grey as Edward's successor; and therefore she became Queen of England. Jane reigned for just nine days before she was deposed by Mary I, daughter of Henry VIII and his marriage to Catherine of Aragon. Jane was imprisoned and executed in 1554 at the age of seventeen. (If you have the desire to follow this further, you might obtain the movie Lady Jane.)

Mary, like her mother, was a devout Catholic. She had suffered years of humiliation after her parents divorced in 1533. After Mary I, had claimed the throne from Jane Grey, she turned England back toward the Catholic beliefs, repealed Protestant legislation, and restored papal supremacy in England.

In March of 1556, William Carmen of Hingham in Norfolk, England—who was a Protestant and who resisted the authority of the Roman Catholic Church, who "had in his possession a Byble, a Testament, and three Salters" in the English tongue—was burned at the stake for being a "contumacious heretic." He committed the crime of owning books of Holy Scripture written in his native tongue. This terrible death would long be remembered. The story would not lose any of its meaning as it passed down from father to son or from mother to daughter. The bitter feelings surrounded William's death may well have started the teachings and beliefs that were to take place fifty years later. Mary I had become known as Bloody Mary, having burned numerous Protestants at the stake for heresy. Mary I died 17 November 1558 at St. James place in London, England.

Elizabeth, the daughter of Henry VIII and wife number two, Anne Boleyn was only three years of age when Mary had Anne executed. Elizabeth, born 7 September 1533, Greenwich Palace was about twenty years of age when; Mary I had her imprisoned, however the imprisonment only lasted for a short while due to Mary's death in 1558. Elizabeth became Queen of England (1558-1603)

A year after Elizabeth became queen, the Protestant Church once again became the dominant religion in England, and their relationship with the Church of Rome was severed. At that time, it was thought best to leave many sections of the doctrine vague, with the intentions of bringing as many people as possible into the new Church of England without offending the conscience. The newly established church spoke of itself as Catholics, yet was called Protestant because it refused to recognize the pope. The most vocal opposition came from those who followed the teachings of Calvin, the French Protestant leader. These people, who became known as Puritans, were attempting to reshape the church along Calvinistic lines. When first used, the name Puritan was one of disgrace. It was a name which Puritans would never use about themselves.

The Puritans believed in predestination, with salvation only for the chosen few. Beliefs, practices, and ceremonies not specifically affirmed in the Scriptures were wrong, superstitious, and heretical in the Puritan's eyes. Carvings, paintings, and idolatrous images, although beautiful, were nothing but a hindrance to man's direct approach to God and therefore should be destroyed. A view expressed by one Puritan who told Bishop Harsnett of Norwich that there was "no Difference between an Alehouse and the Church, till the Preacher be in the Pulpit." Puritans, of course, had no use for bishops, wishing them to be suppressed; and they demanded the right for all people to be allowed the freedom of worship in their own way.

This attitude was not acceptable to the hierarchy of the Church of England, and throughout the reigns of Elizabeth I (1558-1603) and James I (1603-1625), efforts were made to observe the growth of Puritanism in the country. James agreed to meet with some of the leaders in 1604, at which time they presented a petition to him, stating their objections to such matters as the use of the sign of the cross in baptism, the ring in marriage, and the words "priest" and "absolution" in the prayer book. Other demands were made to only allow church music that was considered "moderate" and there should be no objection for the clergy to wear the surplice. James, who thought of himself as a noble theologian, was not ready for these demands and stated, "I will have one doctrine, one discipline, one religion in substance and in ceremony." He then told the Puritan ministers that if they would not conform, "harry them out of the lands." As a result, some three hundred Puritan ministers resigned rather than conform to the prayer book.

Nowhere in the country did Puritanism grow more strongly than in the eastern part of England, where antipope feelings ran so high. Perhaps this is why only the dioceses of London and Canterbury had more people who suffered death for their faith during the reign of Mary I than in the dioceses of Norwich.

It had been forty-nine years since William Carmen died a martyr's death by being burned at the stake for his religious beliefs. There came to Hingham (England) a man whose doctrinal beliefs and teachings were the same for which William Carmen gave his life and which, in one way or another, were going to affect the lives of every man, woman, and child in the parish.3 At this point, we will start to learn a little about Robert Peck Jr., son of Robert Peck and Helen Babbs.

The town of Hingham, in the county of Norfolk, is an ancient settlement going back in history to around AD 925. It is recorded as the property of King Athelstan, grandson of Alfred the Great. It is the home of the fourteenth-century church, Saint Andrew's.4

(To learn more about Saint Andrew's Church, go to your browser and type in Saint Andrew's Hingham. Click on under Norfolk Churches)

On 7 January 1605, Robert Peck, at the age of twenty-five, was appointed rector of the parish of Hingham and St. Andrew's Church. Little did he know that this would be his only parish and, upon his death, fifty-one years later, he would be buried along the side of his family in the churchyard.[sic]

Robert married Anne Lawrence, daughter of Rev. John Lawrence of Elmham, Suffolk, England. Lawrence had preached in the woods and secret places to those who would risk their lives to worship God as their consciences and beliefs dictated. This was the same belief that Robert and his wife were now following and the reason they were so well respected in their new surroundings. Robert served as rector for the next thirty-one years and was a great influence, not only on his parishioners but many other people outside the boundaries of his parish who shared his faith. In later years, his friends and followers referred to Robert as a "godly, loving, painful and peaceable minister, a man so unblamable in his life and doctrine that no just offence in either could ever be found." On the other hand, his enemies found him to be a man of "violent and schismatical [sic] spirit." During the first ten years of his ministry at Hingham, Robert did not allow his Puritanism to drift beyond the boundaries of the diocesan authorities.3

In 1615, Rev. Robert Peck was called before the Consistory Court in Norwich. This court, also known as the Bishop's Court, dealt with ecclesiastical offences; and Robert was to account for an offence, which may seem strange in modern eyes. He was charged with holding prayer meetings (conventicle), not in the church but in the homes of his parishioners. This gathering provided opportunity for treasonable, seditious talk and preaching outside the English doctrine. In 1593 by Act of Parliament, attendance at this type of meeting was punishable by banishment. Robert's defense was that he and others had merely been visiting and had done no more than to sing a psalm and say a prayer before going on their way. Nothing more was said about this matter, but it is certain that Robert Peck was a man to be carefully scrutinized.

In 1633, William Laud became archbishop of Canterbury; and with the wholehearted support of Charles I, the King of England, he was determined to restore the Church of England in a manner which was much to the disliking of the Puritans. Also, by 1633, the children baptized by Rev. Robert Peck were now grown men and women whose early years had been spent under the dominant figure of Robert Peck. Peck's influence had now spread far beyond the confines of his parish and had affected people of all ages. Men who had been unable to adjust to developments in England, both with the church and in civil life, had been leaving the country to make a new life for themselves, both on the continent, particularly in Holland, and in the New World.

By 1633, the Pilgrim Fathers had been settled in America for thirteen years, during which, time other settlements had also begun in Massachusetts Bay Colony, Virginia, Maryland, and Connecticut. During this time, ships returning from America brought letters containing information about the conditions of the New World, and this information would then be passed along to those who might be thinking about making the journey. It was more than likely that some of the letters ended up in Norwich and in the hands of some of Robert's parishioners. It was in 1633 that Edmund Hobart of Hingham gathered fourteen members of his family and, along with seven other Hingham people, set forth on the ship Elizabeth Bonaventure of Great Yarmouth. Records show that they arrived on June 15 of that year at the already-established settlement of Charlestown. Two years later in 1635, another party, led by Edmund Hobart's son, Rev. Peter Hobart, arrived; and the two groups made their way to a location, known at that time as Bare Cove. This name was soon changed to Hingham (Massachusetts), and when the first meetinghouse was built, Peter Hobart became its first pastor.

Things were not improving at home in old Hingham. The death of Richard Corbett, bishop of Norwich, did not help matters. Although Bishop Corbett found the Puritans' outlook rather ridiculous, he tried to meet the Puritan clergy in the Norwich diocese in a spirit of conciliation and friendship; however, the stubborn, unfriendly members of his flock felt the iron hand of his authority.

Bishop Matthew Wren, Corbett's successor, was of a different caliber. Bishop Wren was a High Churchman and, like Archbishop Laude, was a very strong believer of following the prayer book and insuring the ceremony was dignified and reverent when it came to church conduct during services. When Bishop Wren made his initial visit in 1636, he issued orders that the form of services in the prayer book should be followed as outlined and not altered in any manner. Wren was not pleased with the ways of Puritan services or customs, and one such change was to have the altar moved from the central position in the church because it gave members of the congregation every opportunity to treat it with disrespect, throwing their hats and gloves upon it and lolling over it, taking their ease at sermon time. If such behavior was intended to show disrespect, we may be certain that it was disrespect for the Communion table and not for the preacher, for there was no more important time as when the sermon was being preached.3

Puritans would not have thought they were lacking in reverence by keeping their hats on, as a matter of fact, reverent behavior in the church meant little to the Puritan way of thinking. Bishop Wren found it necessary to issue very detailed instructions concerning the administration of Holy Communion and the position of the Communion table, "that no wicker bottles or tavern pots" are brought to the table, indicates the manner or behavior which he was attempting to correct.3

At some churches, it was possible for the parishioners to tell whether or not a sermon was to be preached on that day by the manner in which the bell was rung. Those who wished would wait until after the prayers had been said before attending, just to hear the sermon. These acts continued even after the bishop had issued the order. This, of course, offended the bishop so much that his attitude toward the Puritan lessened considerably. In many parishes where the preacher might be under suspicion of nonconformity, as was the case of Peck, the parishioners were thoroughly questioned by those working for the bishop on all aspects of their church life and life in the parish. The parishioners were asked about the order of services, whether they were reverently conducted strictly in accordance with the directions of the prayer book. They were asked about the condition of the church and the churchyard and the dress of the clergy. They were questioned as to whether or not they attended or knew of any conventicles being held in private homes.3

Robert Peck was already on the "watch list" of Bishop Wren and, again, was in trouble for holding secret prayer meetings in the homes of his parishioners. It was also likely that Peck had refused to read the king's book of sports from the pulpit.

The book of sports, officially titled His Majestie's [sic] Declaration of Lawful Sports, had been issued by James I in 1617. It was originally intended for use in Lancashire County because there had been outbreaks of displeasure caused by the Puritan clergy objecting to the manner in which their parishioners were partaking in sporting activities on Sunday. A year later, because the disagreement had spread throughout entire England, clergy were ordered to read the king's declaration from the pulpit at every Sunday service. Not surprising, this order was met with very strong opposition; and subsequently, it was withdrawn. After Charles I became king, he ordered that the book be republished and repeated his father's command to have it read at Sunday services in every church. Most of the clergy of the Puritan faith refused either outright or just simply failed to obey the king's command, thus committing a punishable offence. For all that we have learned about the character of Robert Peck, it seems extremely likely that he did not read the book of sports at his services in Hingham.

The declaration very clearly lay down which sports and amusements were permissible on Sundays. Archery, "leaping and vaulting," dancing, and other harmless recreations were allowed. Exception was given for the holding of "May games." During the May games, certain dances as well as the setting up of the "maypoles" were allowed; but since the maypole was of pagan origin, the Puritans disapproved of this activity.

The declaration was not only concerned with the pastimes to be allowed on Sundays, but it also enforced restrictions on some of the other most popular sports. The baiting of a bear or bull had been a popular source of entertainment for generations, but now it was no longer allowed on the Lord's Day. Bull or bear baiting was a bloodthirsty event that people would spend their afternoons watching and gambling on the outcome of each event. It was first introduced to England during the medieval period of the 1200s. Arenas or baiting rings would be built for this occasion. The spectators would number about one thousand. The seating was in tiered benches that surrounded the ring with the spectators being protected by a wall that was made of stone. In the bull or bear baiting ring, there would be a stake in the center and the bull or bear would be tied to the stake—the bull with a rope about fifteen feet in length tied around his horns and attached to the stake with an iron ring. This would restrict the bull to a thirty-foot-diameter area. Owners of dogs that participated in this sporting would stand with their dogs just outside the circle and contain their dogs by holding them by their ears. When the event began, one of the owners would let his dog loose on the bull. The baiting lasted for about one hour. Bear baiting was similar except that the bear was attached to the stake with a rope tied to one of its hind leg or by his neck. The whipping of a blinded bear was a variation of bear baiting.

Robert Laneham, an Elizabethan reporter, had to say about one such event:

> It was a sport very pleasant to see, to see the bear, with pink eyes, tearing after his enemies approach; the nimbleness and wait of the dog to take his advantage and the force and experience of the bear again to avoid his assaults: if he were bitten in one place how he would pinch in another to get free; that if he were taken once, then by what shift with biting, with clawing, with roaring, with tossing and tumbling he would work and wind himself from them; and when he was loose to shake his ears twice or thrice with the blood and the slaver hang about his physiognomy.

The performance of plays on Sunday was no longer permitted. These and other restriction continued until the impeachment of Archbishop Laud in 1640 and the rise of the Puritan power at which time the king's declaration was abolished.

In 1636, Bishop Wren became outraged when he learned that some of the parishioners had broken into the church at Hingham and caused a great deal of damage to the inside. The act of vandalism and the possibility of Robert's secret involvement were to have consequences not only for Rev. Robert Peck and the parishioners but the entire parish. This may not have been the first time that such destruction occurred at the church as the reverend was called before a Consistory Court in Norfolk on 9 October 1636 and charged with "contumacious disobedience to the orders and ceremonies of the Church." Such disobedience of this nature was in fact a violation of the oath taken by Peck and other clergymen at the time of their ordination. Disciplining Peck and any other minister who was in violation was simply enforcing the laws of the church, which were within the duties of the archbishop and bishops. Peck failed to obey the orders set forth and was therefore excommunicated "for not appearing in person, but by proctor." Robert probably did not expect such severe punishment, and when he learned that he would have to abide by and subscribe to "certain new articles tendered to him" by the chancellor, he absolutely refused to do so. Since he was excommunicated, he had no way of earning a living. It is believed that he and his family moved to Prittlewell, Essex County, to live with their son, who was also a minister. Although Robert had moved from Hingham, he was not forgotten as was evidenced in a letter written by Dr. Corbett to the Bishop of Norwich. "Although there is a sequestration long since granted and Don [sic] Pecke stands still excommunicated, his parishioners are now so addicted yet to him that they pay their tythes [sic] to him and not to him that hath the sequestration."[3]

A petition dated 14 February 1637 was filed by Edward Ages, who had assumed the duties of curator of Hingham. Ages explained that since his appointment of replacing Peck, he had noticed a great decrease in attendance for Sunday services. He credited this decrease due to the fact that the parishioners did not plan to conform to the new doctrine of the church. The debate as to what to do went on for two years, and on 5 May 1638, Rev. Luke Skippon was appointed rector of Hingham as it had been assumed that Rev. Robert Peck had died since he had been absent and unheard from. On 11 April 1640, Rev. Luke Skippon was again appointed rector as it was assumed that Peck was dead.

Robert Peck was not dead; in fact, he had been in touch with many of the people of Hingham. His son, also a minister, tried to take his father's place in the parish; and having been discovered, Dr. Corbett, in another letter to the bishop, stated, "Young Peck that officiated in his father's church in Hingham . . . I sent an express for him to appear at Wymondham, but he is returned to Essex from whence he came and it is rumoured [sic] that the old fox is kenneled there." This was when Robert decided that it was time for him and his family to join their friends in the New World. Once word reached Hingham, many of his old parishioners elected to travel with him, taking their families with them.

In William Bradford's book, *History of Plimoth Plantation*, he describes the future faced by would-be emigrants of the New World and the spirit which must be maintained during the new and trying life they were choosing. He writes (translated into a newer English, but with spelling unchanged), "All great and honorable actions are accompolished [sic] with great difficulties, and must be both enterprised [sic] and overcome with answerable courages [sic]. The dangers were great, but not desperate; the difficulties were many, but not invincible. For though there were many of them likely, yet they were not certain; it might be sundry of the things feared might never befall; others by provident care and the use of good means might in a great measure be prevented; and all of them, through the help of God, by fortitude and patience might either be borne or overcome."

Leaving England and the security of their homeland had to have been very difficult; but the desire for freedom to worship God, in their own way, was so strongly felt, they were willing to risk it all for this freedom. Once the decision to sail to America was made, there were many problems facing them, problems that demanded a firm and final decision. Arrangement for their passage and approximate sailing date had to be established, a date that was dictated by the winds and tide. This meant that those desiring to leave must be on standby and ready to go at almost a moment's notice. They would probably have to live on board ship for days, possibly weeks while still in the harbor, or at a lodge nearby, waiting for the right time to set sail. The decision on what to take and what to leave behind had to be made. The decision had to be coordinated with the rest of the passengers so that items on board would not be duplicated. Things like household furniture, clothing, arms, and equipment of every kind would be needed to start their new life. Remember, these ships were not very large and did not have the comforts that we have come to enjoy today. Their restroom was nothing more than a bucket or a pot with the contents being tossed over the side. The sleeping quarters were nothing more than a crude bunk down below deck, when the weather would not permit them to sleep on deck. Since they had no refrigeration, some, but very little, livestock had to be brought along and killed for their meals. However, their meals consisted mostly of wheat, oats, barley, rice, and fish caught during the voyage.

The men had to be very much aware of the possible dangers awaiting them upon their arrival. They had heard tales of unfriendly natives who scalped their enemies, flayed them using seashells from the ocean, and boiled them before the eyes of their victims. In preparing for this type of greeting, the men had to concentrate as to what weapons, how much gun power, flint and shot belts, shields, and other armor should be taken. There was much danger awaiting them; but in spite of this, they were willing to risk it all, just for the chance of a new life and religious freedom.

Once they arrived to their New World, they would have to feed off the land, so hunting weapons would be needed to kill what would be strange species of game. A letter from an earlier emigrant had stressed the necessity of taking "shot most for big fowls." As quickly as possible, they had to start clearing the ground and start cultivating; therefore, scythes, sickles, billhooks [sic], mattocks, spades, hoes, rakes, and hayforks would be needed as well as supplies of grain and vegetable seeds. Think of the space that would be needed to store these things during the voyage.

Imagine if you were living in 1630 and planning a voyage to a new and uninhabited land. Look around your house and ask yourself, what you would take, knowing there is a very limited space to store these items. Keep in mind, the year is 1630, so many of the items that you might want to take were not even thought of at the time. Unlike today, anything that you may have forgotten could not be purchased once you arrived at your new home. Since you will be traveling with other people, you would not want to duplicate many items as it would take up too much space. Such items as spinning wheels, kitchen utensils, blacksmith tools, tools for tanning and making shoes and other clothing would be some of the items you would not want to duplicate. Money would be of no use, so you would barter services.

Another consideration would be that such a trip would take as much as six to eight weeks, depending on the tides and winds and the fact that they might drift off their course and get lost. The seas are rough and will cause the ship to sway, roll, and pitch, thus causing much a very uncomfortable feeling and, in most cases, causing queasiness and nauseousness among the passengers. No, this would not be an enjoyable, fun-filled adventure, but an adventure that was necessary for those who would make the journey to a new and free world.

Robert Peck; his wife Anne (Lawrence) and two of his children, Anne and Joseph; and two servants came to America, along with his brother Joseph and his family. In all, a party of 133 departed from Ipswich, England, in June 1638 on the ship *Diligent*, mastered by John Martin.[2]

They arrived at Boston on 10 August 1638. They then traveled from Boston to Hingham where they were greeted by the friend who had arrived before them. Rev. Peter Hobart was the pastor of the newly built church, so on 28 November 1638, Robert was appointed "teacher," meaning he was an ordained minister responsible for giving instructions to the congregation while the pastor preached the sacraments.

John Winthrop, governor of Massachusetts, wrote in his journal about Rev. Peter Hobart, "He did manage all affairs without the Church's advice," which was later supported in the history of Hingham, Massachusetts, thus indicating a "strong-willed" individual. And because Rev. Robert Peck was also known as an equally "strong-willed" person, there may have been a slight conflict, although there is no documentation indicating this. During 1641, Rev. Peter Hobart wrote in his diary this brief entry: "The Reverend Peck left for England this day."

We cannot really be sure why Robert returned to England with his wife and son Joseph. It could have been because Robert and Rev. Peter Hobart were equally "strong-willed" and, thus, both leaders, with neither of them willing to be a follower. It could also have been that they missed the family left behind in England. Or could it have been because the remaining parishioners in old Hingham wanted him back as their minister. Perhaps all of these reasons persuaded Robert to return to his old home in Hingham. Not much had changed during the three years they were in America, Robert still being excommunicated and Skippon still the rector of Hingham. We do not know anything about Robert during the years 1641 to 1646 when he again became the rector at Hingham, where he remained until his death in 1656. Robert and his wife are buried in the churchyard.

Robert Peck attended the University of Cambridge and is listed in the Alumni Cantabrigienses, "a biographical list of all known students, graduates and holders of office at the University of Cambridge, from the earliest times to 1900."

Robert Peck received his BA from St. Catharine's in 1598-9. He was the third son of Robert Peck Sr, and was born at Beccles, Suffolk. He received his MA from Magdalene in 1603 and was ordained deacon and priest (Norwich) on 14 February 1604-5 at the age of twenty-five. He was appointed curator of Oulton, Norfolk, and became rector of Hingham in 1605-38. "A strong puritan; through his influence a number of his parishioners became nonconformists and immigrated to New England where they founded Hingham, Mass., in the year 1635.Under Bishop Wren he was finally forced to flee to New England, 1638. He was Teacher of the Church at Hingham, Mass., 1638-1641. He returned to England and was reinstated at Hingham, Norfolk in 1646.Father of Thomas (1624) and Samuel (1629-30)."[5] (The dates for Thomas and Samuel are the years they graduated from University of Cambridge.)

Rev. Robert Peck was born at Beccles, Suffolk County, England, in 1580. He was the son of Robert and Helen (Babbs) Peck of Beccles. Helen was the daughter of Nicholas Babbs of Guilford. Shortly after Robert's arrival at Hingham, Massachusetts, he was ordained Teacher of the Church (28 November 1638). Robert's name appears throughout the history of Hingham and the town records.[6]

Anne (Lawrence) Peck died and was buried on 30 August 1648 in the churchyard with other family members. Robert's second wife was Martha Bacon, the widow of Rev. James Bacon, rector of Burgate. Robert died in Hingham, England, and was buried in his churchyard. His will was proved at London with the granting of administration on 10 April 1658.

These were the children of Robert and Anne (Lawrence) Peck:

23.	Robert Peck	baptized 23 July 1607
24.	Thomas Peck	baptized 6 September 1608
25.	Joseph Peck	baptized 22 April 1610
26.	Benjamin Peck	baptized 29 September 1611
27	Samuel (1) Peck	baptized 12 March 1612; died prior to 1 March 1616
28.	Nathaniel Peck	baptized 13 September 1614
29.	Samuel (2) Peck	baptized 1 March 1616
30.	Daniel Peck	baptized 8 June 1616
31.	Anne Peck	baptized 18 November 1619; married Major John Mason

Only Thomas, Joseph, Samuel, and Anne were living at the time of Robert's will dated 1651.

23.   Robert was baptized on 23 July 1607. He married Joanna, daughter of Robinson, alderman of Linne. Robert died before July 1651 as he is mentioned in his father's will as being deceased (England). Joanna was the sister of John Robinson, Esq., of Beach in Cambridgeshire, England. Robert and Joanna Peck had several children, two of which were Robert, a clerk, and Joanna.[10]

24. **Thomas** received his BA from Emmanuel College in Cambridge in 1627 and his MA in 1631. He was ordained deacon on 13 February 1629-30 and the next day ordained priest. Thomas was appointed vicar of St. Mary's Church in Prittlewell, Essex County, England, on 2 May 1633 upon the presentation of Robert, Earl of Warwick.[10] He remained in that position until 1622 when he was replaced by his son Samuel, who served until 1671.[5]

25. **Joseph** may have been physically or mentally challenged as evidenced in his father's (Rev. Robert Peck) will.

> *I give to my sonne Joseph Dureinge his natural life the sume of 14 La yearlie to be in the hands of my Sonnes Thomas and Samuel as it shall arise out of my houses lands and chattles for his maintenance with necessarie foode and apparrell duringe the terme of his natural life And I doe wholie comitt my said Sonne Joseph to the care of my twoe sonnes Thomas and Samuell to provide for him in such a way as he may not want things necessary for his livelyhood.*

29. **Samuel** also attended Emmanuel College and received his BA in 1633-34. He received his MA in 1737 and moved to Chelmsford, Essex County, England, where he practiced as a physician.[5]

31. **Anne**, their only daughter, stayed behind in America as she became the wife of Major John Mason (see Mason chapter).

The following is a transcription of Rev. Robert Peck's will: I have attempted to leave the spelling as I found it, along with the lack of periods at the end of the sentences. Those not mentioned are assumed deceased: Robert (sixteen), Benjamin (nineteen), Nathaniel (twenty-one), and Daniel (twenty-three).

July the xxiiij th 1651

> *I Robert Pecke Minister of the word of God at Hingham in the couutye of Norff beinge in bodilye health and perfect memory knowinge the unceartainety of mans life, doe dispose of that worldly estate God hath given me in manner and form followinge*

> *Imprimus I give and bequeath unto Thomas my Sonne and Samuel my Sonne and their heirs forever All that my messuage wherein I now dwell situate and lyenge in Hingham a forsaid with all the edifices yards and*

orchards thereunto belonginge As alsoe the Inclose and Barnes adioyninge As also one Inclose now devided called The Lady close conteyninge about eight acres be it more or less As olso one pightell at the end thereof conteyninge twoe acres and did uppon condicons followinge, and for the paiement of such legacies as are herein expressed

First I will and bequeath unto Robert Pecke sonne of my sonne Robert deceased the sume of 20 pounds at his age of 23 years

Item   I give unto John Pecke sonne of the said Robert deceased To be paid to him at his age of 22 years

Item   I give unto Beniamin Pecke the youngest sonne of the said Robert deceased at his age of 22 years 20 La

Item   I give to the children of Anne Mason my daughter wife of captain John Mason of Seabrooke on the river Connecticut in new England the sume of Forty pounds to be devided. equally unto them and to be sent to my sonne John Mason to dispose of it for their use within 2 years after my death

Item   I give to my sonne Joseph Dureinge his natural life the sume of 14 La yearlie to be in the hands of my Sonnes Thomas and Samuel as it shall arise out of my houses lands and chattles for his maintenance with necessarie foode and apparrell during the terme of his naturall life And I doe wholie comitt my said Sonne Joseph to the care of my twoe sonnes Thomas and Samuell to provide for him in such a way as he may not want things necessary for his livelyhood

Item   I give to the children of Thomas and Samuell my sonnes which shall be liveinge at my decease the sume of Five pounds apiece at their severall. ages of 21 years

Item   I give to my now wife Martha Pecke 40 La To be paid within twoe months after my decease

Item   I give to the poore of Hingham 5 La To be destrubted at the discrecon of my Executors Thomas Pecke and Samuel Pecke whome I do ordeyne and make Executors of this my last will and Testament

confiding that they will faithfully fulfill and performe this my last
will according to my trust reposed in them

All my other goods cattells debts moneys household stuffe or whatsoever
ells belongeth unto me I give and bequeath to my said Executors, towards
payeinge of my legacies already bequeathed and towards the bringinge of
my body to buriall. which I desire if I depart this life in Hingham may be
entered in the church yard near unto Anne my wife deceased

In witness whereof I have written this my last will and testament
with my own hand the day and yeare above written

Robert Peck's will was proved at London before the judges for probate of
wills and "granting of Administrations the tenth day of April in the year of our
Lord God One thousand six hundred fiftye and eight." (Note the spelling of
the Peck name in the above will.)

Notes

1.   Plantagenet Somerset Fry, *The Kings and Queens of England and Scotland,* Gross Press, New York 1990

2.   *History of the Town of Hingham, Massachusetts*, Vol. I, II & III, published by the town in 1893.

3.   M. E. Lonsdale *The Heyday of Their Strength,* The 17th Century emigration from Hingham, Norfolk, England printed 1979.

4.   M. E. Lonsdale *Hingham in History* For the St. Andrew's Hingham Heritage Fund

5.   *Alumni Cantabrigienses* Part I, Volume III, printed in Cambridge at the University Press in 1924, page 333.

6.   Ira B. Peck *Genealogical History of the Descendants of Joseph Peck who Immigrated with his Family to the Country in 1638 and Records of His father and Grandfather's Families in England*, Originally published in 1868.

7.   Clarence Almon Torrey Prepared for publication by Elizabeth P. Bentley; *New England Marriages Prior to 1700*; Genealogical Publishing Company, Baltimore, Maryland 1985.

8.   "The Old Ship Church" brochure, printed by the Old Ship Church.

9.   The Dedham Historical Register, Volume III, 1892 and Volume VII, 1896, published by Dedham Historical Society.

10. Philip Benton, *The History of Rochford Hundred,* Vol. II, from the former authors *Ancient Manuscript and Church Registers*; published by A. Harrington printed 1888.

TEN

John Dwight

(See Appendix J)

———————◆◆◆———————

Professor Theodore W. Dwight of Columbia College and the author of the book *The History of the Descendants of John Dwight of Dedham, Mass.*, which is used as one of the references in this chapter, in 1887, did a massive amount of research in England concerning the Dwight family. The name Dwight is plainly derived from Doit or Doyt or Doito as early form. The final *o* in the form Doito was probably attached to it in order to give distinct expression and significance to the final *t*, which would have otherwise been left silent, according to the custom in French pronunciation.[1] The name is of Norman origin. As early as the year 1185, there were families in Normandy that bore the names Ranald, Ralph, and Richard de Doito. These names are all found in the Great Rolls of the Exchequer of Normand*y*.

John Dwight was born in Dedham, Oxfordshire County, England, and came to America in 1634 along with his wife Hannah (last name unknown) and their three children: John, Timothy, and Hannah. They lived in Watertown, Massachusetts, where, on 2 May 1638, he became a freeman.

John, like most of those of the *Mayflower*, was motivated to come to America because of his religious beliefs. A strong religious spirit is observable in his character and life; and this spirit was from the beginning, and uniformly, a conspicuous trait of the family founded by him.

John and his family stayed in Watertown for only a short period of time before relocating to what is now known as Dedham, Massachusetts.[1] In 1635 John was one of twelve to receive from the General Court the town grant of

Dedham, which on September 1 of that year became the settlement of Dedham.[1,] [2] While living in England, as is the tradition of this family, John followed in his father's footsteps and became a wool comber. John not only brought his family to America with him, but he also brought a valuable estate and became a wealthy farmer, and extremely a very useful citizen and Christian of Dedham.

In the book *History of Dedham*, page 32 and 33, "a John Dwight therefore came not hither, to enjoy institutions already formed, or quietness already secured, but to plant with others, the first germs of our national prosperity and renown." John spent the rest of his life in Dedham. According to the town records of Dedham, John is described as having been publicly useful and a great peacemaker. He was one of those who conveyed the town's first water mill and was one of the founders of the Church of Christ (1638) and was one of the original trustees of the Dedham school, which in 1645 was the first free educational institution in America to be supported by local tax.[3] John was a selectman for sixteen years (1639-1655). In the Dedham town records "the said inhabitants, taking into consideration, the great necessity of providing some means for the education of the youths of said town, did with unanimous consent declared by vote their willingness to promote that work, promising to put to their hands, to provide maintenance for a free school in our said town."

Hannah died 5 September 1656. Following Hannah's death, John married the widow, Elizabeth Ripley. Elizabeth had been widowed twice; her first marriage was to Thomas Thaxter who died 20 January 1658/9. Following Thomas' death, Elizabeth married William Ripley who came to America in 1638 with his first wife, also named Elizabeth, and their four children. They lived in Hingham, Massachusetts. William Ripley died 20 January 1656. Elizabeth Dwight died 17 July 1660.

John Dwight, our immigrant ancestor, died in January 1660/61. Following is the will of John Dwight (without corrections):

> *I John Dwight of Dedham, yeoman, being in perfect health, the 16th June 1658, doe [sic] make this my last will.*
>
> *To my wife Elizabeth, that now is, £50 sterling, to be payd [sic] her by my executors in currant country pay, at my now dwelling house in Dedham, within 3 monethes [sic] after my decease, as my covenant before our marriage appeareth; also all he wearing Apparell both linin and woolen; also that my said wife shall have dyet allowed her, at my said dwelling house in Dedham, during ye space of three monethes after my decease, if she shall desire it, that soe she may more comfortably provide for y° removeall of her habitation to some other place.*
>
> *I give to my sonne Nathaniell Whiting 20s; ynto my sonne Henrie Phillips, 20s; unto sonne Nathaniel Reinolds, 20s. My will is that my*

dwelling-house, land and moveables, in y town of Dedham or elsewhere, which shall be founde to my estate at my decease, be equally divided into five pts.; two pts. Whereof I give unto my sonne Timothy Dwight, and one part, unto y children of my sonne Nathaniell Whiting and of Hannah his wife or soe many of them as shall be surviving at my decease, to be payde by my executors, as in his discretion will best endure for their benefit.

I give vnto my Grand Child Eliazar Phillips, sonne of my sonne Henry Phillips and of Mary, his wife, my dau, one part of ye five; and if ye said Eliazar shall not be surviving at my decease, then my will is, that my executor at his discretion shall dispose of that one part of y five, vnto ye rest of y children of my sonne Henry Phillips, and my dau, Mary, his wife.

The fifth part remaining of y five, I give vnto my daughter Sarah Reynolds or to her child or children, as my executor shall see cause to dispose of. Alsoe my will is, that my sonne Timothy Dwight shall enjoy all that house and land which I gave him at his first marriage with Sally Sibbey.

Also that my sonne Nathaniel Whiting shall enjoy all that six acres of land, be it more or lesse, which lyeth in y low playne and Y 2 Acres of meadow lyeing in foule meadow, which I bought from Lieut. Joshua Fisher.

My will is that it shall be my executors liberty to pay said legacyes, either in land or currant country pay, and to pay them at y same prise, as they were valued at by y prises at my decease. Alsoe is that my executor shall not be ingaged to pay y said legacyes to any of y said children vnder age, untill they canne legally give a discharge for y receipt of y same. I appoint my sonne Timothy Dwight to be the executor of this my last will.

In presence of John Dwight
Peter Woodard
Wm. Avery

                                                    Peter Woodard

Deposed 5 March 1660/1

The poor spelling of the above instrument must of course be credited to the legal hand that drew it up (probably Peter Woodard). The Timothy Dwight Sr., one of the above appraisers, must have been Timothy of Medfield who was, without doubt, his brother.[4]

John and Hannah had the following children:[1]

I.	Hannah Dwight	born 1625, England
II.	Timothy Dwight	born 1629, England
III.	John Dwight	born 1632, England

IV.	Mary Dwight	born 25 July 1635, Dedham, Massachusetts
V.	Sarah Dwight	born 17 June 1638, Dedham, Massachusetts

The following are the descendants in the line of Hannah Dwight, daughter of John and Hannah Dwight, the emigrant ancestors:

I. **Hannah Dwight** (1625-1714), daughter of John and Hannah Dwight, according to the town records of Dedham, married Nathaniel Whiting (?-1683) of Dedham (see appendix C) 4 November 1643 although in another source (*Savage's Genealogy Dictionary*, vol. 4, p. 519), it is given as 4 March 1643.[1a,8] In 1638, Nathaniel received a land grant of fifteen acres in Lynn, Massachusetts; but in 1641, he moved to Dedham where he joined the church 30 July 1641. Nathaniel resided there until his death. History reveals that Nathaniel was not only a man of purity and with a great deal of integrity but also an honorable and quite successful merchant. Nathaniel had a vision of one day developing an area of Boston into an establishment of the manufacturers' exchange. This vision became a reality when a residential area once known for its stylish residences, had become a "vast nuisance in the heart of the city," was torn down and leveled. Nathaniel was up against great odds as the destruction and leveling of Fort Hill, as it was known, had been opposed several times due to the fact that no one could demonstrate the benefit of replacing Fort Hill. Because of Nathaniel's wisdom, foresight, and energy, this enormous area in the business center of Boston was reclaimed and turned into the manufacturers' exchange. Nathaniel died 15 January 1682. Hannah never remarried and continued to live in Dedham until her death 4 November 1714 at the age of eighty-nine.

Hannah (Dwight) and Nathaniel Whiting of Dedham had the following children:

1.	Nathaniel Whiting	born 7 September 1644; married 29 March 1664 Joanna Gay (born 23 March 1645, daughter of John and Joanna Gay)
2.	John Whiting	born 29 September 1646; died soon after birth
3.	`John (2nd) Whiting	born 9 October 1647; died soon after birth
4.	Samuel Whiting	born 20 November 1649
5.	Hannah Whiting	born 17 February 1651
6.	Timothy Whiting	born 5 January 1653

7.	Mary Whiting	born 8 July 1656; died soon after birth
8.	Mary (2nd) Whiting	born 12 October 1658
9.	Sarah Whiting	born 3 December 1660
10	Abigail Whiting	born 7 June 1663
11	John (3rd) Whiting	born 19 July 1665; died 1732; married Mary Billings of Wrentham, Massachusetts, who died 4 January 1728.
12	Jonathan Whiting	born 9 October 1667; married Rachel Thrope
13	Judah Whiting	born 30 March 1670
14	Anna Whiting	born 23 February 1672

In the 1600s, there were three families with the name Whiting: Nathaniel Whiting of Dedham, William Whiting of Hartford, and the Whiting family of Virginia.[1a] Most of those who bear the name of Whiting—originating in Dedham, Wrentham, Hingham, and Plymouth—have descended from Nathaniel and Hannah (Dwight) Whiting. To date, tying the Whiting families together has yet to be accomplished (see the Whiting chapter in this book).

II.   **Timothy Dwight**, born in 1629, son of John and Hannah Dwight, was four or five years of age when he came to America with his family. In later years, Timothy was referred to as Captain Timothy Dwight. There were no schools in Dedham until around 1645 when Timothy was about the age of sixteen. Another source says that the first schoolhouse was not built until 1648, so whatever education Timothy received was from his mother. "Mrs. Hannah Dwight was a woman of superior intelligence and character, and both faithful and successful in the right training of her household, is manifest from ability and thoroughness with which her son Timothy executed the many public trusts committed to him."

Captain Dwight was one of the most forceful and distinguished characters of his time in Massachusetts. He was admitted into the church of Dedham in 1632 and, for more than fifty years, was one of the church's chief members and supporters. He served as town clerk for ten years. Existing today are some of the records, still clear and in his own handwriting just as he had left them. Captain Dwight was a selectman for twenty-five years (1664-1689) and a representative of the town in the General Court in 1691-2. He also served as agent of the town in much import business and especially in transactions with the Indians relating to lands. He was cornet in his younger years. (Cornet was the third and lowest grade of a commissioned officer in a British Cavalry troop. The cornet carried the troop standard, flag, also known as a cornet of a troop of horse, cavalry. On

10 October 1683, he was promoted to lieutenant of the "troop of horse" [*sic*] in Boston and, in 1693, captain of a foot company, infantry)

In the church records of Dedham, Captain Dwight is referred to as Timothy Dwight, Esq., a gentleman truly serious and godly, one of an excellent spirit, peaceable, charitable, and a great promoter of the true interest of the church and town.[1] In 1738, on the one-hundredth annual anniversary of the First Church of Dedham, he is mentioned by Rev. Samuel Dexter as one of three men of principal renown in the history of the community.

Captain Timothy Dwight was married six times;[2] his first marriage was 11 November 1651 to Sarah Perman who died in 1652. They had one child who died in infancy and whose name is unknown.

Captain Dwight's second wife was Sarah Powell, who was the daughter of Michael Powell of Dedham. They were married 3 May 1653. Sarah Powell died 27 June 1664.

Captain Timothy Dwight and Sarah Powell had the following children:

15.	Timothy Dwight	born 26 November 1654
16.	Sarah (1st) Dwight	born 2 April 1657; died 9 February 1659
17.	John Dwight	born 31 May 1661; left no children
18.	Sarah (2nd) Dwight	born 25 June 1664; died 10 July 1668

Captain Dwight married (3) 9 January 1665 Anna Flint (1643-1685) of Braintree, daughter of Rev. Henry Flint (Flynt) of Braintree, Massachusetts, and Margery Hoar, who was the sister of Leonard Hoar, president of Harvard College.

Rev. Henry Flint came to America in 1685, supposedly from Derbyshire, England, and who was ordained the pastor of the church in Braintree in 1639. Flint was described as a gentleman remarkable for piety, learning, wisdom, and fidelity in office. His wife, Margery Hoar, was the daughter of Charles Hoar, the sheriff of Gloucester, England, and Joanna Hincksman.

Charles Hoar died in 1638. After the death of Charles, Joanna and her children came to America (see Hoar chapter). Anna died 29 January 1685 (see Flint chapter).

Captain Timothy Dwight and Anna Flint had the following children:

19.	Josiah (1) Dwight	born 8 October 1665; died in infancy
20.	Nathaniel Dwight	born 20 November 1666; settled in Hatfield
21.	Samuel Dwight	born 2 December 1668
22.	Josiah (2) Dwight	born 8 February 1670 or 1671 (see below)
23.	Seth Dwight	born 25 July 1673
24.	Anna Dwight	born 12 August 1675; died 15 October 1675
25.	Henry Dwight	born 10 December 1676

26. Michael Dwight   born 10 January 1679
27. Daniel Dwight   born 23 September 1681
28. Jabez Dwight   born 1 September 1684; died 15 June 1685

Captain Dwight married (4) 7 January 1686 Mrs. Mary Endwind or Edwards of Reading. She died 30 August 1688. Captain Dwight married (5) 31 July 1690 Esther Fisher, daughter of Daniel Fisher of Dedham. Esther died 30 January 1691. Captain Dwight married (6) 1 February 1692 Bertha Morse. Bertha died 6 February 1718, the same day of the funeral for Captain Dwight.[2] Captain Timothy Dwight and his fourth, fifth, and sixth marriages produced no children.

Captain Dwight was made a freeman in 1655. He died 31 January 1718 at the age of eighty-eight. The inscription on Captain Timothy Dwight's tombstone reads:

Here lyes the body of
Timothy Dwight, Esq.,
Who departed this life Jan. 31st
Anno Domini 1718,
Aged 88 years

The Ancestor
of the Dwight Family in America.
A Family like himself,
Truly serious and godly;
Of an excellent spirit,
Faithful and upright;
Among men of renown
In Church and State, In Halls of Learning
and, in War.

20. Nathaniel Dwight, son of Captain Timothy and Anna (Flint) Dwight, was born 20 November 1666 in Dedham, Massachusetts. He removed from Dedham to Hatfield, Massachusetts. Around 1695, he moved to Northampton, Massachusetts, and remained until his death 7 November 1711. He was trader, farmer, and surveyor of land on a large scale; and he held the office of justice of the peace. Justice Nathaniel Dwight, 9 December 1693, married Mehitable, daughter of Colonel Samuel and Mehitable (Crow) Partridge of Hatfield, Massachusetts. She was born 26 August 1675 and died 19 October 1756 (see Partridge chapter).

Justice Nathaniel Dwight and Mehitable (Partridge) Dwight had the following children:[1]

29.	Timothy Dwight	born 19 October 1694, Hatfield (see below)
30.	Samuel Dwight	born 28 June 1696, Northampton; married Mary Lyman (They lived in Suffield and Middletown and settled in Summers, Connecticut.)
31.	Mehitable (1) Dwight	born 11 November 1697, Northampton; died 22 December 1697
32.	Daniel Dwight	born 29 April 1699, Hatfield: graduated Yale College 1721; died 28 March 1748
33.	Seth Dwight	born 3 March 1703, Northampton; died September 1703
34.	Elihu (twin) Dwight	born 17 February 1704, Northampton; died Philadelphia 1728; no children; occupation was that of a cordwainer
35.	Abia (twin) Dwight	born 17 February 1704, Northampton; married 28 February 1722 Samuel Kent of Suffield, Connecticut
36.	Mehitable (2) Dwight	born 5 November 1705, Northampton; married 31 January 1728 Abraham Burbank of Suffield (see Burbank chapter)
37.	Jonathan Dwight	born 14 March 1708, Northampton; married Mary Lane; settled in Boston; had children: died at Halifax, Nova Scotia
38.	Anne Dwight	born 20 July 1710, Northampton; married Abel Caldwell
39.	Nathaniel Dwight	born 20 June 1712, Northampton (posthumous); lived in Belchertown Massachusetts; married Mary Lyman

22. **Rev. Josiah (2) Dwight**, born 8 February 1670 and fourth child of Timothy and Anna (Flint) Dwight, graduated from Harvard College in 1687. He was ordained and installed as the first minister of Woodstock, Connecticut, in 1690, where he continued serving for thirty-six years. He subsequently served as pastor of the Third Parish Church of Dedham. On 4 December 1695, he married Mary Partridge, daughter of Colonel Samuel Partridge and Mehitable (Crow) Partridge. Mary was the sister of

Mehitable Partridge, who was the wife of Rev. Mr. Dwight's elder brother, Nathaniel (see 20 above).

III. **John Dwight**, son of John and Hanna Dwight, was born in England in 1632. According to "The Early Records of Boston," John, at the age of seven, went wandering into the wood and became lost. He was never found, and so his date of death is recorded as 24 March 1638.[4]

IV. **Mary Dwight**, the fourth child of John and Hanna Dwight, was born 25 August 1635 in Dedham, Massachusetts. Mary is mentioned in the town records as the first child born in Dedham. At the age of sixteen or seventeen (1652), Mary became the third wife of Henry Phillips (?-1686). Henry was considered a freeman at Watertown in 1637. Henry is mentioned in the will of John Dwight dated 16 June 1658. This marriage produced twelve children, born between the years 1653 and 1672. Mary died about 1693.[8]

V. **Sarah Dwight**, the fifth and last child of John and Hannah Dwight, was born 17 June 1638 in Dedham, Massachusetts. Sarah married Nathaniel Reynolds of Boston 30 December 1657,[9] with Governor Endicott performing the ceremony.[4] Nathaniel was the son of Robert Reynolds of England and later of Watertown, Massachusetts. Nathaniel, like his father, was a shoemaker. Sarah died 24 January 1664. Nathaniel's second wife's name was Priscilla.[4]

Sarah Dwight and Nathaniel Reynolds had two children:

| 40. | Mary Reynolds | born 20 November 1660 |
| 41. | Nathaniel Reynolds | born 3 March 1662 |

Nathaniel and his second wife Priscilla had four sons:[4]

42. John Reynolds
43. Peter Reynolds
44. Phillip Reynolds
45. Joseph Reynolds

29. **Timothy Dwight**, born 19 October 1694 in Hatfield, Massachusetts, and son of Justice Nathaniel and Mehitable (Partridge) Dwight, later became known as Colonel Timothy Dwight. He was a lawyer by profession and was noted for his disposition to discourage litigation, persuading litigants to settle their differences before referees. He was looked upon as one of the

leading men in the community and was very successful in his undertakings and thus acquired considerable wealth. He was a selectman of the town for a number of years; judge of probate, 1734-41; judge of the county court, 1748-57, a portion of the time serving as chief justice; for many years represented Northampton in the General Court; and was colonel of a regiment. In 1724, he superintended the building of Fort Drummer, now known as Fort Drummer in Brattleboro, Vermont. He was first commander of the fort and maintained that position until 1726.

It was Timothy who obtained the Dwight coat of arms from the Heralds' College in England and had it engraved on a silver tankard. Underneath the arms, the initials T. E. D. were engraved, which stood for Timothy, Experience Dwight.

On 16 August 1716, Timothy married Experience, daughter of Lieutenant John King Jr. of Northampton and his wife, Mehitable (Pomeroy) King.

Colonel Timothy died 30 April 1771 at the age of seventy-six.[1,2] One source (*Encyclopedia of Connecticut Biography*) shows his date of death as 15 December 1763, which of course is the date of death of Experience Dwight, who died at the age of seventy-one. They had the following children:[1]

47.	Eleanor Dwight	born1717; married Phineas Lyman of Suffield, Connecticut, who later became General Lyman
48.	Gamaliel Dwight (1)	born 1718; died in infancy
49.	Gamaliel Dwight (2)	born 1720; died young
50.	Timothy Dwight	born 19 October 1726

32. **Daniel Dwight,** born 29 April 1699 in Hatfield, Massachusetts, and son of Justice Nathaniel and Mehitable (Partridge) Dwight, graduated from Yale College in 1721 and was an Episcopal clergyman near Charleston, South Carolina. Rev. Daniel Dwight went to England to take orders in the Episcopal Church and received his ordination as a priest 1 June 1729. While in England, Dwight also received 29 July 1729 his MA from Oxford University. Upon returning to America, he became the rector of Strawberry Chapel, St. John's Parish in Berkeley County, South Carolina, where he remained for the rest of his life. His first marriage was to Christina, daughter of Governor Thomas Broughton of South Carolina and Anne Johnson, daughter of Governor Nathaniel Johnson. There were no children by this marriage.[2] Daniel's second marriage was to Esther Cordis. This marriage produced five children. Daniel died 28 March 1748.

36. **Mehitable Dwight (2)**, born 2 November 1705, was the daughter of Justice Nathaniel and Mehitable (Partridge) Dwight. She married 31 January 1728 Captain Abraham Burbank of Suffield, Connecticut. Abraham Burbank was a captain in the trainband and was the son of John Burbank Jr. and Mary Granger (see Burbank chapter). Mehitable died 20 November 1767.

37. **Jonathan Dwight**, born 4 March 1708 and son of Justice Nathaniel and Mehitable (Partridge) Dwight, married Mary, the daughter of Thomas Boylston and Mary (Gardner). Jonathan was a hotelkeeper from 1730 to 1750 at which time he moved to Halifax, Nova Scotia, where he died.[4] Jonathan's widow, Mary, according to the book *The History of the Descendants of John Dwight of Dedham, Mass*, married a third husband, "a Mr. Hubbard." Jonathon and Mary (Boylston) Dwight had the following children:

51.	Mary Dwight	born about 1730, probably Boston
52.	Nathaniel Dwight	died young
53.	Samuel Dwight	died young
54.	Sarah Dwight	married Parker of Halifax, Nova Scotia

39. **Nathaniel Dwight** was born 20 June 1712, Belchertown, Massachusetts, seven months after the death of his father, Justice Nathaniel Dwight (7 November 1711). He removed from Northampton in 1733 and settled in to look after the various interest of his older brother, Colonel Timothy Dwight, in addition to those of Governor Jonathan Belcher of Massachusetts.[1] Captain Dwight was a permanent resident of Belchertown and was a prominent man in all civil and religious affairs and, at the same time, performed a creditable part of the military service as did so many of the Dwight families. He served as the Hampshire County surveyor, whose work at that time included the entire western part of Massachusetts.

He was commissioned captain 10 September 1755 and, with his company of troops, traveled to Crown Point where he assisted in building Fort William Henry. He maintained a journal which was published in 1902, outlining the erection of the fort and a description of the Battle of Lake George. On 9 August 1757, he was ordered to march immediately, without delay, to the relief of Fort William Henry, which had been attacked by an army of French and Indians under Montcalm. He mustered his company the same day and proceeded as far as Kinderhook, but upon learning that the fort had been surrendered to the French, Captain Dwight and his company returned home.[1]

50. **Timothy Dwight** was born 19 October 1726, North Hampton, Massachusetts, and was the son of Colonel Timothy and Experience Dwight. He married Mary Edwards, daughter of the Rev. Jonathon Edwards who at that time was the pastor of the church at Northampton and, in 1758, became the president of the College in New Jersey (now known as Princeton University). (If you wish to learn more about this very important man in the history of America, please go to your "search engine" and type in Rev. Jonathon Edwards.) Timothy Dwight, Esq., died 10 June 1777 in Natchez at the age of fifty-two. Mary (Edwards) Dwight died in Northampton 28 February 1807 at the age of seventy-three. They had the following children:

55.	Timothy Dwight	born 14 May 1752
56.	Sereno Edward Dwight, Jr.	born 10 December 1754
57.	Erastus Dwight	born 13 September 1756; died 1825; never married
58.	Jonatha Dwight	born 29 January 1759; married Wright
59.	Sarah Dwight	born 29 May 1761; married Storrs
60.	Mary Dwight	born 9 January 1763
61.	Theodore Dwight	born 16 December 1764; married Abby Alsop of Middletown, Connecticut (a highly respected lawyer, moved to Hartford, and later settled in New York); died 1846
62.	Maurice William Dwight	born 15 December 1766
63.	Fidelis Dwight	born 7 August 1768; married Justice Jonathon Edward Porter of Hadley, Massachusetts, 16 January 1793
64.	Nathaniel Dwight	born 31 January 1770; married 20 June 1798 Rebecca Robbins, daughter of Appleton Robbins, Esq., of Wethersfield, Connecticut (Rebecca Dwight died 28 April 1848 at the age of seventy-seven)
65.	Elizabeth Dwight	born 29 January 1772
66.	Cecil Dwight	born 20 June 1770; married Mary Clapp
67.	Henry Edwin Dwight	born 20 September 1770; married Electra Centre

51. **Mary Dwight** was born about 1730 and was the daughter of Jonathan and May (Boylston) Dwight. According to the records of her uncle, Nathaniel

Dwight of Belchertown, Massachusetts, "Mary was a most beautiful young woman in shape and features." Mary was an avid reader and was very much interested in history and the study of religion. Although only twenty-two years of age when she died, she was well versed in business matters and would feel very comfortable around the "best of gentlemen."[4]

55. Timothy Dwight was born 14 May 1752 in Northampton, Massachusetts,[6] and was the son of Major Timothy and Mary (Edwards) Dwight. He graduated from Yale College in 1769 and was the principal of the Hopkins Grammar School from 1769 to 1771. During the period of 1771-77, he was a tutor at Yale while at the same time he studied law. He was licensed to preach in 1777 and served in Parson's brigade of the Connecticut line in 1777-78. Parson's brigade was a force of about 2,500 men under the command of Brigadier General Samuel Holden Parsons. Due to the death of his father (1777), as soon as was possible, Timothy Dwight returned home and took charge of the family farm.

In addition to the farm responsibilities, Timothy found time to preach in the local churches. Timothy ran a day school and had in his care several British refugee Yale students. Timothy Dwight was a representative in the Massachusetts legislature in 1782, but refused a nomination in Congress. He was pastor of the church in Greenfield Hill, Fairfield, Connecticut, from 1783 to 1795; and it was there that he established a highly acclaimed academy and became the pioneer of higher education for women, putting both sexes on equal footing in his school.[6] He was president of Yale College from 8 September 1795 to 11 January 1817 and Livingston professor of Divinity (pro tempore) from 1805 to 1817 by election. Because his influence, the college's bitterness between the students and faculty and between the freshmen and upperclassmen was soon changed, the enrollment went from just over one hundred to over three hundred; thus, the college became one of the most modern university schools in America.

Dr. Dwight—as he became known—received from the college in New Jersey (Princeton) his degree of STD (doctor of sacred theology) in 1787. In 1810, he received his LLD from Harvard College. His master dissertation was "History, Eloquence and Poetry of the Bible." One of his greatest works was his epic *The Conquest of Canaan* and his most popular pastoral poem was "Greenfield Hill," which was written in 1794.

Timothy died in New Haven, Connecticut, 11 January 1817 and is buried in Grave Street Cemetery in New Haven.

* As early as 1631 in order to become a freeman, it was required that the applicant produce evidence that he was a member of the Congregational Church. This regulation was modified in 1664. Freemen were admitted by the General

Court of the colony. A freeman was entitled to exercise the right to vote and to hold office.

There was another Timothy Dwight, probably the brother of John, our emigrant ancestor and who also lived in the same household. He was known as Timothy of Medfield.[1] This Timothy Dwight was also a man of considerable and prominence, serving in various offices. He appears to have first resided in Dedham. He was wounded by the Indians at the burning of Medfield in 1677 and died a few days later at Dedham. He was married twice. His second wife, Dorcas Watson, had three sons which, according to Historic Families of America, the male line of the Timothy Dwight of Medfield branch of the Dwight family is now extinct although there are various lines of descent in female branches.

Notes

1a. William Whiting, former president of the New England Historical Genealogical Society, and author of *War Powers Under the Constitution of the United States; Memoir of Rev. Samuel Whiting, D. D. and of his wife, Elizabeth St. John; with reference to some of their English Ancestors and American Descendants.*

1. Walter W. Spooner, editor *Historic Families of America* Historic Families Publishing Company, New York

2. Nathaniel Goodwin, *Genealogical Notes of Contributions to the Family History of some of the First Settlers of Connecticut and Massachusetts,* Genealogical Publishing Company Baltimore, Maryland 1987.

3. Dedham town records.

4. Benjamin W. Dwight, *The History of The Descendants of John Dwight of Durham, Mass.,* Vol. I John W. Trow and Son New York 1874

5. New. England Historic Genealogical Society, vol. X (1856) p. 263

6. Encyclopedia of Connecticut Biography, the American Historical Society, NY 1917

7. John Dwight's "Last will and testament"

8. Clarence Almon Torrey, Prepared for publication by Patricia P. Bentley, *New England Marriages Prior to 1700* Genealogical Publishing Company, Baltimore 1985.

9. Melinde Lutz Sanborn *Third Supplement to Torrey's New England Marriages Prior to 1700,* Genealogical Publishing Company, Baltimore 2003.

ELEVEN

William Partridge and Mary Smith

(See Appendix K)

The Partridge name is one that has been easily traced back to the time of William the Conqueror in the year 1066 when the Battle of Hastings was fought. William was crowned King of England, following the defeat of King Harold II (1017-1066). It was King Harold II that added his Duchy of Normandy to the Partridge lands. The men, who assisted William the Conqueror in the Battle of Hastings, were given grants of land, with the degree of services rendered, determining the amount of grants given. In the Abbey Roll, the name is spelled de Pertiche, the Norman. Later the family moved to Gloucestershire. Being given grants showed "recognition as being in high favor of the court and at once marked it as an ancient family."[5]

William Partridge was born in Berwick upon Tween in England. He was one of the earlier settlers of Hartford, Connecticut, and was a member of the First Church of Hartford at the time of Rev. Thomas Hooker and Rev. Samuel Stone. It was during Stone's pastorate that William was considered one of the "strict Congregationalists" and became a "withdrawer" of the church.

On 18 April 1659, William Partridge and fifty-nine members entered into articles of agreement for the settlement of the new community. The town of Hadley, Massachusetts, was laid out; and thus, in 1659 William Partridge moved to Hadley where he spent the remainder of his life working as a trader. William became a freeman 14 March 1638.[6] He was one of the first auditors (1661) and was selectman in 1668. He also served in other local offices.[2] William married 12 December 1644, Mary Smith.[3] William died 27 June 1668.[1] Mary was born in 1625. She died 20 July 1680 at the age of fifty-five.[1]

William and Mary(Smith) Partridge had two children:

I.   Colonel Samuel Partridge born 15 October 1645, Hartford
II.   Mary Partridge   born about 1646/7

I.   **Colonel Samuel Partridge** was born 15 October 1645 in Hartford,
Connecticut. His family moved to Hadley, Massachusetts, in 1659 when
Samuel was around the age of fourteen. He "became at an early age, a man
of commanding influence." At the age of thirty-six (1681), Samuel was third
on the list of taxpayers. In 1687, Samuel changed his residence to Hatfield
that had just become a new community and was set apart from Hadley.

Samuel married 24 September 1668, Mehitable Crow, daughter of John
Crow of Hartford and Elizabeth Goodwin, daughter of Elder William Goodwin.
Both John Crow and Elder William Goodwin were among the founders of
Hartford.

Colonel Partridge was a merchant, and from 1692 to 1740, he served as
judge of the Court of Connecticut. During that time, Colonel Partridge was
chief justice (1706-1736).

In the days, liquor was sold, but only by a select few. To sell liquor, one
must be licensed. It appeared that the time period was a short one (1679-1692).
This license allowed the holder to sell to his neighbors and to retail wine and
strong drink. "Retailers were required to sell only on necessary occasions and
at a moderate price—not allowed to sell to children, servants and extravagant
persons, or to have customers sit tippling in their houses."[1]

Colonel Partridge also served as probate judge, and in 1685-6, he represented
the town. He also held the rank of colonel of a regiment and one of His
Majesty's (King James II) Council. Following the death of Colonel Pynchon,
"Col. Partridge became the most important man of all the western part of
the province." Samuel Partridge was quite wealthy and was one of the three
Connecticut River Gods—the other two being John Pynchon of Springfield
and Colonel John Stoddard of Northampton. In the book *History of Western
Massachusetts*, written by Dr. J. G. Springfield, "in the civil and military affairs of
his native town and country, Colonel John Stoddard stood at the head—forming
one of that great trios which had John Pynchon of Springfield as its first member,
and Colonel Samuel Partridge of Hatfield, for its second, and which ruled or
led Western Massachusetts through an entire century of its history."[1]

Mehitable (Crow) Partridge died on 8 December 1730 at the age of seventy-
eight. Colonel Partridge married on 28 December 1731 Hanna Edwards. They
did not have any children. Colonel Samuel Partridge died on 25 December
1740 at the age of ninety-five.

Colonel Samuel and Mehitable (Crow) Partridge had the following children:

1.	William Partridge	born 16 November 1669; graduated Harvard 1689; was a minister; died September 1693 at Wallingford, Connecticut, at the age of twenty-three: never married
2.	Samuel Partridge Jr.	born 21 January 1672
3.	Mehitable (1) Partridge	born 1 May 1674; died 16 May 1674
4.	Mehitable (2) Partridge	born 26 August 1675
5.	Mary Partridge	born 1678
6.	Jonathan (1) Partridge	born 5 April 1681; died 11 September 1684
7.	Edward Partridge	born 26 April 1683
8.	Jonathan (2) Partridge	born 18 September 1685; died 24 January 1686
9.	John Partridge	born 1686
10.	Elizabeth Partridge	born 7 October 1688

II. **Mary Partridge**, daughter of William and Mary (Smith) Partridge, was born about 1646/7 at Hartford, Connecticut. Mary married (1) 12 November 1663, John Smith, son of Lieutenant Saul Smith. John Smith died 30 May 1676. In September 1679, Mary married (2) Peter Montague. Peter was born in 1651 and died in 1725. Mary died 20 May 1680.

Mary (Partridge) and John Smith had one child, Mary Smith, born at Hadley in 1677. Mary Smith, the daughter of Mary (Partridge) Smith, married Major John Day of Springfield. John was born in 1673 and died in 1752. He was the son of Thomas Day (1638-1711) of Springfield and Sarah Cooper (1642-1726). Mary (Smith) Day died in 1742.

Mary (Smith) and Thomas Day had one child, a daughter named Thankful who born in 1721 and died in 1803. Thankful Day married Hon. Eldad Taylor of Westfield, Massachusetts.[1]

2. **Samuel Partridge Jr.**, second son of Colonel Samuel and Mehitable Partridge, born 21 January 1672, Hadley, Massachusetts. He married 2 May 1695, Mary (1670-1729) (Cotton) Atwater, daughter of Rev. Seaborn Cotton (1633-1688) and Dorothy Bradstreet (?-1672) and widow of John Atwater.[4] Samuel and Mary had eight children.[1,4]

11.	William Partridge	born 9 January 1696; died young
12.	Samuel Partridge	born 1 June 1697

13. Mary Partridge	born 15 June 1698; married Isaac Mattone of Northfield
14. Elizabeth Partridge	born 22 September 1701; married Ezekiel Kellogg of New Salem
15. Dorothy Partridge	born 7 March 1703; died soon after
16. Cotton Partridge	born 13 October 1705
17. Mehitable Partridge	born 8 October 1707; married Thomas Barnard of Tolland, Connecticut
18. William Partridge	born 15 September 1710; graduated from Yale 1729; secretary of state in Nova Scotia

4. **Mehitable Partridge (2)**, daughter of Colonel Samuel and Mehitable (Crow) Partridge, married 9 December 1693 Nathaniel Dwight (1666-1711) of Hatfield.[1,3] Nathaniel Dwight was the son of Captain Timothy and Ann (Fitch) Dwight (see Dwight chapter).[2]

5. **Mary Partridge**, daughter of Colonel Samuel and Mehitable (Crow) Partridge and sister of Mehitable (above), married 5 December 1695, Rev. Josiah Dwight of Woodstock (1671-1748). He was the brother of Nathaniel Dwight (see Dwight chapter).[1,4]

7. **Edward Partridge**, son of Colonel Samuel and Mehitable (Crow) Partridge, married 14 May 1707 Martha Williams, daughter of Rev. William Williams of Hatfield, Massachusetts. Edward died 26 December 1757.[1]

Edward and Martha (Williams) Partridge had the following children:

19. Elizabeth Partridge	born 14 October 1708
20. Martha Partridge	born 9 October 1710
21. Oliver Partridge	born 13 June 1712

9. **John Partridge**, son of Colonel Samuel and Mehitable Partridge, graduated from Harvard in 1705 and died in Springfield, Massachusetts, 19 May 1717.[1]

10. **Elizabeth Partridge** was born 7 October 1688 and was the daughter of Colonel Samuel and Mehitable (Crow) Partridge. She married 4 May 1709 John Hamlin Jr. who was born 16 July 1687 and was the son of Judge John Hamlin of Middletown, Connecticut. After the death of John, Elizabeth married another Hamlin. Following the death of the second Hamlin, Elizabeth married a Mr. Johnson of Woodstock, Connecticut. Following

Mr. Johnson's death, Elizabeth married a fourth time to a Mr. Payton of Middletown, Connecticut.[1]

16. **Cotton Partridge**, the son of Samuel and Mary (Cotton) Partridge, was born 13 October 1705 and lived in Hadley, Massachusetts. Cotton married Margaret Cook, daughter of Captain Moses and Mary (Barnard) Cook. Margaret was born 18 March 1711. Cotton Partridge died 28 September 1733. They had two children:

22.	Samuel Partridge	born 3 July 1730
23	Sybil Partridge	born 7 October 1732; married Josiah Dickinson

21. **Oliver Partridge**, son of Edward and Martha (Williams) Partridge, was born 13 June 1712 and resided at Hatfield. He married Anna Williams, daughter of William Williams of Weston, Massachusetts. There were thirteen children born of this marriage. Oliver was a member of the Continental Congress (1765).

22. **Samuel Partridge**, son of Cotton and Margaret (Cook) Partridge, was born 3 July 1730 and lived in Hatfield. During the French and Indian War, he held the rank of lieutenant and was connected to a foot company (infantry) under the command of Colonel William Williams. He participated in the reduction of Canada and was present at the fall of Quebec.[2]

Lieutenant Samuel Partridge 18 January 1754, married Abigail Dwight who was born 19 September 1733. She was the daughter of Captain Seth and Abigail (Strong) Dwight, granddaughter of Captain Henry and Lydia (Hawley) Dwight, and great-granddaughter of Captain Timothy and Anna (Flint) Dwight. Lieutenant Samuel Partridge died 4 April 1809.[2]

Samuel and Abigail (Strong) Partridge had the following children:

24.	Esther Partridge	born 26 March 1761; died 22 December 1834; married John Allis of Hartford
25.	Cotton Partridge	born 1 December 1675
26.	Samuel (1) Partridge	born 1767; died young
27.	Samuel (2) Partridge	born 1776; died 1858

25. **Cotton Partridge**, son of Samuel and Abigail (Strong) Partridge, was born 1 December 1765. He married (1) Sophia Arms, daughter of Deacon Arms of Deerfield, Massachusetts. Samuel and Sophia resided in Hatfield, Massachusetts. Sophia died 29 June 1793. Cotton married (2) 23 June 1796 Hannah Lyman. Hannah was born 20 June 1773 and was the daughter

of Rev. Joseph and Hannah (Huntington) Lyman. Hannah died 10 May 1835. Samuel died 13 November 1864.

Cotton and Sophia (Arms) Partridge had several children.

27. **Samuel Partridge**, son of Samuel and Abigail (Strong) Partridge, was born in 1776. His residence was Hatfield, Massachusetts. He married 8 September 1796 Mable Dickinson. Mable was born about 1776, and she died 4 November 1841 at the age of sixty-five. She was the daughter of General Lemuel Dickinson. They had one child:

    28. Hepsey Dickinson Partridge born in 1797; married Israel Billings, Esq., of Hatfield; had six children
    29. Samuel Dwight Partridge born 1806

29. **Samuel Dwight Partridge** was born in 1806 and was the son of Samuel and Abigail (Strong) Partridge. He graduated from Amherst College in 1827. He married Lucretia Andrews Warner. Samuel and Lucretia had the following children:

    30. Mary Ann Ward Partridge married Peter Meyer (banker and broker in New York)
    31. Harriet Holms Partridge married Henry I. Bliss

Notes

1. Benjamin W. Dwight, The *History of the Descendants of John Dwight of Dedham, Mass.*, Vol. I, pg 110; John Trow and Son New York 1874.

2. Walter W. Spooner, Editor *Historic Families of America*, Vol. II, Historic Families Publishing Association, New York.

3. Nathaniel Goodwin, *Genealogical Notes or Contributions to the Family History of some of the First Settlers of Connecticut and Massachusetts*, 1st published 1856 Hartford; reprinted 1987 Genealogical Publishing Company, Baltimore

4. Clarence Almon Torrey, *New England Marriages Prior to 1700* Prepared for publication by Elizabeth P. Bentley; Genealogical Publishing Company, Baltimore 1985.

5. William Cutter and William Frederick Adams, Genealogical and Personal Memoirs of Massachusetts Families

6. New England Historical and Genealogical Register Vol. 3, pg. 99

TWELVE

Henry Flynt (Flint) and Margery Hoar

(See Appendix L)

Henry (2) Flynt (or Flynt) was born in 1613 in Matlock, Derbyshire, England. He was the son of Henry (1) Flynt—his mother's name is unknown. Henry (2) graduated from Jesus College at Cambridge, England, and received his AB in 1634/5. He came to New England in 1635 and was admitted to the church at Boston on November 15 of the same year. He was made a freeman of the colony 25 May 1636. On 11 August 1639, Henry Flynt left the church in Boston and joined the church at Mt. Wollaston (Braintree) (now Quincy) Massachusetts where he became the religious teacher of the church with Rev. William Tompson as pastor. He continued in that capacity until 1659. When Tompson became incapacitated, Flynt began officiating alone and did so until his death in 1668. Flynt gave the Artillery Election Sermon in 1657.

Rev. Henry Flynt married before 1642 in Braintree, Massachusetts, Margery Hoar (Hoare),[6] eldest daughter of Charles Hoare Jr. who was the sheriff of Gloucester, England, and who died in 1638. Margery's mother was Joanna Hinkesman (or Henchman as sometimes spelled). Joanna continued to live in England for two years following the death of her husband. After two years as a widow, in 1640, Joanna (Hinkesman) Hoare came to America with five of her children.

I.	Thomas Hoare	baptized 15 June 1612; stayed in England
II.	Charles Hoare	born 1613
III.	Daniel Hoare	came to America in 1640*

IV.	Leonard Hoare	came to America in 1640*
V.	Margery Hoare	came to America in 1640*
VI.	John Hoare	came to America in 1640*
VII	Joanna Hoare	came to America in 1640 as a widow and childless,*

Rev. Henry Flynt was the brother of Thomas Flynt of Concord who was in Boston in 1637 and settled in Concord where he died 8 October 1653. Thomas married Dorothy (last name unknown) of Matlock, Derbyshire County, England.

Flynt lived in Quincy, next to the Reverend Tompson; and on 27 January 1639/40, Flynt was granted an eighty-acre lot by the Town of Boston. It became exempt from taxes when Boston and Braintree separated. In 1644, he had an additional grant in the Three Hill marsh, now known as Broad Meadows. Flynt divided this new grant with Tompson. The eighty-acre land was known as the Flynt farm, which was bordered on the east side by Weymouth, Massachusetts, and was bordered on the west side by Smelt Brook. In the will of Rev. Henry Flynt, this lot was left to his son, Seth, who died in 1673, and then reverted to his mother, Margery, who at that time was a widow. In 1680, Margery sold thirty acres to Ephraim Hunt of Weymouth.[1]

A stone in the form of a monument lies over the remains of Mr. Flynt and his wife, with another at the head, on which is the following inscription[2,3] (no changes in spell or punctuation):

Here lies interred the body of the Rev. Mr. Henry Flynt, who came to New England in the year, 1635, was ordained the first teacher of the Church of Braintrey 1639, and Died April 27, 1668.

He had the character of a gentleman remarkable for his piety, learning, wisdom, and fidelity in his office. by him, on his right hand, lies the body of Margery, his beloved consort, who died March 1686-7, her maiden name was Hoar. She was a gentlewoman of piety, prudence, and perhaps peculiarly accomplished for instructing young gentlewomen, many being sent to her from other towns, especially from Boston.

They descended from antient [sic] and good familys [sic] in England [2,3]

Rev. Henry Flynt died on 27 April 1668; Margery died on 10 March 1687. They had the following children:[1]

| 1. | Dorothy Flynt | born July 1642; married 30 April 1666, Rev. Samuel Shepard of Rowley (Both died in the year 1668—within two years of marriage.) |

2.	Anna Flynt	born 11 September 1643
3.	Josiah Flynt	born 24 August 1645
4.	Margaret Flynt	born 20 June 1647; died soon afterward
5.	Joanna Flynt	born February 1649; married 30 December 1669 Rev. Noah Newman
6.	David Flynt	born 11 January 1652; died soon afterward
7.	Seth Flynt	born 2 April 1653; died at Dedham, 12 May 1673 during his second year at Harvard College
8.	Ruth Flynt	born 31 January 1655; Ruth died June 1673
9.	John (twin) Flynt	born 16 June 1656 (may have been born in November records not clear); died soon after birth
10.	Cotton (twin) Flynt	born 16 June 1656 (may have been born in November records not clear); died soon after birth

2. **Anna Flynt** first married John Dassett in Braintree, Massachusetts, 15 November 1662. John was born about 1630. Ann's second marriage was to Captain Timothy Dwight, 9 January 1665. Anna was Captain Dwight's third wife. Anna and Timothy's son, Nathaniel, married Mehitable Partridge (see Partridge chapter). Captain Dwight died on 31 January 1717, and Anna died on 29 January 1685/6 (see Dwight chapter).[4]

3. **Josiah Flynt**, the eldest son of Rev. Henry and Margery (Hoar) Flynt, was born in Braintree, Massachusetts, 21 September 1645. Josiah graduated from Harvard College in 1664 and was ordained successor of Rev. Richard Mather at Dorchester 27 December 1671, where he made it his home from 1671 until his death 16 September 1680 at the age of thirty-five. Rev. Josiah Flynt also had the honor of preaching the Artillery Election Sermon in 1677.

Josiah married Esther Willett 24 January 1672, Swansea, Massachusetts. Esther was the daughter of Captain Thomas Willett, the first mayor of New York City.[5] Esther was born in Plymouth, Massachusetts, 10 July 1649. She died in Dorchester 26 July 1737.

Josiah and Ester (Willet) Flynt had the following children:

11.	Henry Flynt	born 5 May 1675, Dorchester, Massachusetts
12.	Dorothy Flynt	born 11 May 1678, Dorchester

11. **Henry,** later referred to as Tutor Flint, was born 5 May 1675 and was named after his grandfather Henry Flynt. He graduated from Harvard College in 1693 with AB and MA; Fellow at Harvard College from 1700-1760. He settled in Norwich, Connecticut, from 1696-1699. He became a Tutor at Harvard 7 August 1699 and resigned 25 September 1754, fifty-five years later. Josiah, Henry's father, was secretary to the board of Overseers at Harvard until 1758. Flynt died at Cambridge, Massachusetts, 13 February 1760 at the age of eighty-five.[5] As far as I can tell, Henry never married.

12. **Dorothy Flynt** married Edmund Quincy 20 November 1701, Dorchester, Massachusetts. Edmund was born 21 October 1681 (another source shows 14 October 1681) in Braintree, Massachusetts. Edmund was the son of Edmund Quincy (1628-1698) and Elizabeth Gookin Eliot Quincy (1645-1700). Edmund was a merchant of Braintree and Boston. He graduated from Harvard in 1699 and was selectman, justice of the peace, colonel of militia, representative in the General Court, and member of Council, and justice of the Superior Court of Judicature. He married in 1701 Dorothy Flynt (1678-1737). The house in which she lived was built by Colonel Edmond Quincy in 1685. At the time of his death, he had an estate of over £14,000

Edmund died in London, England, of smallpox 23 February 1738. Dorothy died 29 December 1737, Dorchester. They had the following children:

> Edmund Quincy (Justice)
> Elizabeth Quincy (17 October1706-2 March 1746) married John Wendell of Boston.
> Dorothy Quincy (1709-1762) married Edward Jackson; their daughter married Judge Oliver Wendell whose daughter, Sarah Wendell married Rev. Abiel Holmes and was the mother of Dr. Oliver Wendell Holmes.

Notes

1. James Savage, *A Genealogical Dictionary of the First Settlers of New England, before 1692,* Vol. 2, Boston, Little Brown and Company 1860.

2. New England Historical and Genealogical Register for the year 1855, Vol. IX, pg. 151

3. Henry Stedman Nourse, *The Hoar Family in America and its English Ancestry, from the collection of the Hon. George Frisbie Hoar,* Boston, David Clapp & Son, Printers,1899.

4. The American Historical Society. *Encyclopedia of Connecticut Biography. New York 1917.*

5. Frederick Lewis Weis, *The Colonial Clergy and The Colonial Churches of New England* pages 85 & 86. Genealogical Publishing Company, Baltimore, Maryland 1977

6. Melinde Lutz Sanborn *Third Supplement to Torrey's New England Marriages Prior to 1700,* Genealogical Publishing Company, Baltimore 2003.

THIRTEEN

Charles Hoar Sr. and Margery

(See Appendix M)

———◆◆◆———

The Hoar name—at times spelled Hoare or Hore or Hoore—has been found in the histories of England and Ireland. As early as 1300 and up to 1700, there were thirteen members of Parliament that came from six different countries, who bore the name of Hoare or some variation of the spelling.[1]

Charles Hoare Sr. of Gloucester, England, was married to Margery (sometimes spelled Margerie, last name unknown). His will was written on 29 May 1632, and his occupation was that of a sadler [*sic*] (maker of saddles). In his will, the following people are mentioned:

> Wife—Margery
> Son—Charles Hoare Jr
> Son—Thomas Hoare
> Thomas Hore and John Hore, sons of Charles Hoare Jr
> Margery, daughter of Charles Hoare Jr
> Charles Hoare and Johan Hoare, sons of Thomas Hoare
> Son-in-law—Thomas Hill, wife not mentioned, assumes deceased
> Son-in-law—Leonard Tarne, wife not mentioned, assumes deceased
> (Both Thomas Hill and Leonard Tarne are referred to as sons in the will.)

In some records, the spelling of a family's last name will differ in order to distinguish the different families within that family, even though the males were brothers. John *Hore* and Johan *Hoare* were cousins. Their fathers were brothers, Charles Hoare Jr. and Thomas Hoare.

On 21 December 1599, Charles Jr., by an act of an Indenture, agreed that for a period of eight years he would become an apprentice to Charles Sr. and his wife Margerie [*sic*]; and at the end of the eight-year period, Charles Sr. and his wife Margerie [*sic*] would pay Charles Jr. forty shillings. Even though Charles Jr. had studied under his father as an apprentice, learning the trade of a saddler, he did not follow in his father's footsteps, instead his occupation became that of a brewer.[1]

Charles Hoare Jr. married Joanna Hincksman in England, prior to 1612, when their first child Thomas was born.[5]

Following is the will of Charles Hoare Jr. of Gloucester (1638).[1] Although sometimes difficult to understand, because of the spelling; nevertheless, the spelling in his will has not been edited.

Prerogative Court of Canterbury

> *In the name of God Almightie Creator of all thinges and in Jesus Christ his deare and only son my most bountifull loveing Saviour and in the blessed spiritt my comforter Amen.*
>
> *I Charles Hoare of the cittie of Gloucester being weake in body but perfect in memory blessed be my good god therefore, Doe hereby declare that my last will and testament as followeth ffirst I bequeath my soule into the handes of God that created it and my deare Saviour that soe dearlie ransom'd it with full confidence thorough his merrittes that after the end of his life it shall rest with him everlastingly. And my bodie to the earthe from whence it came with full assurance that at the last daie when my Saviour shall appeare in glory it shalbe by his power raised up to the resurrection of the just.*
>
> *And for the estate it hath pleased god to lend unto me of the things of this world I thus dispose ffirst that with as much convenient speede as may well be all my rentes and debtes sett downe under my hand and all other if any be and can appeare to be due shalbe paid.*
>
> *Item I give to my brother Thomas Hoare twentie poundes, to my sister Elinor Bailies fortie shillinges, to my brother William Hincksman and Walter Hincksman and Edward Hincksman and my sister ffounes twentye shillinges a peece in gould, also I give to my brother Thomas Hincksman five poundes and to my servant John Sponar at presberie five markes and to hie wife five nobles and to Thomas Prichard my servant fortie shillinges and to Thomas Ade my servant tenn shillinges,*

Alsoe I give to Mr. Thomas Vell and to Alderman Hill and Mr. Leonard Tarne my brother lawes and my brother too new rings for my sake, and to good Mr. Workman our faithfull watchman forty shillings.

Alsoe I give unto my welbeloved wife Joane Hoare ye some of three hundred and fiftie poundes and to my sonne John Hoare twoe hundred poundes and to my son Daniell Hoare one hundred and fiftie poundes and to my daughter Joane Hoare a hundred poundes and to my son Leonard Hoare one hundred poundes and my will is that my wife shall have the furniture of houshold that I have in all places at her disposing during her life and after to come indiferentlie amongst my children except the goodes at Thornebery which was delivered me by the sheriffe by vertue of an elegit, all which I give unto my daughter Margerie Mathewe presentie after my decease.

Alsoe I give unto my sonn Thomas Hoare twentie poundes.

Alsoe I give to the said Margery my daughter and her sonne Charles Mathewe twoe hundred poundes and my will is that soe longe as this twoe hundred poundes remanies in the stocke which I shall leave (which shalbe till my executors and overseers shall allowe thereof for her good to lett him have it.) there shalbe unto her and her sonne sixteene poundes a yeare quarterly paid and my will and desire is that the stocke I shall leave unto my wife and the foure first named children with the twoe hundred poundes given my daughter shalbe used and imployed uppon the three bargaines I have taken at Encombe, Presbery and Slimbridge and my wife and the foure children to have their maintenance out of it, and my will is that my sonne Leonard shalbe carefullie kept at Schoole and whem hee is fitt for itt to be carefullie placed at Oxford, and if ye Lord shall see fitt, to make him a Minister unto his people and that all ye charge thereof shalbe discharged out of the proffitt which it shall please god to send out of the stocke and that all the rest of my estate unbequeathed all debtes and expence being discharged shalbe equallie devided betweene my wife and my twoe sonnes Daniell and John, and Joane, and the profittes of the said stocke to accrewe unto them alsoe untill my executors and my overseers shall agree for their good to lett any of them have their porcons for their preferment.

Only this excepted that my sonne Leonard shall have accrue and dewe unto him out of this estate six poundes a yeare to be paid unto him by the foresaid hundred poundes when my executors and overseers shall allowe of it to be for his preferment and if anie of my children shall die before they come to make use of their porcons my will is that porcons soe falling out shalbe equallie devided amongst my five children nowe with me and my sonne Thomas aforesaid and if it shall soe happen that the stocke bequeathed be not founde fitt to be imployed as I have directed but I trust ye Lord will soe blesse that happie trade of life unto them that some of them will never give over but if soe should be then my will is that my executors pay in ye porcons unto them if they bee att age or els to paie it in or good securitie to my overseers and my will is that as I have agreed with Mr. Thoms Vell and promised there shall alwaies be really upon the groundes at Encombe which I have taken of him for Eight yeares eight hundred of the best ewes to stand for his securitie untill all rentes and dewes whatsoever shalbe really paid unto him, and now deare saviour spreade thy armes of mercie over me purge away my synnes though they are many and greate and my faith weake lett thy power be seene in my weaknes and thy strength in my manifould infirmities keepe me from that evill one and Receive me to thy mercy to whom with god the father and the holie spiritt be all glorie and power and thankes giveinge both nowe and for evermore Amen this 25th day of September 1638.

By me Cha: Hoare: ffurther I give unto my sonne John Hoare fortie poundes more which shall accrewe unto him when all the other are satisfied out of the estate. Admon granted 21 Dec. 1638—to Joane Hoare the relict

According to one source, sometime in 1640, Joanna Hoare journeyed to America with her five children. Joanna had been a widow for two years, having been married to Charles Hoare Jr., sheriff of Gloucester, England.

Charles Hoare Jr. died in 1638 in England. His will was written in England and was dated 25 September 1638. Joanna (Henchman) Hoare died in Braintree, Massachusetts, on 21 September 1651.

Charles Hoare and Joanna Hincksman had the following children:

1.	Thomas	baptized 15 June 1612
2.	Charles	born 1613
3.	Daniel	
4.	Leonard	married Bridget Lisle
5.	Margerie	
6.	John	born 1622 in Gloucester, England; died 2 April 1704, Massachusetts
7.	Joanne	born 1622/3; married Edmund Quincy
8.	Ruth	died 1625

1. **Thomas Hoare,** probably the oldest of the surviving children of Charles, did not accompany his brothers and sisters to New England. According

to the register of St. Mary de Crypt, he was baptized on 15 June 1612. Following is a translation of the apprenticeship agreement with his father dated 2 February 1625: "Thomas Hoare son of Charles Hoare of the city of Gloucester, Brewer, binds himself apprentice to said Charles, his father by indenture dating the day of the Feast of Purification of St. Mary the Virgin (Feb. 2,) in the year of the reign of King Charles now of England the first, for the term of twelve years etc. paying at the end of the term two suites of clothes" (King Charles I, 1625-1649). There was a Thomas Hoare in the records of the early settlers of Norfolk, Massachusetts, but he could not be linked to Charles Hoare.

3. **Daniel** traveled to Massachusetts with the rest of the family; however, records cannot be found as to him being a resident or real estate owner.[1] On 2 October 1650, he was licensed "to export to New England birding fowling peices [sic] and muskets upon giving security that they will not be used to the prejudice of the Commonwealth." One source says that Daniel died in London. Daniel's wife Mary, who was living in Hull, England, wrote a letter to her sister-in-law (Leonard Hoar's wife) asking her if they would "receive her son into their own family"; however, it was not clear as to whether or not Daniel was still alive.[1]

4. **Leonard Hoar** (1630-1675) (educator) was born in Gloucester, England. He married Bridget Lisle who died on 25 May 1723. She was the daughter of Lord John Lisle, president of the High Court of Justice and Lord Commissioner of the Great Seal, who was one of the judges at the trial of King Charles I and therefore one of the judges to sentence Charles to death in 1649.[2,3] On 11 August 1664, as Lord John Lisle was leaving a church service at Lausanne, he was shot to death by an Irish Royalist by the name of Thomas Mac Donnel. His wife was Alice Lisle, also referred to as Dame or Lady Alicia. She was the daughter of Sir White Beconshaw of Moyles Court at Ellingham in Hampshire, England, and Edith Bond. On 20 July 1685, Lady Alicia agreed to provide shelter to John Hicks, a well-known nonconformist minister. Traveling with Rev. John Hicks was Richard Nelthorpe, also a nonconformist. Lady Alicia allowed them to spend the night at her residence. The following morning, the sheriff knocked on the door and questioned Lady Alicia about Hicks and Nelthorpe. She denied that they spent the night at her residence. Somehow, the fugitives were caught and arrested. Lady Alicia was also arrested for denying that the men were at her residence. She was charged with harboring traitors. At her trial, she was found guilty and thus sentenced to be burned at the stake. Judge Jeffreys ordered that the sentence be carried out the same day as the trial, but a few days' delay was subsequently granted. King James II ruled that beheading was to be substituted for burning; and so on 2

September 1685, in Winchester marketplace, Lady Alicia was executed. She is buried in a tomb on the right-hand side of the porch at St. Mary's Church, Ellingham, Hampshire, England.[2]

Leonard matriculated at Oxford in England but never got the chance to attend because that was the year he traveled to America with his mother. Leonard, however, attended and graduated from Harvard in 1650. He returned to England and became a minister at Wanstead, Essex. In 1662, he was ejected for being a nonconformist. After he was released from the church, he continued his education and, in 1671, received the degree of MD from Cambridge University.[1] Leonard and his wife Bridget returned to Massachusetts on 8 July 1672, and he became the assistant pastor to Rev. Thomas Thatcher at the South church in Boston. Leonard, on 10 December 1672, was elected and became the first graduate of Harvard to become the president of that college. On 15 March 1675, Dr. Hoare resigned from his position as president and died in Braintree, Massachusetts, on 28 November 1675.

On 29 November 1676, Bridget Hoare married for a second time. Her husband was Hezekiah Usher who was quite eccentric in his ways and was considered unsuited for the lifestyle Bridget had become accustomed. She continued to live unhappily until 12 July 1687 when she returned to England with her only surviving child, Bridget Hore, and stayed there until the death of Hezekiah, which was in Lynn, Massachusetts, on 11 July 1697. In his will, he wrote the following:[1]

> *And to my dear wife, whom I may count very dear but her love to what I had but not a real love to me, which should accounting it more worth than any other outward Enjoyment; and for her covetousness & overreaching & cunning Impression that has almost ruinated [sic] me by a gental behaviour,[sic] having only words but as sharp swords to me, whose Cunning is like those to be as an Angel of Light to others but wanting Love and charity for me . . . And therefore I do cut her off from the benefit of all my Estate & do not bestow anything upon her but what the law doth allow . . . But as to her daughter Bridget if her mother had not been so undermining and overreaching for her I should have been willing to have done what I could for her. And do give her the Tumbler with the Arms of a Spread Eagle with two heads. (but I think one head for a body is enough.) And the Table Cloth of the best Damask, and the napkins thereto. And this will I make to be a Warning to those women that have no Love for their Husbands, but to what they have.*

Judge Samuel Sewall served as Madame Usher's attorney while she stayed in England. Regardless of the will, Bridget was awarded the house and grounds and, thus, moved back to Massachusetts, which became her residence. On 9 May 1700, Judge Sewall declared that "Madame Usher obtained judgment for her Dower in the Mansion House against the Town House yesterday. Brick Shops and ware house are of the same title and will follow the Dwelling-house." Bridget had the reputation and respect of friends and those that knew her. They praised her and commented on her lifestyle as being one of a charitable and blameless life. Rev. Thomas Foxcroft, pastor of the Old Church in Boston, preached a sermon upon "the character of Anna the prophetess considered and applied," which was printed with a preface by Benjamin Wadsworth, president of Harvard College in which he calls Madame Usher "a wonderful example of Christian Patience under great Pains and Bodily Afflictions." Bridget died on 25 May 1723, probably in Lynn, Massachusetts.

5. **Margery (a.k.a. Margaret) Hoare** was married to John Matthews at St. Nicholas Church in Gloucester on 25 December 1633 and had a son, Charles (1642-?), who is mentioned, in his grandfather Hoare's will. She was a widow, and probably childless, when she came to New England. Margery married (2) before 1642 in Braintree, Massachusetts, Rev. Henry Flynt (Flint) (ca 1615-1668) of Braintree.[6] According to some records, Flint was born at Matlock, Derbyshire, England. In politics, he was of the party of Sir Henry Vane; and his theological views led him to take, for a time at least, the unpopular side in the Antinomian controversy (see Henry Flint and Margery Hoar chapter).

6. **John Hoare** (?-1704); On 11 May 1633, John agreed to an apprenticeship with his father, Charles Hoare of the city of Gloucester, brewer, for a term of ten years. He was to receive at the end of his term, six shillings. His apprenticeship lasted only five years as his father died in September 1638. John was living in Scituate, Massachusetts, in 1643. He married Alice (last name unknown). Their first child was in 1650. Alice died in 1696.[5]

According to Samuel Deane, the historian of Scituate, John Hoare was always engaged in working for the town—drafting deeds, bonds, and whatever documents might be needed—and, at times, was referred to as "lawyer." John moved to Concordin 1659, having sold his land that adjoined Mosquasheut pond, to the lawyer, John Saffin. His ability, vigor, and originality of thought and action soon made him one of the prominent figures in Concord and vicinity; but he was found often at odds with the ecclesiastical oligarchy of the times. Whether like his sometime neighbor at Lancaster, John Prescott sympathized with the Presbyterian criticisms of the theocratic restriction of political and religious privileges in the colony, is not known; but he strongly resembled Prescott in his persistency, enterprise, and altruistic spirit. He was not only independent in speech but rashly sharp of tongue and pen and suffered accordingly at the hands of jealous authority. The story of his disbarment is best told by the original documents:[1]

Jonathan Prescott, born ca. 1645 and son of John Prescott, married (2) 23 December 1675 in Concord, Massachusetts, Elizabeth Hoar who was born ca. 1650 and was the daughter of John Hoare. Elizabeth died in 1687.[5]

7.   **Joanna Hoare (Hoar)** was the daughter of Charles Hoare Jr., granddaughter of Charles Hoare Sr., sister of Leonard Hoare, third president of Harvard College, and Margery Hoare. According to the book *New England Marriages Prior to 1700,* Joanna married on 26 July 1648 Edmund Quincy (1627/8-1698).

Edmund and Joanna (Hoare) Quincy had the following children:

Mary Quincy (1650-1676)	married Ephraim Savage (1645-1731) before 1671[5]
Daniel Quincy (1651-1690)	married (1682)[5] Anna Shepard (and their daughter Elizabeth Quincy married Rev. William Smith, whose daughter Abigail Smith married John Adams, our second American president and whose son, John Quincy Adams, became the sixth president of the United States)
John Quincy	died young
Joanna Quincy (1654-1695)	married (June 1680) David Hobart (1651-1717) (They were married in Hingham, Massachusetts.)[5]
Judith Quincy (1655-1679/80)	married (1673) Rev. John Rayner Jr. (?-1675/6)[5]
Elizabeth Quincy (?-1691)	married October 1682 Rev. Daniel Gookin (?-1718)[5]
Edmund Quincy	died as an infant
Ruth Quincy (1658-1748)	married 19 October 1686 John Hunt (1654-1724)[5]
Experience Quincy	married 24 November 1698 William Savil (?-1700)[5]

The following is found in the Records of the Massachusetts Bay Colony, 1628-1686:vol. IV, part II, p. 291, 1665

In answer to the peticon or remonstrance of John Hoare, the Court finding that severall of the magistrates, and some others, are impeached for not doing justice and other complaints of a very high nature, doe therefore order that a hearing be granted to the peticoner, and that due notice be given to the complaynant to appeare to make good his severall charges, or otherwise to give reason for the same. Notice was given accordingly to the sayd Hoare, and the sayd John Hoare appearing in Court, his peticon or remonstrance being read with such evidences as he produced, the Court proceeded as followeth:—Whereas John Hoare, of Concord, hath presented to this Court a petition or remonstrance, wherein he complains of great wrongs and injuryes he hath susteyned as his brother's agent, by reason he could not obteyne justice in some of our Courts of judicature in severall actions depending betweene himself, as agent and Lieut Richard Cooke, of Boston, the Court having affoorded him large liberty and oppertunity to make good his charges, and having heard all his allegations together wth such witnesses as were produced to proove the same and duely weighed the case, doe judge his complaints to be groundless and unjust, and his offences to be of a very high nature, tending not only to the dishonour of God, but to the scandall and reproach of severall of our Courts, honer'd magestrates, and officers of Court. That due witnes may be borne against such sinfull practises, and goverment of this jurisdiccon under his majestyes royall charter, may be upheld and mayntayned, this Court doeth order, that the sayd Hoare shall find suertyes bound in one hundred pounds for his good behavior during the Court's pleasure, and that henceforth he shall be disabled to plead any cases but his owne in this jurisdiction, and also that he pay as a fine the sume of fifty pounds for such his miscarriages, and be imprisoned till it be payd, or security given for the same. Whereas John Hoare, contrary to express order of the Court, hath withdrawn himself from the Court before his sentence was declared, the secretary is appointed by the Court to send for him, and require the performance of the sentence of this Court to all intents and purposes therein conteyned.

(Massachusetts Records, vol. IV, part II, p. 301, 1666)

In answer to the peticon of John Hoare, humbly desiring the favour of this Court to release him of his bonds of good behaviour and to make such abatement of his fine as their wisdomes shall judge meete. The Court judgeth it meete, and orders, the peticoner be released his bonds of good behaviour, and that twenty pounds of his fine be abated him.

(Massachusetts Records vol. IV, part II, p. 387, 1668)

In ans'r to the petition of Alice, the wife of John Hoare, of Concord,
the Court judgeth it meete, on the petitioner's satisfying and paying in to
the Treasurer to his content the sume of tenn pounds to abate the remainder
of her husband's fine yet remaining and unpaid.

In 1668, John Hoare was charged before the county court of saying at the public house of Ensign William Buss "that the Blessing Master Bulkeley pronounced in dismissing the pubilque Assembly in the meeting-house was no better than vane babbling." Upon conviction of what the law of 1646 calls "the disparagement of the Lord's holy ordinance and making God's ways contemptible and ridiculous," he was fined ten pounds. He was also called upon to answer to the Court on two occasions "for neglecting the public worship of God on the Lord's day" (County Court Files, 1668-1675).

Notes

1.   Henry Stedman Nourse, *The Hoar Family in America and its English Ancestry*, A Compilation From Collections Made by The Hon. George Frisbie Hoar; Boston, David Clapp & Son, Printers 1899.

2.   Wikipedia, the free Encyclopedia.

3.   Plantagenet Somerset Fry, *The Kings and Queens of England & Scotland*, Grove Press, New York pg 134.

4.   The will of Charles Hoare, Jr.

5.   Clarence Almon Torrey, *New England Marriages Prior to 1700*, Prepared for publication by Elizabeth P. Bentley, Genealogical Publishing Co. Baltimore 1985.

6.   Melinde Lutz Sanborn *Third Supplement to Torrey's New England Marriages*

FOURTEEN

William Goodwin

(See Appendix N)

The English ship, the *Lyon*, under the command of William Peirce—with close to 350 passengers of which 150 were named—50 being children, set sail from London, England, for America. The voyage started on 22 June 1632 with the first four weeks sitting at the docks, waiting for the right time (weather) to depart. Everyone had to be on board and ready to go at a moment's notice. This was not a cruise of luxury but rather a journey that would take the passengers to a New World and a new way of life. The passengers had to give up their homes and most of their belongings. The ship was not a big ship, in fact, it was about the size of the *Mayflower*; and if you have ever been on board the *Mayflower* replica, you might wonder how 350 got on board. The number of 350 passengers comes from a passenger list with comments by John Corley's 1984 version. Depending on which version you use, and there a couple, the number changes. It is as low as 123 and as high as 350. A lot of the names on the 123 list are omitted. That list only contains the names of the head of house, omitting names of the spouses and children. The smaller lists also may not include names of servants; rather the list might show "two servants" or whatever number of servants took the voyage. The voyage ended in Boston on 16 September 1632.[1]

Rev. Thomas Hooker graduated from Emanuel College in Cambridge in England. He started preaching in England, continuing in Holland, and then returning back to England—running into the same problems that faced Rev. Robert Peck (see Peck chapter). And like Peck, Rev. Thomas Hooker, Rev. Samuel Stone, and some of their parishioners fled England. They arrived in

Boston sometime in 1633 and immediately traveled to Newe Towne (also spelled Newtowne) (Cambridge) where the congregation was eagerly awaiting their arrival. Hooker was chosen their pastor and Stone their teacher of the Church. Soon after, a house of worship was erected, but Hooker and Stone's stay did not last long. Because of certain conflicts between Hooker's company and the arrival of another group of people known as the Griffin's company, certain uneasiness arose—causing the entire membership of the church to move to a new area, now known as Hartford, Connecticut. Cambridge is located just outside of Boston, so the trip to Hartford was not an easy one, especially for families that were not used to trudging through the forest and creating their own paths and roadways. This group of people, for the most part, was of a refine and delicate lifestyle.

In 1630, the people of the Massachusetts Bay Colony selected a site on the north side of the Charles River for their new home that at first was named Newe Towne—later (1638) named Cambridge.[5] In 1636, Cambridge became the home of Harvard College, one of the oldest colleges in America.

In 1636 (some historians say 1635), Rev. Thomas Hooker and one hundred of his group, with one hundred or so cattle, left Cambridge and headed toward what is now known as Hartford, Connecticut. Some say they started by heading toward Springfield, Massachusetts, then south to Hartford. There would have to be an advanced party—a group of men that would choose the right path to follow and prepare the woods to allow passage of such a large group. The advanced party had to cut down trees and move them out of the way or go around them. They had to clear enough of a path to allow for the wagons and animals that they took with them.

Remember, this was still the wilderness, with hostile (and some friendly) Native Americans and wild animals. There were hills to climb, rivers and streams to cross. The woods they had to travel through were not marked, and the only thing they had to use was probably just a compass and, of course, the stars.

I am sure that it just wasn't man, woman, and child. They surely had most, if not all, of their belongings. Of course, their travel required wagons that had to be pulled by horse or oxen. History indicates the direction that they may have traveled was from Newe Towne to Springfield, which is almost due north of their destination, Hartford, Connecticut. They would have had to cross the mighty Connecticut River; so barges, rafts, and boats had to be built.

The area around what was to be later known as Hartford already had one settlement established by the Dutch. Upon arriving, the first order of business was to purchase the land that was to become their home, from the Indians. The first structure to be built would have been their meetinghouse, and according to history, it was erected in 1638.

In 1622, William was a sidesman [sic] of his church in Braintree, Essex, England. He was churchwarden in 1630 and 1631.

On 25 June 1632 and, again, on 16 July 1632 and on 4 August 1632, William and several other members of the church of Braintree were charged in the Commissary Courts of Essex and Herts [sic] County for "not receiving the Holy Communion at Easter nor since in his parish church."[7] William Goodwin of Braintree, Essex, England (some records indicate Bocking, Essex, England), his wife Elizabeth (White), and their only child, Elizabeth—along with William's brother Ozias and his wife Mary and their son William and fellow parishioners of their church—were on their way to a New World as passengers on the *Lyon*. William and Ozias were instrumental in the organization the voyage.

At first a member of a Massachusetts Bay church, probably in Watertown, before 6 November 1632, he soon transferred his membership to the Cambridge church and served as elder of the church. Mr. Winthrop reported to the General Court held on 3 September 1634, "Mr. Goodwin, a very reverend and godly man, being the elder of the congregation of Newtown, having, in heat of argument, used some unreverend [sic] speech to one of the assistants, and being reproved for the same in open court, did gravely and humbly acknowledge his fault, etc."

William Goodwin, shortly after his arrival to America, was made a freeman on 6 November 1632. He became a member of the First General Court of Delegates of the colony on 14 May 1635. [7]

Ozias settled in Newtowne [sic], later known as Cambridge (Massachusetts) and finally Hartford, Connecticut. William also took the same path of residency.[1] Both William and Ozias were among the group of followers that left Newtowne, Massachusetts, with Rev. Thomas Hooker.

Ozias Goodwin, according to a deposition given by him in 1674, stated that his age was seventy-eight years, thereby making his date of birth in the year 1596.[3] Ozias married Mary (Woodward) in England, prior to 1629.[2] Upon reaching Boston in 1632, Ozias, Mary, and their oldest child, William, settled in Newtowne [sic], now known as Cambridge, Massachusetts. It appears that the Ozias Goodwin family left with Rev. Thomas Hooker and company in 1635 or 1636.

In 1630, the settlement of Massachusetts and, for a period of three years thereafter, the affairs of the settlement was managed by the people under the administration of the Court of Assistants by means of meetings. Because the colony was experiencing a rapid growth, the governing body soon changed from the Court of Assistants to the General Court of Delegates. Membership required that there be two delegates from each town and that they would attend an annual meeting chaired by the governor and the Court of Assistants.

William Goodwin was known as Elder Goodwin and was a member of the First Church of Christ in Hartford, under the leadership of Rev. Thomas Hooker. Following Hooker's death on 7 July 1647, Stone then became the minister of the church, and that was when the difference of opinion between Rev. Samuel

Stone and Mr. Goodwin, the ruling elder, became evident. This controversy lasted several years and became such a problem that in 1659, under the leadership of Elder Goodwin and Governor John Webster, "the Withdrawers" withdrew from the church and moved to Hadley, Massachusetts, where Elder Goodwin continued his role as ruling elder of the church in Hadley (see more about the controversy in the Whiting chapter).

William Goodwin (1591-11 March 1673) married on 7 November 1616 in Shalford, Essex, England,[2] Elizabeth White (1591-1669/70) who was the daughter of Robert White of Messing, Essex, England.[7] Elizabeth died before January 1669. William married (2) Susannah (Garbrand) Hooker (1616-1676), widow of Rev. Thomas Hooker.

William and Elizabeth (White) Goodwin's only child, Elizabeth (?-1686), married John Crow (1606-1686). Elizabeth (daughter) was John's second wife (see Crow chapter).

Notes

1.   John Corley, Passenger List of the LYON that sailed in 1632,

2.   Clarence Almon Torrey, Prepared for Publication by Elizabeth P. Bentley, *New England Marriages Prior to 1700*, Genealical Publishing Co. Baltimore 1985.

3.   Nathaniel Goodwin, *Genealogical Notes or Contributions to the Family History of some of the First Settlers of Connecticut and Massachusetts*, 1st published 1856 Hartford; reprinted 1995 Genealogical Publishing Company, Baltimore

4.   Society of the Descendants of the Founders of Hartford (Printed information).

5.   Cambridge Historical Commission.

6.   Edwin Pond Parker, *History of The Second Church of Christ in Hartford*, Hartford, Connecticut, Belknap & Warfield Hartford 1892.

7.   Robert Charles Anderson, *The Great Migration, Immigrants to New England 1634-1635*, Volume III, G-H, Great Migration Study Project, New England Historic Genealogical Society, Boston 2003.

FIFTEEN

Major John Mason

(See Appendix O)

—————◆◆◆—————

Many researchers have attempted to discover the actual date of birth, place of birth, and the parents of John Mason, but to no avail. He was probably born in England around the year 1600. The date is based on his date and age at which he died.

The first sign of Mason was when he served as a lieutenant in the French army under the command of Sir Thomas Fairfax and while fighting in the Netherlands, on behalf of the Dutch patriots, who at that time were fighting against Spain. However, Thomas Fairfax was not much older than John Mason, so it is more probable that the two of them fought beside each other.[9] In 1645, Sir Thomas Fairfax wrote to Mason, requesting that he return to England and accept a commission as a major general in the Parliamentary army under the command of Lord Fairfax.

He supposedly sailed from Plymouth, England, on 20 March 1630 and landed in Nantasket, Massachusetts, on May 30.[1] A few sources claim that John Mason was on the ship *Mary & John*, but according to all the records that I could find, the original passenger list was never found and, therefore, his coming to America in 1630 is only speculative. Passenger lists were not mandatory until around 1635.

Lieutenant John Mason cannot actually be found in America until 1632. The magistrates, having a problem with pirates, commissioned Captain John Gallup, a well-versed skipper, who had sailed up and down the Maine coast many times along with twenty volunteers. This crew was to be under the command of John Mason and now became the first American naval task force.[4] The purpose of this union was to cruise the seas in search of Dixy [*sic*] Bull. Dixy Bull was an English sea captain who later became a pirate and earned the reputation of preying on other ships off the New England coast. Dixy had a crew of twenty to twenty-five men and not only attacked other ships but also attacked the settlement of Pemaquid, a coastal settlement in Maine. This act earned Dixy the title of the Dreaded Pirate.[3] A couple of attempts were made to find Dixy, but to no avail. In December, the expeditions ran in headwinds, blizzard, ice, and what turned out to be quite a severe storm, so much so the search had to be discontinued until early spring. They never did catch Dixy, but they must have frightened him so much so that he took up harassing those in Virginia. He was captured in Virginia and sent back to England where he stood trial and met his just fate, the gallows.[4]

It was not long after the Dixy Bull tour that Mason was promoted to the rank of captain. In 1634, the charter of the Massachusetts Bay Colony was revoked. King Charles I appointed a governor-general to rule and enforce the established church (Church of England) on the colonist. This news did not settle well with the settlers; therefore, a debate took place among the clergy, magistrates, and citizens as to how they should act in the event of an emergency. They began to prepare for an attack, should one occur. Captain Mason was appointed by the General Court to inspect the land on the Boston peninsular and was to find a suitable location for fortification for the protection of Charlestown and Dorchester.[5] Work on the fort did not advance fast enough to suit the magistrates; so in September 1635, almost one year since the beginning of this project, Captain Mason was authorized to increase the labor force and manner of work in order to complete the fort at Castle Island as quickly as possible. John Mason's reputation was becoming well-known, first for his part in the search for Dixy Bull and again in his appointment as engineer and superintendent in the selection of the site and overseeing the construction of the fort.

John Mason was one of the three renowned professional soldiers who came to America with the earliest of settlers. The other two were Miles Standish (*Mayflower*, 1620) and Lion Gardiner. Mr. Gardiner was hired by John Winthrop Jr. to oversee the construction of the fort at Saybrook, Connecticut.

After the Dutch settlers of Manhattan Island heard of the fertile soil along the Connecticut River, they laid claim to the land, but the Puritans had also learned of this rich land, and they too laid claim. (The Connecticut River is the largest river in New England. It flows from the Connecticut Lakes in Northern New Hampshire, along the border between New Hampshire and Vermont, through Western Massachusetts and down past Hartford and into Long Island Sound, at Saybrook.)

In October 1633, a small vessel sailed from Plymouth, with plans to build a trading house on the banks of the Connecticut River. As they sailed up the river toward what is now the city of Hartford, they discovered that the Dutch had already settled there and actually had erected a fort. The Dutch gave warning and threatened to fire upon them if they continued up the river. The English ignored the threats and continued to a spot near what is now known as Windsor, Connecticut. There, the English constructed a trading house. In July 1635, another settlement was constructed. This time it was at Wethersfield, just south of Hartford. Windsor was still just a trading post, so Wethersfield became the first English settlement in Connecticut, which was five years after the Massachusetts Bay Colony had begun and fifteen years after the founding of the Plymouth Colony.

The next settlement in Connecticut was at the Plymouth trading house location. The following year, Rev. Thomas Hooker and his company departed from Cambridge, Massachusetts, and founded the town of Hartford. The English were now in settlements of Windsor, Wethersfield, and Hartford and, due to their close proximity to each other, chose magistrates to regulate their common interests. At about the same time, John Winthrop Jr. was hired by Lords Saye, Brooke, and Sele to establish a colony at the mouth of the Connecticut River. Junior, as he was often called, employed Lion Gardiner to oversee the construction of the fort. The colony was named Saybrook of which John Winthrop Jr. became its first governor.

The Pequot Indians, at one time, lived together with the Mohegan tribe along the Hudson River in lower New York. However, sometime around the year 1590, the Pequot tribe decided to separate and head north to what was to become their new territory in Connecticut. While doing so, they began to raid other tribes along the way. These skirmishes added to clashes with the English settlers, which began, what has gone down in history as the Pequot War. One such clash occurred when the Pequot Indians raided the settlement of Wethersfield. Several settlers were killed, and two young girls were carried off. On 1 May 1637, the General Court in Hartford declared war on the Pequot nation. Captain John Mason was appointed commander of the Connecticut forces. Captain Mason was living in the settlement of Windsor at that time and was instrumental in plotting the expedition, preparing the plans for war, and following through with the entire event, which wrote the history of the war with the Pequot Indians. At the time of the war, there were only 250 settlers in Connecticut, mostly in the settlements of Wethersfield, Hartford, and Windsor. Of those 250 settlers, John Mason recruited forty-two men from Hartford, thirty from Windsor and eighteen from Wethersfield. Along with these ninety men were an additional six hundred warriors from the Mohegan and Narragansett tribes. They marched into the heart of hostile territory, charged the Pequot's fortress, and completely destroyed the fort, killing about half of the entire Pequot nation. This expedition took three weeks and two days to accomplish. During one of the skirmishes,

John Mason's life was saved by Sergeant William Hayden of Windsor. Just as a Pequot warrior taking aim at Mason and was about to shoot an arrow, Sergeant Hayden reached out with his knife and cut the string of the warrior's bow.

In 1620, the settlement in Plymouth, Massachusetts, was established. The Indians provided most of the work, with Squanto and Massasoit being the leaders—Squanto on account of his ability to speak English and Massasoit as he was the chief of the Wampanoag tribe. Massasoit had a son named Metacom (Metacomet or Pometacom) and soon became known by the English as King Philip.

As more and more English came to America and settlements were sprouting up into territories that once belong to the Indians, tension also built. The main tribes at that time were the *Wampanoag, Nipmuck, Narragansett, Mohegan*, and *Pequot*. There were other tribes but not quite as large. They were all treated individually; however, most were enemies of the English. By 1675, there were many small towns between Boston and the Connecticut River, so many in fact that the Indians were running out of goods to trade to the colonist. The Indians were losing their territory and felt that they had to fight for what was once theirs. When Metacom became chief, he and other chiefs joined together and became less friendly to the Englishmen.

John Sassamon was an early graduate of Harvard and an Indian converted Christian and translator and advisor to Metacom. Sassamon passed on to the officials of Plymouth Colony a report stating that Metacom was planning attacks on smaller settlements. Before the colonial officials could investigate this report, John Sassamon was murdered, allegedly by a few of Metacom's Wampanoag warriors. After a further investigation, three of the warriors were arrested, tried, and hanged for the murder of John Sassamon. The Wampanoags felt that both the trial and court's sentence were an insult to Indian sovereignty; and in response, on 20 June 1675 (twelve days after the hangings), a small band of Pokanoket Indians attacked a small settlement, setting the town on fire and killing several settlers. One thing led to another and thus the beginning of King Philip's War.

There were two very decisive battles in which the Pequot nation was destroyed, one being (1637) at the Pequot Fort in Mystic, Connecticut, and the other (1675) at the Great Swamp Fight in Fairfield, Connecticut, which was an important battle that took place during the King Philip's War. The colonial militia, a combined force of one thousand or more men, including about 150 Pequot and Mohegan Indians, attacked the Narragansett tribe while living near Narragansett Bay, which runs along the borders of Rhode Island, Massachusetts, and Connecticut. The Narragansetts were not at war at that time and, in fact, were allies of the English. They were, however, found to have been harboring warriors of King Philip. King Philip was at war with the

English, so the Narragansetts became the enemy and, according to history, had to be destroyed.[3]

The settlements in the colonies had to be protected from hostile Indians, so a trainband was formed. The trainband was simply a group of settlers, or band of men, within the settlement to be militarily trained to ward off hostile attacks, thus the name "trainband."

The trainband was not a new concept as it dates back to the sixteenth century, during the period Elizabeth was Queen of England (1558-1603). In 1636, the General Court ordered that each able-bodied man between the age of sixteen and sixty serve in a unit that required military training once a month. This was known as the trainband or, as later referred to, as the militia. The exceptions were church officers, whether past or present, and commissioners. It was also stipulated that any man, who missed a training session, would be fined five shillings. The training was not just for fighting but included other duties such as guarding the town twenty-four hours a day and standing guard during church services.[2]

In 1637, Mason was appointed by the General Court, the chief military officer of the colony and whose duty it was to train the military men of the several settlements. For the entire period from 1637 to 1672, he was the only major in the entire colony of Connecticut.[4]

Also, in 1637, while living in Windsor, John Mason's wife, whose name is unknown and who was referred to as the captain's wife, passed away, leaving Mason with a young daughter named Isabel.[6] According to the book *Major John Mason of Connecticut* (1600-1672), Captain Mason had talked a lot with his wife about going to the Connecticut Valley; and at that time, Isabel was only a year old.

Part of the duties, as commander in chief of the military forces of Connecticut, was to visit several of the settlements from time to time. One such trip was to Hingham, Massachusetts, where he met Anne Peck, the daughter of Rev. Robert Peck and Anne Lawrence of Hingham, England (see the Peck chapter). In the book *The Life and Times of Major John Mason*, it is suggested that their meeting was love at first sight. Of course, we will never be certain if that was the case, but it was not long after they met that John and Anne were engaged.

To marry without the consent of Ann's parents would have been a breach of a law; and that would mean a possible fine, imprisonment, or punishment by a whipping in the town square in front of the townspeople. Their marriage took place in Hingham in July 1639 and was probably performed by one of the magistrates of the town as ministers of the gospel were forbidden by law to act in that capacity. The Peck family was a very noble and highly respected family. With Rev. Robert Peck being the teacher of the church at Hingham and

Major John Mason being the commander of the military forces and having the reputation of a great warrior, it must have been quite a wedding.

There were customs then that we have revised a bit but nevertheless used today, and there were customs that were used then that we have ignored today. Once the bride's garters were removed, there would be a scramble, and the lucky person finding them would be assured a good and happy future. "Sack possett" [*sic*] was often consumed in the bridal chambers, afterward a psalm was read and a prayer offered.[6] In some cases, the groom was dressed in a nightgown and led by the bridesmaids and groomsmen to the bride's bed, and then the wedding couple was put to bed. Then, as a common practice, the guests entered the bridal chamber, and they all drank to their health.

A few days after the wedding, Major Mason and his wife Anne left for their home in Windsor, Connecticut. Today, if we were to travel by automobile, the distance would be about one hundred and twenty-two miles, but that would be by automobile and on a paved road. Let's go back to 1639 where we would have to travel by horseback or wagon, but probably horseback. We would not have paved roads, only paths made mostly by Indians. There were very few, if any, settlements between Hingham, Massachusetts, and Windsor, Connecticut. Horses can travel about twenty miles a day, so the trip might take us a week to reach our final destination, that is, if we did not run into hostile Indians. We would have had to stop, make camp, and eat before darkness as there were no motels or streetlights. John and Anne probably had an escort of military men, so even twenty miles a day might be stretching it a bit.

After the completion of the fort at Saybrook, Major Mason was requested by the settlers to come to Saybrook and take command of the fort and watch over the new colony. Being the military man that he was, Major Mason, with his wife Anne and their three children, relocated to Saybrook where they made their home for the next twelve years.[10]

During his residence at Saybrook, the colony of New Haven was born. But the settlers at this new settlement were not entirely happy with their location, so a committee was developed with the task of investigating a piece of land on the Delaware River. In 1651, they approached Major Mason with the idea of him relocating with them and taking over the management of their town—just that fact alone shows the high respect and admiration for Major Mason. The offer by the settlers was so enticing that Mason was about to accept, but the legislature of Connecticut had different ideas. They strongly suggested that he not accept the generous offer, but rather stay put at his post as the safety of Connecticut was at stake. This strong request was accepted by Major Mason, and therefore, the offer made by the New Haven group was declined.[10]

Major Mason held several public offices. He was Indian agent, Indian umpire, and the counselor of the government for all Indian matters. He was captain of the fort, justice of the peace, and had the authority and power to hold courts as a judge. He was a member of the Connecticut legislature and the Board of Commissions of the United Colonies. Mason held the position of major general of the militia and acting commander of all expeditions abroad. In 1660, Major Mason was appointed deputy governor and was reelected each year for eight years, three of which were under the king's charter, which united Connecticut with New Haven.

Norwich was founded in 1659 by settlers from Old Saybrook, led by Major John Mason and Rev. James Fitch. They purchased the land that would become Norwich from the local Native American Mohegan tribe. There were sixty-nine founding families, and they soon divided up the land which was used for farming and businesses. In 1660, Major John Mason became deputy governor of Connecticut and major general of its fighting forces and held this position until 1669.

The book *Story of New London, Connecticut with Biographical Sketches of Many of Its Pioneers and Prominent Men* breaks down the life of Major Mason as follows:

> Beginning at Dorchester; for the first five and one-half years, lieutenant and captain
>
> The conqueror of the Pequots; magistrate and major at Windsor, twelve years
>
> Captain of the fort and commissioner of the united colonies at Saybrook, twelve years
>
> Deputy Governor and assistant at Norwich, twelve years

There are a couple of sources that say Anne (Peck) Mason died just prior to John's death, and other reports say she died shortly after his death. Anne's son-in-law, Rev. James Fitch, in giving a memorial sermon, had this to say, "Gifted with a measure of knowledge above what is usual in her sex. I need not tell you what a Dorcas you have lost; men women and children are ready with weeping to acknowledge what works of mercy she hath done for them."[10] Major John Mason died on January 30, 1671/72 at Norwich, Connecticut.

John and Anne (Peck) Mason had the following children:[5]

1.	Priscilla Mason	born October 1641, Windsor, Connecticut
2.	Samuel Mason	born July 1644, Windsor, Connecticut
3.	John (2) Mason	born August 1646, Windsor, Connecticut
4.	Rachael Mason	born October 1648, Saybrook, Connecticut
5.	Anne Mason	born June 1650, Saybrook, Connecticut
6.	Daniel Mason	born August 1652, Saybrook, Connecticut

7.   Elizabeth Mason   born August 1654, Saybrook,
                                          Connecticut

1. **Priscilla Mason** married in October 1664 Rev. James Fitch. This was the
    second marriage for Fitch. His first marriage was to Abigail Whitfield
    who was born 1 September 1622, Ockley, Surrey, England. She was the
    daughter of Rev. Henry and Dorothy (Sheaffe) Whitfield of Guilford, New
    Haven County, Connecticut. Abigail died 9 September 1659, Saybrook,
    Connecticut (see Fitch chapter).[7]
2. **Samuel Mason** married 20 January 1670, Hingham, Massachusetts, Judith
    Smith. [11] Judith was born in 1650. They settled in Stonington where
    Samuel held the rank of major of the militia as well as the assistant of the
    colony. Judith died in Stonington. The date of Judith's death is unknown,
    but it had to be before 1694 when Samuel married a second time.

Samuel and Judith's children were the following:

8.   John Mason   born 19 August 1676; died 20 March
                                          1705; unmarried
9.   Anne Mason   married her first cousin, Captain John
                                          Mason (son of Captain John Mason and
                                          Abigail Fitch)
10.   Sarah Mason   born about 1687; died in February
                                          1720, Lebanon, Connecticut; married
                                          her first cousin, Joseph Fitch, who was
                                          born November 1681 (After the death of
                                          Sarah, Joseph married Anne Whiting.)

On 4 July 1694, Samuel married Elizabeth Peck of Rehoboth.[11] Elizabeth
was born 26 November 1657 and was the daughter of Joseph Peck Jr. and Joseph's
second wife Deliverance (last name unknown) [8,11] Joseph Peck Jr. came to America
in 1638 at the age of fifteen. He was born in England and baptized 23 August
1623.[8] Joseph Peck's will was written 5 July 1697; but in his will, there is no mention
of a wife, which would lead one to believe that his wife died before his will was
written (see Peck chapter). In Joseph's will, Elizabeth is mentioned as the third
daughter and the wife of Captain Mason.[8] Samuel reached the same military rank
as his father, John Mason, and was also known as Major Mason. He was one of the
four purchasers of Lebanon, Connecticut but, rather than relocating there, stayed
in Stonington until his death 30 March 1705, leaving four daughters: Anne and
Sarah by his first wife and Elizabeth and Hannah by his second marriage. His son,
John, died ten days before him at the age of twenty-eight and was unmarried.

These were the children of Major Samuel Mason and Elizabeth Peck:

11.	Samuel Mason	born 26 August 1695, Stonington; died 28 November 1701
12.	Elizabeth Mason	born 6 May 1697, Stonington; married Rev. William Worthington
13.	Hannah Mason	born 14 April 1699, Stonington; died November 1724; unmarried

3. **John Mason (2)** married Abigail Fitch, daughter of Rev. James and Abigail (Whitfield) Fitch (see Fitch chapter). John Mason, now Captain Mason, and his wife Abigail settled at Norwich where he spent the rest of his very short life.[5] John Mason, the second son of Major John Mason, followed in his father's footsteps. He fought in the Great Swamp Fight at Narragansett and, on 19 December 1675, was wounded and brought home by his fellow Mohegan warriors where several months later he died as a result of the wounds never healing. He was in his thirties at the time of his death, but in those short thirty years, he was highly respected both in civil and military arenas. He had represented the town at three sessions of the legislature and was chosen an assistant the year of his death. In the probating of his estate, before the County Court, he was referred to as "the worshipful John Mason." Bradstreet of New London said this of him, "My hon'd and dear friend Capt. Jno. Mason one of ye magistrates of the Colony, and second son of Major Jon. Mason dyed." His date of death was 18 September 1676.[1] John left two young children, John (Junior) and Anne, both born in Norwich, Connecticut. John (Junior), the son of the second John (3), was born in 1673 and was later referred to as Captain John Mason, making him the third in lineal succession that carried the name as John Mason. John (3a) was best known as an Indian claimant, visiting England to assert the rights of Major Mason to those lands, which the latter purchased as agent of the colony.

Their children were the following:

14.	John (3) Mason	whose first wife was Anne Mason, his first cousin and daughter of Major Samuel Mason and Elizabeth Peck (Following the death of Anne, John married the widow, Anne—Sanford—Noyes.)
15.	Anne Mason	married John Denison

4. **Rachael Mason** married 12 June 1678, New London and became the second wife of Charles Hill of New London. Charles was the son of George Hill of Derbyshire, England. Rachael died on 4 April 1679, less than one year after her marriage, while giving birth to twins, who also died with her. Charles Hill died 1684.[11]

5. **Anne Mason** married 8 November 1672, Captain John Brown of Swansey, Massachusetts. John Brown was born in September 1650 and died in March 1709.[11] He was the grandson of Mr. John Brown of Rehoboth who was born in England and was one of the assistants of the Plymouth Colony. Mr. John Brown, the grandfather, died 10 April 1662, Rehoboth.

6. **Daniel Mason** was an early schoolmaster in Norwich, Connecticut. He married (1) before 8 February 1673/4, Margaret Denison of Roxbury, born 15 December 1650 [11, 12] Margaret was the daughter of Edward Denison and Elizabeth Weld. Daniel sent his wife Margaret and son Daniel to Roxbury for safety reasons as it was during the time of the King Philip's War (1675-1676). Margaret died in 1679.[11]

Daniel and Margaret had two children:

| 16. | Daniel Mason | born 26 November 1674, Stonington |
| 17. | Hezekiah Mason | born 3 May 1677, Stonington |

Daniel Mason married (2) 10 October 1679 Rebecca Hobart, daughter of Rev. Peter Hobart of Hingham, Massachusetts. Rebecca died 8 April 1727, Stonington. Lieutenant Daniel Mason died at Stonington, Connecticut, 28 January 1736/7 at the age of eighty-five.

Daniel Mason and Rebecca Hobart had the following children:

18.	Peter Mason	born 9 November 1680, Stonington; married Mary Hobart
19.	Rebecca Mason	born 10 February 1682, Stonington; married February 1707 Elisha Cheeseboro
20.	Margaret	born 21 December 1683, Stonington
21.	Samuel	born 11 February 1686, Stonington; married Elizabeth Fitch and then Rebecca Lippincot
22.	Abigail	born 3 February 1689, Stonington
23.	Priscilla	born 17 September 1691, Stonington
24.	Nehemiah	born 24 November 1693, Stonington; married Zerviah Stanton

Daniel's oldest son, also Daniel (16), married Dorothy Hobart and settled in Lebanon where he died 4 July 1706, thirty years before his father's death. He left one son, Jeremiah, named after his grandfather, Rev. Jeremiah Hobart.[10]

7.   **Elizabeth Mason** married in January 1670 in Norwich, Connecticut, Major James Fitch. Fitch was born in 1649 and died in 1727. He was the son of Rev. James and Abigail Fitch (see Fitch chapter).

In 1889, the State of Connecticut erected a monument on Pequot Hill, which is located near the Indian fort that was destroyed. This monument was to commemorate the victory over the Pequot Indians. The inscription reads, "The Heroic Achievement of Major John Mason and his comrades."[9] Sometime around 1993, possibly a year or so earlier, the town council, after pressure from the Pequots, agreed to move the statue from Pequot Hill as it was near the graves of those that were killed in the Pequot War and, therefore, an insult to the Pequots. After a couple of years of meetings and suggestions trying to determine a suitable location, Marcus Mason Maronn, a tenth-generation descendant of Major John Mason, formed a group of other Mason descents and filed a report claiming possession of the statue. The new group was called the Mason Family Memorial Association. Many local citizens weighed in on the relocating of the statue; and finally in May 1995, it was agreed that after many emotional debates over how Connecticut's most important colonial history should be remembered, the new location would be Major John Mason's hometown of Windsor. The forty-five-ton monument, today, proudly stands at the Palisado Green within three hundred feet of John's original home site in Windsor, Connecticut.

Notes

1.   Francis Manwaring Caulkins, *History of Norwich, Connecticut, From its possession by the Indians, to the Year 1866, Published by the Author 1866*

2.   Todd L. Gerlander, *Descendants of the Founders of Windsor, Connecticut Newsletter* Volume XIX, Number 2, pages 4-7 Winter 2001-2002.

3.   Wikipedia, the free encyclopedia

4.   William Haynes, *Connecticut's Own Major* reprinted from the *Connecticut Antiquarian*, Volume VII, No. 2 December 1935.

5.   *New England Historical Genealogical Register for the Year 1861*, Vol. XV, Pg 117-121, Boston, Samuel S. Drake, Publisher 1861

6.   Louis B Mason, *The Life and Times of Major John Mason of Connecticut 1600-1672*, G. P. Putnam's Sons, New York and London1935

7.   John T. Fitch, with the assistance of Patricia M. Geisler, *Descendants of the Reverend James Fitch, 1622-1702*, Vol. 1, The First Five Generations, Picton Press, Camden, Maine 1997

8.   Ira B. Peck, *Genealogy History of the Descendants of Joseph Peck who Emigrated with His Family to this Country in 1638 and Records of His father's and Grandfather's Families in England, Originally published Boston 1868, Reprinted for Clearfield Company, Genealogical Publishing Co., Baltimore, Maryland 2000.*

9.   *National Genealogy Society Quarterly*, Vol. XX, No. 3, September 1932

10. Janece Streig (transcribed), *Story of New London, Connecticut with biographical Sketches of Many of its Pioneers and prominent Men.*

11. Clarence Almon Torrey, Prepared for Publication by Elizabeth P. Bentley, *New England Marriages Prior To 1700, Genealogical Publishing Company, Baltimore, Maryland 1985.*

12. Robert Charles Anderson, *The Great Migration Begins: Immigrants to New England, 1620-1633*, Vol. 2, pg 1228 New England Historical Society.

SIXTEEN

John Crow
(See Appendix P)

While researching the family of John Crow (1), I ran into many inconsistencies. Some of which may never be corrected; others were corrected by the printing of *The Great Migration*'s publications by NEHGS. To learn more about *The Great Migration* project, you can do a search on the Internet. I purposely omitted writing much about John (1) Crow-Crowe-Crowell line as there are too many conflicting and ambiguous statements and so-called facts. I have, however, given a brief outline of that family.

Early New England records indicate there were two John Crows: John Crow (1) at times spelled with an *e* and at times spelled Crowell. John Crow (2) was one of the founders of Hartford, Connecticut, and settled there in 1639.

John Crowe (1) was born about 1590 and died about 1651 in Yarmouth, Massachusetts.[7] "Records for the name John Crow after 1652 do not include the honorific 'Mr.' so it may be that the immigrant died about this time." John (1) married Elishua (last name unknown) around 1615. Some say Elishua came to America one year before John (1).[9] John (1) arrived from England in 1634 and settled in Charlestown, Massachusetts, but in 1638 moved to Yarmouth. Church membership for the church in Charlestown show that Elishua Crowe was admitted on 4 January 1634/5.[7]

According to *The Great Migration : Immigrants to New England: 1634–1635*, vol. II, C-F, John Crow (1) and his wife Elishua had four children:

1a.	Yelverton,	born about 1615
2a.	Elizabeth,	born abt. 1617

3a.	John,	born abt. 1635
4a.	Moses.	Baptized 24 June 1637, Charlestown

1a. **Yelverton Crow,** son of John (1) and Elishua Crow, was born about 1615 and married about 1642 Elizabeth (last name unknown). Elizabeth died in 1703. They lived in Yarmouth, Massachusetts. Their firstborn was born in 1642.[4]

5a.	John Crow	born 1642
6a.	Edward Crow	
7a.	Thomas (twin) Crow	born 9 May 1649; married Deborah ___; died 1722, Yarmouth[4]
8a.	Elizabeth (twin) Crow	born 9 May 1649; married 12 February 1689 Thomas Clark Sr.; lived in Plymouth[4]

2a. **Elizabeth Crow,** daughter of John (1) and Elishua, was born ca. 1617. She married (1) Arthur Perry born 20 December 1637, Boston Massachusetts. Elizabeth's second husband was John Gillet whom she married about 1654. John was born 12 October 1654, Boston, Massachusetts. Her third marriage was to William Wardwell on 4 December 1657, Boston.[7]

The gap in dates of birth between John and Elishua's first two children (Yelverton and Elizabeth) and the last two may indicate that there may have been a second wife.[7]

3a. **John Crow,** son of John (1) and Elishua, was born about 1635 and married about 1656, Mehitable. Mehitable is stated in several sources that her last name was Miller and that she was the daughter of Rev. John Miller; however, the evidence has not yet to be discovered as to her parents.[7]

4a. **Moses Crow,** son of John (1) and Elishua, was baptized on 24 June 1637 in Charlestown. (No other information is available.)

5a. **John Crow,** (did not follow his father's spelling of Crowe) son of Yelverton and Crowe, was born ca. 1642. He died in 1732. John married Hannah, and they lived in Yarmouth.[4]

John Crow (2)
(See Appendix P)

This John Crow family is pretty well documented; and therefore, I have written as much as I was able to find, that is, with the exceptions of various land purchases and sales.

John Crow (2) was born in 1606 in England and came to New England in 1634. In *New England Marriages Prior to 1700*, it shows that his first wife (name unknown) died in year 1644. It does not show her name or anything else about her.

John Crow's second wife was Elizabeth Goodwin, daughter and only child of Elder William Goodwin (see Goodwin chapter). They were married in 1645

John was one of the first settlers of Hartford, Connecticut, and the largest landholder in Hartford.[2] He is listed on the Founders Monument located in Hartford's ancient burial ground behind the center church that was established in 1632.

In 1659, John and his family moved to Hadley, Massachusetts, with his father-in-law, Elder William Goodwin. He was made a freeman in Massachusetts in 1666. Around 1675, John and his wife Elizabeth returned to Hartford. They were admitted to the South Church on 31 March 1678.[6]

The Second Church of Hartford (South Church) was organized 12 February 1699 (OS) or (NS) 22 February 1670 (OS is for "Old Style"; NS is for "New Style").

The Julian calendar was the "Old Style" calendar that dates back to Julius Caesar in 46 BC. It was designed to approximate the tropical year (solar year) and had twelve months with 365 days. A leap day was added to the month of February every four years. The Julian calendar remained in use into the twentieth century in some countries as a national calendar but, for the most part, has been replaced by the Gregorian calendar.

The Second Church of Hartford was formed by former members of the First Church of Hartford. For the first eleven years, the First Church of Hartford "flourished in harmony and peace" under the direction of Rev. Thomas Hooker who died in 1647 and was succeeded by Rev. Samuel Stone. During the next ten or so years, a controversy arose that soon became the major topic of discussion and that led to the dissension of several members, one being Rev. John Whiting.

The controversy concerned the differences of opinion concerning baptism and the rights of those who had been baptized, but were not communicants or "the new qualifications for baptism and church membership." The problem involved the right of baptized persons who were not members of the church in "full communion" to have their children baptized.

There has been an entire book written on the breaking up between the two churches; and for the reader that has a true and deep interest, I suggest that you try to obtain a copy of said book, *The History of the Second Church of Christ in Hartford*, by Edwin Pond Parker. Over the years, the Second Church of Hartford has gone through name changes, the current name is South Congregational Church or South Church located at 277 Main Street Hartford, Connecticut. This is the church founded by Rev. John Whiting (see Whiting chapter).

John Crow died 16 January 1686. John and his 1st wife (name unknown) had the following children:

1b.	Esther Crow	born 1628
2b.	John Crow	lived in Fairfield
3b.	Mary Crow	died 12 October 1720
4b.	Nathaniel Crow	lived in East Hartford
5b.	Elizabeth Crow	born 1644

John Crow and Elizabeth (Goodwin) had the following children:

6b.	Sarah Crow	born 1 March 1646
7b.	Anne or Hannah Crow	born 13 July 1649
8b.	Mehitable Crow	born about 1652
9b.	Ruth Crow	married William Gaylord of Hadley
10b.	Samuel Crow	married Hannah Lewis
11b.	Daniel Crow	born about 1656; lived in Hartford; died 12 August 1693

1b. **Esther Crow**, daughter of John Crow and his first wife, was born in 1628. She married Giles Hamlin, Esq., (1622-1689) in 1654. Esther died in 1700.

2b. **John Crow**, son of John Crow and his first wife, was a merchant in the West India trade. He died at sea in 1667. As far as we know, he was not married and did not have any children.

3b. **Mary Crow**, daughter of John Crow and his first wife, married 27 December 1666 Noah Coleman. Noah died in 1676. Mary married (2) 16 September 1680 Peter Montague (1651-1725). This was Peter's second marriage, his first being to Mary (Partridge) Smith who died in 1680. Mary (Crow) (Coleman) Montague died 12 October 1720.

4b. **Nathaniel Crow**, (date of birth unknown), son of John Crow and his first wife, married Deborah Leffingwell. Nathaniel died 30 July 1695. Deborah then married Andrew Warner before 1697 and moved to Windham, Connecticut.

5b. **Elizabeth Crow**, born in 1644, daughter of John Crow and his first wife, Elizabeth married William Warren of Hartford. Following William's death (date unknown), Elizabeth married Phineas Wilson, a very wealthy merchant from Dublin. Phineas died May 22, 1692 (possibly 1691). Elizabeth must have learned something about Phineas's business because after his death, she continued his business and became the main extensive banker in the colony. She not only loaned money on mortgages to citizens of Hartford, but would also loan to those in nearby towns. She handled her affairs with wisdom and good judgment. Elizabeth died 9 or 19 July

1727 at the age of eighty-six, leaving a large amount of property and many legacies.[2]

6b. **Sarah Crow**, daughter of John and Elizabeth (Goodwin) Crow, was born 1 March 1646 in Hartford, Connecticut. She married 1 November 1661 Daniel White of Hatfield who died in 1713. They lived in Hadley, Massachusetts. Sarah died 29 June 1719 at the age of seventy-two.

7b. **Anna or Hannah Crow**, daughter of John and Elizabeth (Goodwin) Crow, was born 13 July 1649. She married Thomas Dickinson 7 March 1667/8. Thomas Dickinson was one of the first settlers of Hadley, but moved to Wethersfield in 1679. Thomas died in 1716.

8b. **Mehitable Crow**, daughter of John and Elizabeth (Goodwin) Crow, was born about 1652. She married Colonel Samuel Partridge of Hadley and Hatfield 24 September 1668. Mehitable died 8 September 1730 at the age of seventy-eight.

9b. **Ruth Crow**, daughter of John and Elizabeth (Goodwin) Crow; (birth date unknown); married 21 December 1671, William Gaylord. William died in 1680, and Ruth married John Haley who died in 1688. They lived in Windsor, Connecticut. There were other Gaylords also living in Windsor.

10b. **Samuel Crow**, son of John and Elizabeth (Goodwin) Crow, (birth date unknown) 17 May 1671 married Hannah Lewis, daughter of Captain William Lewis of Farmington who was killed at Falls Fight 18 May 1676. Following the death of Samuel in 1676, Hannah married Daniel March in 1676.

11b. **Daniel Crow**, son of John and Elizabeth (Goodwin) Crow, was born about 1656. He lived in Hartford and died 12 August 1693.

Notes

1. John Farmer, reprinted with Additions and Corrections, by Samuel G. Drake, *A Genealogical Register of the First Settlers of New-England*, Genealogical Publishing Co., Baltimore

2. Mary F. Talcott, *The Original Proprietors of Hartford*, From "Memorial History of Hartford County" first published 1866, Pg. 235, Tuttle Antiquarian Books, Inc. Rutland, Vermont.

3. S. V. Talcott, *Genealogical Notes of New York and New England Families*, Weed, Parsons and Company 1883

4. Clarence Almon Torrey, Prepared for publication by Elizabeth P. Bentley, *New England Marriages prior to 1700*, Genealogical Publishing Co., Baltimore1985.

5. Benjamin W. Dwight *The History of the Descendants of John Dwight of Dedham, Massachusetts*, Vol. I, John F. Trow and Son New York 1874

6. Edwin Pond Parker *The History of the Second Church of Christ in Hartford, Hartford, Connecticut, Belknap & Warfield 1892.*

7. Robert Charles Anderson, George F. Sanborn Jr., and Melinde Lutz Sanborn, *The Great Migration 1634-1635*, Vol. II C-F, New England Historical Genealogical Society, Boston 2001.

8. Melinde Lutz Sanborn, *Third Supplement to Torrey's New England Marriages Prior to 1700*, Genealogical Publishing Co. Baltimore 2003.

9. Charles Henry Pope, *Pioneers of Massachusetts*, 1900 Archives CD Books *www.ArcivesCDBooksUSA.com* ISBN 1-933828-45-5

GLOSSARY

The following glossary is presented with the spelling and definitions provided by several resources.

&c.   Of the like kind and the rest; Used to point out that other things which could be mentioned are to be understood. Usually abbreviated in etc. or &c.

annual parochial   Church meeting and receiving guidance in their duties from the churchwardens.

abbey roll   The roll was a list of William the Conqueror's companions who stood by William during the Battle of Hastings and his victory over Harold.

Alumni Oxonienses   A biographical dictionary of all known students who attended the University of Oxford at Oxford, England, from the earliest times to 1900.

Alumni Cantabrigienses   A biographical dictionary of all known students who attended the University of Cambridge in Cambridge, England, from the earliest times to 1900.

Anglican   Relating to the Church of England or any church in communion with it.

Apprentice	One learning a trade or a profession, bound by a contract or other legal agreement to work for a specified period of time under the direction or a master workman in exchange for instruction and learning in the trade, some additional education and support.
armory	The art and science of the hereditary system of symbols centered around the shield.
barony	Is an administrative division of a country, usually of lower rank and importance than a county. Countries or their counties can include baronies. Originally, a barony was the land subject to a baron. Just as counties are no longer necessarily connected with a noble earl or count, there are baronies which are not connected with a baron anymore.
census	A count of a population. Federal Censuses, those taken by the U.S. government, occur every ten years on the decade (i.e., 1900, 1910, 1920), while state censuses occur every ten years mid decade (ex: 1905, 1915).
ca.	Calendar year as used in genealogy when exact date is unknown.
consort	A wife, husband, or companion. Usually used as identification of the deceased, i.e., Ann, consort of Shem. Meaning, Ann died first. See "relict."
cordwainer	(or cordovan) Somebody who makes shoes and other articles from fine soft leather.
couplet	Two successive rhyming lines of verse.
Dorcas	Dorcas was a disciple of Joppa and is found in the book of Acts (9:36—42). She made clothes for the poor in her village. After her death, the people of the village prayed to Saint Peter to raise her from the dead.
forefather	Ancestor
foremother	Ancestor

fowling piece	A light shotgun for shooting birds and small animals. For firing shot at short ranges.
freeman	See "freemen."
freemen	As early as 1631, in order to become a freeman, it was required that the applicant produce evidence that he was a member of the Congregational Church. This regulation was modified in 1664. Freemen were admitted by the General Court of the colony. A freeman was entitled to exercise the right to vote and to hold office.
grantee	The one receiving. The person to whom the grant is made. The party in a deed to whom the conveyance is made.
grantor	The person who makes the grant. The party in a deed who makes the conveyance.
gristmill	A place to mix grains.
herald	All that which pertains to the office of herald, including the recording, granting, and regulations of armory as well as precedence, state ceremonial, tournaments, diplomacy, genealogy, and pedigree.
King Philip's War	Sometimes called Metacom's War or Matacom's Rebellion, this war was an armed conflict between Native American inhabitants of present-day southern New England and English colonists and their Native American allies from 1675-1676. Colonial historian Francis Jennings estimated that the war killed nearly seven of every eight Native Americans and six of every thirteen English settlers. King Philip's War was proportionately one of the bloodiest and costliest in the history of America. More than half of New England's ninety towns were assaulted by Native American warriors. The war is named after the main leader of the Native American side, Metacomet, Metacom, or Pometacom, known to the English as King Philip.
league	A measure of distance equal to about three miles.

lineage	Ancestry or pedigree.
magistrate	A civil officer who administers the law, especially one who conducts a court concerned with minor offenses and holds preliminary hearings for more serious ones.
matronymic	Is a personal name based on the name of one's mother. It is the female equivalent of a patronymic. In patriarchal societies, matronymic surnames are far less common than patronymics. In the past, matronymic last names were often given to children of unwed mothers.
messuage	In law, the term "messuage" equates to a dwelling-house and includes outbuildings, orchard, curtilage or courtyard, and garden. At one time, "messuage" supposedly had a more extensive meaning than that comprised in the word "house" or "site"; but such distinction, if it ever existed, no longer survives.
naturalization	A process by which one receives citizenship or nationality as a foreigner which allows those granted, the privileges of citizenship and to hold lands and invest in them as the same as those natural born of said Province.
Nave	The central space in a church, often flanked by aisles.
orrery	An orrery is a mechanical device that illustrates the relative positions and motions of the planets and moons in the solar system in heliocentric model. They are typically driven by a large clockwork mechanism with a globe representing the sun at the centre and with a planet at the end of each of the arms.
relict	Belongs to former or ancient times. Old or in an old-fashioned style. A widow (archaic).
Pedigree	A person's lineage or ancestry; Succession in pedigrees
Progenitor	A direct ancestor; Forefather

sachems	A chief of a Native American tribe or confederation, especially an Algonquian chief.
Sendschoffen	The church councilmen (Sendschoffen/Synodali) were elected by the church membership and confirmed by the priest. It was their duty to care for the poor and needy in the community and to determine the identity of the father of an illegitimate child.
selectman	In most New England communities, somebody, especially a man, who is a member of an elected administrative board that manages local affairs.
shalop	Also spelled "shallop," a large open boat.
sidesman	A sides person, correctly known as an usher, in the Anglican Church and is responsible for greeting members of the congregation, overseeing seating arrangements in church, and for taking the collection. In England they, are usually appointed by the Annual Parochial Church Meeting members and usually will assist the churchwardens.
Sizar	In Cambridge University, A poor scholar whose assize of food is given to him Sizars used to have what was left at the fellows' table because it was their duty at one time to wait on the fellows at dinner. Each fellow had his sizar.
tabard	A tunic worn by a knight over his armor.
TAG	The *American Genealogist*, an independent quarterly journal dedicated to the elevation of genealogical scholarship through carefully documented analyses of genealogical problems and through short compiled genealogies.
tallow	A hard fatty substance made from rendered animal fat used in making candles and soap.
trainband	A small colonial troop maintained by the town for emergencies, drilled, equipped, and trained in the basics of

military techniques. A company of trained militia in England or America from the sixteenth to the eighteenth century.

tarry	Stay longer than intended (archaic). Delay in leaving a place.
tribute	A payment by one ruler or nation to another as an act of submission or price of protection; (2) an excessive tax, rental or levy exacted by a sovereign or superior; (3) a gift or service showing respect, gratitude, or affection. Also, praise.
vital record	Data pertaining to the life of a person, namely birth, marriage, and death.
yeoman	Farmer who owns his own land.

Appendix

Introductory

On the following pages, you will find appendixes of various people in the line of Charles R. Looney or LaVanchie Margaret Cool. You will notice certain dates under each name. These dates represent date of birth, date coming to America, and date of death in that order.

Take Rev. Henry Flint (Flynt) (Appendix L) for example; Henry was born about 1613 and came to America in 1635. He died in 1668. LaVanchie is self. Her mother was Lydia Elizabeth Ackley; her grandfather was Robert O. Ackley; her great-grandmother was Anne Burbank; her second great-grandfather was Shem Burbank and continuing up the line to Rev. Henry Flint—her sixth great-grandfather.

Appendix A

A Word about Calendars*

---◆---

The *Julian calendar* was a makeover or improvement of the Roman calendar, dating back to 46 BC, when Julius Caesar was in power. After meeting with the astronomer Sosigenes of Alexandria, the calendar was designed to a year consisting of 365 days divided by twelve months, with a leap day added to February every four years, Hence, the Julian year is on average 365 days long.[1]

Although the Julian calendar remained in use well into the twentieth century in some countries and, in fact, is still used by many national Orthodox churches. It has, in most part, been replaced for civil use by the modern Gregorian calendar.

The notation "Old Style" (OS) is sometimes used to indicate a date using the Julian calendar, as opposed to "New Style" (NS) which either represents the Julian date with the start of the year as January 1 or a full mapping onto the Gregorian calendar.

The Gregorian calendar is a revision of the Julian calendar, which was introduced in a papal bull by Pope Gregory XIII in 1582. The reason for the stated calendar change "was to correct for the drift in the dates of significant religious observations (primarily Easter) and to prevent further drift in the dates."

The important effects of the change were the following:

- Drop ten days from October 1582 to realign the vernal equinox with 21 March.

---

*   Wikipedia, the free encyclopedia

- Change leap year selection so that not all leap years ending in "00" are leap years.
- Change the beginning of the year to 1 January from 25 March.

Catholic countries immediately changed to the new calendars. On the other hand, the Protestant countries did not accept the change until much later. England finally changed over to the new calendar in 1752, with eleven days moved from September. The additional day came because the two calendars disagreed on whether 1700 was a leap year, so the Julian calendar had to be adjusted by one more day.

Appendix B

John Looney

---

5. Looney, John of Crowcreen, born 1700, probably Isle of Man; died 28 July 1769, Isle of Man; married Margaret Kelvie; their son was:

4. Looney, John (Yack) of Boshin, born 1748, Isle of Man; died 1835, Maughold, Isle of Man; married Isabel Camaish 17 September 1788; their son was:

3. Looney, Robert of Maughold, christened 2 April 1799, Isle of Man; buried 30 March 1853, Isle of Man; married Isabella Lewin, born about 1803; died 17 July 1850; their son was:

2. Looney, James H., born 31 January 1842, Isle of Man, came to America in the spring of 1855; served for the Union during the Civil War (4 June 1862-31 July 1865); died 15 January 1917; married Mary Kane 17 August 1873 Kansas City, Missouri; Mary died 30 March 1877 just twenty-one days after giving birth to twins, one of which was the son:

1. Looney, Charles Robert, born 9 March 1877, Kansas City, Missouri; died 15 March 1943; married 3 July 1907 Windsor, Ontario, Canada, LaVanchie Margaret Cool, born 11 May 1882, died 11 November 1935. Charles was raised by his Aunt Elizabeth (Looney) and John Wark and used the name Wark throughout his life, except when it came to legal matters.

Appendix C

Johann Paul Kuhl
1700-1730(^{1})-1784

---

6. Kuhl, Johann Paul, born 24 March 1700, Maxsain, Germany; came to America and was naturalized 8 July 1730 [1]; died 1784, Amwell Township, New Jersey; married before 1735 Eva Maria Kaes, born England, died 1783, Hunterdon, New Jersey; their son:

5. Kuhl Sr., Wilhelm/William, born 18 July 1738, Hunterdon, New Jersey; died November 1815, Knowlton, New Jersey; married before 1759 Maria (last name unknown), born 18 July 1738, Hunterdon, died November 1815, Knowlton, New Jersey; their son:

4. Cool, Paul, born 6 May 1768, Hunterdon, New Jersey; died 6 March 1845, Hunterdon; married before 1793 Susan Raub, born 23 December 1773, Knowlton, died 8 July 1838, Knowlton, New Jersey; their son:

3. Cool, John Friese, born 27 August 1815, Knowlton, New Jersey; died 29 April 1863, Albion, Michigan; married 6 December 1845 Sarah Ann Snover, born 14 April 1826, died 23 July 1904, Albion, Michigan; their son:

2. Cool, Crittenden Irelius, born 8 May 1849, Columbia City, New Jersey; died 22 January 1933, Albion, Michigan; married 25 February 1880 Lydia

Elizabeth Ackley, born 3 August 1856, Fort Ann, New York, died 13 September 1943, Albion, Michigan; their daughter:

1.   Cool, LaVanchie Margaret, born 11 May 1882, Albion, Michigan; died 11 November 1935, Valparaiso, Indiana; married Charles Robert Looney.

Appendix D

John Burbank
1600-1638-1682

---

8. Burbank, John (1), born 1600, England; died 1682, Haverhill, Massachusetts; married Susannah Merrill, born 1640, Newbury, Massachusetts, died 10 October 1690, Suffield, Connecticut; their son was:

7. Burbank, John (2), born August 1670, Haverhill, Massachusetts; died 25 March 1727, Suffield, Connecticut; married Mary Granger, born 1670, died 18 May 1737; their son was:

6. Burbank, Abraham, born 8 September 1703, Suffield, Connecticut; died 20 November 1767, Suffield; married Mehitable Dwight, born 2 November 1705, died 20 November 1767; their son was:

5. Burbank, Shem Thomas, born 21 May 1736, Suffield, Connecticut; died 31 January 1800, Granville, Massachusetts; married Anne Fitch, born 12 July 1737, Lebanon, Connecticut, died 4 February 1813, Fort Ann, New York; their daughter was:

4. Burbank, Anne, born 15 December 1782, Suffield, Connecticut; died 29 March 1872, Albion, Michigan; married Joseph Ackley of Fort Ann, New York; their son was:

3.　Ackley, Robert O., born 21 January 1826, Fort Ann, New York; died 17 November 1882, Albion, Michigan; married Lydia Osborn; their daughter was:

2.　Ackley, Lydia Elizabeth, born 3 August 1856, Fort Ann, New York; died 13 September 1943, Albion, Michigan; married Crittenden I. Cool; their daughter was:

1.　Cool, LaVanchie Margaret, born 11 May 1882, Albion, Michigan; died 11 November 1935, Valparaiso, Indiana; married Charles Robert Looney.

Appendix E

Rev. James Fitch
1622-1638/9-1702

———◆◆◆———

7. Fitch, James (Rev.), born 24 December 1622, Bocking, England; died 18 November 1702, Lebanon, Connecticut; married Pricilla Mason, born October 1641, Windsor, Connecticut, died after 1714, Norwich, Connecticut; their son was:

6. Fitch, Joseph, born November 1681, Norwich, (New London County), Connecticut; died 9 May 1741, Lebanon, Connecticut; married Anne Whiting; their daughter was:

5. Fitch, Ann, born 12 July 1737, Lebanon, Connecticut; died 4 February 1813, Fort Ann, New York; married Shem Thomas Burbank; their daughter was:

4. Burbank, Anne, born 15 December 1782, Suffield, Connecticut; died 29 March 1872, Albion, Michigan; married Joseph Ackley of Fort Ann, New York; their son was:

3. Ackley, Robert O., born 21 January 1826, Fort Ann, New York; died 17 November 1882, Albion, Michigan; married Lydia Osborn; their daughter was:

2.   Ackley, Lydia Elizabeth, born 3 August 1856, Fort Ann, New York; died 13 September 1943, Albion, Michigan; married Crittenden I. Cool; their daughter was:

1.   Cool, LaVanchie Margaret, born 11 May 1882, Albion, Michigan; died 11 November 1935, Valparaiso, Indiana; married Charles Robert Looney.

Appendix F

Three Whitings

There were three Whiting families that came to America in the 1600s: Whitings of Dedham, Whitings of Lynn, and Whitings of Hartford.

I.   Nathaniel Whiting of Dedham came to America about 1638 and became very successful in the Boston and Dedham area. He was born in England in 1609 and died in Dedham, Massachusetts, on 15 January 1682. He married on 4 November 1643 Hannah Dwight, daughter of John and Hannah Dwight of Dedham. Hannah (Dwight) Whiting died on 4 November 1714.

II. Rev. Samuel Whiting was born in 1597 at Boston, Lincolnshire, England. He graduated from Emanuel College in Cambridge and became the chaplain in the villages of Norfolk and King's Lynn. Whiting, like several other ministers of his time, was not willing to conform to the religious ways of England; and because of his nonconformist behavior, he left the villages and moved to the Skirbek rectory. The complaints against him did not cease; and in 1663, he resigned his position and sailed to the New World, arriving in Boston, Massachusetts, where he stayed but a short while before removing to Lynn, Massachusetts, where he officiated as minister until his death in 1679.

Whiting married on 6 August 1629 Elizabeth St. John, who was born 1 December 1605 in Bedford, England, and died on 3 March 1676 in Lynn, Massachusetts.

III.   The third family was that of the Major William Whiting outlined in chapter 7 of *Ancestral Roots and Descendants of Charles Robert Looney and LaVanchie Margaret Cool.* Major William Whiting married Susanna (last name unknown) and had six children of which one was John Whiting who married Sybil Collins. Their son was Rev. Samuel Whiting, born 1670 in Hartford—seventy-three years after the birth of Rev. Samuel Whiting (in number II above) and seven years after his arrival to America.

To the best of my knowledge, many genealogist have attempted to discover any type of connection between the above three families. So far, all have been unsuccessful.

Reference:

Pishey Thompson's *History and Antiquities of Boston, England.*

Appendix G

William Whiting
1605-before 1632-1647

—◆◆◆—

8. Whiting, William, born 1605, Suffolk, England; died July 1647, Middleton, Connecticut; married Susan (last name unknown), born 1609; died 8 July 1673; their son was:

7. Whiting, John (Rev.), born 1635, probably Massachusetts; died 8 September 1689, Hartford, Connecticut; married Sybil Collins, born November 1637, died 3 June 1672; their son was:

6. Whiting, Samuel (Rev.), born 24 April 1670, Hartford, Connecticut; died 27 September 1725, Enfield, Connecticut; married Elizabeth Adams, born 23 February 1681, died 3 June 1672; their daughter was:

5. Whiting, Anne, born 2 January 1698, Windham, Connecticut; died 23 September 1778, Windham, Connecticut; married Joseph Fitch, born November 1681, died 21 December 1766; their daughter was:

4. Burbank, Anne, born 15 December 1782, Suffield, Connecticut; died 29 March 1872, Albion, Michigan; married Joseph Ackley of Fort Ann, New York; their son:

3.   Ackley, Robert O., born 21 January 1826, Fort Ann, New York; died 17 November 1882, Albion, Michigan; married Lydia Osborn; their daughter was:

2.   Ackley, Lydia Elizabeth, born 3 August 1856, Fort Ann, New York; died 13 September 1943, Albion, Michigan; married Crittenden I. Cool; their daughter was:

1.   Cool, LaVanchie Margaret, born 11 May 1882, Albion, Michigan; died 11 November 1935, Valparaiso, Indiana; married Charles Robert Looney.

Appendix H

William Bradford
(*Mayflower*)
1589-1620-1657

The following is from William Bradford of the *Mayflower* to LaVanchie Margaret Cool:

10. William Bradford of the Mayflower, baptized 19 March 1589, England (Austerfield, York County); died 9 May 1657, Plymouth, Massachusetts; married Alice (Carpenter) (Southworth); their son was:

9. Bradford, William, born 17 June 1624, Plymouth, Massachusetts; died 20 February 1703/3, Plymouth, Massachusetts; married Alice Richards; their daughter was:

8. Bradford, Alice, born 1659, Plymouth, Massachusetts; died 15 March 1745/46, Canterbury, Connecticut; married Rev. Williams Adams; their daughter was:

7. Adams, Elizabeth, born 23 February 1680/81, Dedham, Massachusetts; died 21 December 1766, New Haven, Connecticut; married Rev. Samuel Whiting of Windham, Connecticut; their daughter was:

6.   Whiting, Ann, born 2 January 1698, Windham, Connecticut; died 23 September 1778, Lebanon, Connecticut: married Joseph Fitch; their daughter was:

5.   Fitch, Ann, born 12 July 1737, Lebanon, Connecticut; died 4 February 1813, Fort Ann, New York; married Shem Thomas Burbank; their daughter was:

4.   Burbank, Anne, born 15 December 1782, Suffield, Connecticut; died 29 March 1872, Albion, Michigan; married Joseph Ackley of Fort Ann, New York; their son was:

3.   Ackley, Robert O., born 21 January 1826, Fort Ann, New York; died 17 November 1882, Albion, Michigan; married Lydia Osborn; their daughter was:

2.   Ackley, Lydia Elizabeth, born 3 August 1856, Fort Ann, New York; died 13 September 1943, Albion, Michigan; married Crittenden I. Cool; their daughter was:

1.   Cool, LaVanchie Margaret, born 11 May 1882, Albion, Michigan; died 11 November 1935, Valparaiso, Indiana; married Charles Robert Looney.

Appendix I

Rev. Robert Peck
1580-1638-1656

9. Peck, Robert (Rev.), born 1580, Beccles, Suffolk County, England; died 24 July 1656, Hingham, Norfolk County, England; married Anne Lawrence, born in England, died 1648, Hingham, England. Both are buried in St. Andrew's Church cemetery in Hingham, England. Peck, his wife Anne, their son Joseph, and their daughter came to America on the ship *Diligent*, leaving England June 1638 and arriving in America on August 10. They stayed for a short period of time, leaving America and returning to their homeland; their daughter was:

8. Peck, Anne, born 1619, Hingham, Norfolk County, England; died after 30 January 1672, Norwich, Connecticut; married Major John Mason; their daughter was:

7. Mason, Pricilla, born October 1641, Windsor, Connecticut; died after 1714, Norwich, Connecticut; married Rev. James Fitch; their son was:

6. Fitch, Joseph, born November 1681, Norwich (New London County), Connecticut; died 9 May 1741, Lebanon, Connecticut; married Anne Whiting; their daughter was:

5. Fitch, Ann, born 12 July 1737, Lebanon, Connecticut; died 4 February 1813, Fort Ann, New York; married Shem Thomas Burbank; their daughter was:

4. Burbank, Anne, born 15 December 1782, Suffield, Connecticut; died 29 March 1872, Albion, Michigan; married Joseph Ackley of Fort Ann, New York; their son was:

3. Ackley, Robert O., born 21 January 1826, Fort Ann, New York; died 17 November 1882, Albion, Michigan; married Lydia Osborn; their daughter was:

2. Ackley, Lydia Elizabeth, born 3 August 1856, Fort Ann, New York; died 13 September 1943, Albion, Michigan; married Crittenden I. Cool; their daughter was:

1. Cool, LaVanchie Margaret, born 11 May 1882, Albion, Michigan; died 11 November 1935, Valparaiso, Indiana; married Charles Robert Looney.

Appendix J

John Dwight
1600-1634-1660

———◆———

9. Dwight, John, born about 1600, Oxfordshire, England; died 24 January 1660, Dedham, Massachusetts; married Hannah (last name unknown), born about 1600; died 24 January 1660; their son was:

8. Dwight, Timothy (Captain), born about 1629, England; died 31 January 1718, Dedham, Massachusetts; married 9 January 1665, Anna Flint, born 11 September 1643, Braintree, Massachusetts, died 29 January 1689, Dedham, Massachusetts; their son was:

7. Dwight, Nathaniel (Justice), born 20 November 1666, Dedham, Massachusetts; died 7 November 1711, Springfield, Massachusetts; married Mehitable Partridge, born 26 August 1675, died 19 October 1756; their daughter was:

6. Dwight, Mehitable, born 2 November 1705, Northampton, Massachusetts; died 20 November 1767, Suffield, Connecticut; married Abraham Burbank; their son was:

5. Burbank, Shem Thomas, born 21 May 1736, Suffield, Connecticut; died 31 January 1800, Granville, Massachusetts; married Anna Fitch, born 12 July 1737, Lebanon, Connecticut; their daughter was:

4.   Burbank, Anne, born 15 December 1782, Suffield, Connecticut; died 29 March 1872, Albion, Michigan; married Joseph Ackley of Fort Ann, New York; their son was:

3.   Ackley, Robert O., born 21 January 1826, Fort Ann, New York; died 17 November 1882, Albion, Michigan; married Lydia Osborn; their daughter was:

2.   Ackley, Lydia Elizabeth, born 3 August 1856, Fort Ann, New York; died 13 September 1943, Albion, Michigan; married Crittenden I. Cool; their daughter was:

1.   Cool, LaVanchie Margaret, born 11 May 1882, Albion, Michigan; died 11 November 1935, Valparaiso, Indiana; married Charles Robert Looney.

Appendix K

William Partridge
1610-before 1638-1680

———◆◆◆———

9. Partridge, William born 1610, Berwick-on-the-Tweed, England; died 27 June 1688, Hadley, Massachusetts; married Mary Smith, born 1625, England, died 20 July 1680: their daughter was:

8. Partridge, Samuel (Colonel), born 15 October 1645, Hartford, Connecticut; died 25 December 1740, buried Hadley, Massachusetts; married Mehitable Crow, born 1652, died 8 December 1730, Hartford, Connecticut. Their daughter was:

7. Partridge, Mehitable, born 26 August 1675, Hatfield, Massachusetts; died 19 October 1756, Northampton, Massachusetts; married Justice Nathaniel Dwight, born 20 November 1666, England, died 7 November 1711, West Springfield, Massachusetts; their daughter was:

6. Dwight, Mehitable, born 2 November 1705; died 20 November 1767, Suffield; married Abraham Burbank, born 8 September 1703, Suffield, Connecticut, died 20 November 1767, Suffield; their son was:

5. Burbank, Shem Thomas, born 21 May 1736, Suffield, Connecticut; died 31 January 1800, Granville, Massachusetts; married Anne Fitch, born 12 July 1737, Lebanon, Connecticut, died 4 February 1813, Fort Ann, New York; their daughter was:

4. Burbank, Anne, born 15 December 1782, Suffield, Connecticut; died 29
    March 1872, Albion, Michigan; married Joseph Ackley of Fort Ann, New
    York; their son was:

3. Ackley, Robert O., born 21 January 1826, Fort Ann, New York; died 17
    November 1882, Albion, Michigan; married Lydia Osborn; their daughter
    was:

2. Ackley, Lydia Elizabeth, born 3 August 1856, Fort Ann, New York; died
    13 September 1943, Albion, Michigan; married Crittenden I. Cool; their
    daughter was:

1. Cool, LaVanchie Margaret, born 11 May 1882, Albion, Michigan; died 11
    November 1935, Valparaiso, Indiana; married Charles Robert Looney.

Appendix L

Rev. Henry Flint
1613-1635-1668

———————◆◆◆———————

9. Flint, Henry (Rev.), born about 1613, Matlock, Derbyshire, England; died 27 April 1668; came to America in 1635; married before 1642 Braintree, Massachusetts, Margery Hoar, daughter of Charles Hoare Jr., sheriff of Gloucester, England; their daughter was:

8. Flint, Anna, born 11 September 1643, Braintree, Massachusetts; died 29 January 1689, Dedham, Massachusetts; married (2) 9 January 1665 Captain Timothy Dwight; their son was:

7. Dwight, Nathaniel (Justice), born 20 November 1666, Dedham, Massachusetts; died 7 November 1711, Springfield, Massachusetts; married Mehitable Partridge; their daughter was:

6. Dwight, Mehitable, born 2 November 1705, Northampton, Massachusetts; died 20 November 1767, Suffield, Connecticut; married Abraham Burbank; their son was:

5. Burbank, Shem Thomas, born 21 May 1736, Suffield, Connecticut; died 31 January 1800, Granville, Massachusetts; married Anna Fitch, born 12 July 1737, Lebanon, Connecticut; their daughter was:

4.   Burbank, Anne, born 15 December 1782, Suffield, Connecticut; died 29
      March 1872, Albion, Michigan; married Joseph Ackley of Fort Ann, New
      York; their son was:

3.   Ackley, Robert O., born 21 January 1826, Fort Ann, New York; died 17
      November 1882, Albion, Michigan; married Lydia Osborn; their daughter
      was:

2.   Ackley, Lydia Elizabeth, born 3 August 1856, Fort Ann, New York; died
      13 September 1943, Albion, Michigan; married Crittenden I. Cool; their
      daughter was:

1.   Cool, LaVanchie Margaret, born 11 May 1882, Albion, Michigan; died 11
      November 1935, Valparaiso, Indiana; married Charles Robert Looney.

Appendix M

Joanne (Hincksman) Hoar
Unk.—1640-1651

---

10. Hoar, Joanne (Hincksman), date of birth unknown; following the death of her husband, Charles Hoar Jr. (December 1638), spent time in England before coming to America in 1640; died 21 September 1651, Braintree, Massachusetts; her daughter was:

9. Hoar, Margery, date of birth unknown; came to America with her mother in 1640; married (2) Rev. Henry Flint (Flynt) of Braintree, Massachusetts; their daughter was:

8. Flint, Anna, born 11 September 1643, Braintree, Massachusetts; died 29 January 1689, Dedham, Massachusetts; married (2) 9 January 1665 Captain Timothy Dwight; their son was:

7. Dwight, Nathaniel (Justice), born 20 November 1666, Dedham, Massachusetts; died 7 November 1711, Springfield, Massachusetts; married Mehitable Partridge: their daughter was:

6. Dwight, Mehitable, born 2 November 1705, Northampton, Massachusetts; died 20 November 1767, Suffield, Connecticut; married Abraham Burbank; their son was:

5. Burbank, Shem Thomas, born 21 May 1736, Suffield, Connecticut; died 31 January 1800, Granville, Massachusetts; married Anna Fitch, born 12 July 1737, Lebanon, Connecticut; their daughter was:

4. Burbank, Anne, born 15 December 1782, Suffield, Connecticut; died 29 March 1872, Albion, Michigan; married Joseph Ackley of Fort Ann, New York; their son was:

3. Ackley, Robert O., born 21 January 1826, Fort Ann, New York; died 17 November 1882, Albion, Michigan; married Lydia Osborn; their daughter was:

2. Ackley, Lydia Elizabeth, born 3 August 1856, Fort Ann, New York; died 13 September 1943, Albion, Michigan; married Crittenden I. Cool; their daughter was:

1. Cool, LaVanchie Margaret, born 11 May 1882, Albion, Michigan; died 11 November 1935, Valparaiso, Indiana; married Charles Robert Looney.

Appendix N

Elder William Goodwin
1591-1632-1673

---

10. Goodwin, William, born 1591, Braintree, Essex, England; came to America 1632 (*Lyon*); died 11 May 1673, Farmington, Massachusetts; married (1) Elizabeth White, born ca. 1591, Messing, England, died before January 1669; their daughter was:

9. Goodwin, Elizabeth, came to America with her parents (1632), unknown birth date; died 1686, probably Hartford; married John Crow; their daughter was:

8. Crow, Mehitable, born 1652; died 8 December 1730, Hartford, Connecticut; married Partridge, Samuel (Colonel), born 15 October 1645, Hartford, Connecticut, died 25 December 1740, buried Hadley, Massachusetts; their daughter was:

7. Partridge, Mehitable, born 26 August 1675, Hatfield, Massachusetts; died 19 October 1756, Northampton, Massachusetts; married Justice Nathaniel Dwight, born 20 November 1666, England, died 7 November 1711, West Springfield, Massachusetts; their daughter was:

6. Dwight, Mehitable, born 2 November 1705; died 20 November 1767, Suffield; married Abraham Burbank, born 8 September 1703, Suffield, Connecticut, died 20 November 1767, Suffield; their son was:

5. Burbank, Shem Thomas, born 21 May 1736, Suffield, Connecticut; died
    31 January 1800, Granville, Massachusetts; married Anne Fitch, born 12
    July 1737, Lebanon, Connecticut, died 4 February 1813, Fort Ann, New
    York; their daughter was:

4. Burbank, Anne, born 15 December 1782, Suffield, Connecticut; died 29
    March 1872, Albion, Michigan; married Joseph Ackley of Fort Ann, New
    York; their son was:

3. Ackley, Robert O., born 21 January 1826, Fort Ann, New York; died 17
    November 1882, Albion, Michigan; married Lydia Osborn; their daughter
    was:

2. Ackley, Lydia Elizabeth, born 3 August 1856, Fort Ann, New York; died
    13 September 1943, Albion, Michigan; married Crittenden I. Cool; their
    daughter was:

1. Cool, LaVanchie Margaret, born 11 May 1882, Albion, Michigan; died 11
    November 1935, Valparaiso, Indiana; married Charles Robert Looney.

Appendix O

Major John Mason

1600-1632-1672

---

8. Major John Mason, among founders of Windsor, Connecticut, defeated the Pequot Indians; born about 1600, probably England; died 30 January 1672, Norwich, Connecticut; married Anne Peck, daughter of Rev. Robert Peck: their daughter was:

7. Mason, Pricilla, born October 1641, Windsor, Connecticut; died after 1714, Norwich, Connecticut; married Rev. James Fitch; their son was:

6. Fitch, Joseph, born November 1681, Norwich (New London County), Connecticut; died 9 May 1741, Lebanon, Connecticut; married Anne Whiting; their daughter was:

5. Fitch, Ann, born 12 July 1737, Lebanon, Connecticut; died 4 February 1813, Fort Ann, New York; married Shem Thomas Burbank; their daughter was:

4. Burbank, Anne, born 15 December 1772, Suffield, Connecticut; died 29 March 1872, Albion, Michigan; married Joseph Ackley of Fort Ann, New York; their son was:

3. Ackley, Robert O., born 21 January 1826, Fort Ann, New York; died 17 November 1882, Albion, Michigan; married Lydia Osborn; their daughter was:

2.   Ackley, Lydia Elizabeth, born 3 August 1856, Fort Ann, New York; died
      13 September 1943, Albion, Michigan; married Crittenden I. Cool; their
      daughter was:

1.   Cool, LaVanchie Margaret, born 11 May 1882, Albion, Michigan; died 11
      November 1935, Valparaiso, Indiana; married Charles Robert Looney.

This would make Major John Mason the fifth great-grandfather of LaVanchie
Margaret Cool.

There is a plaque under the statute of Major John Mason Palisado [*sic*] Green in
Windsor, Connecticut, that reads, "Major John Mason, born 1600 in England,
immigrated to New England in 1630; a founder of Windsor, Old Saybrook and
Norwich; Magistrate and Chief Military Officer of the Connecticut Colony
Deputy Governor and acting Governor of Connecticut; A patentee of the
Colonial Charter died 1672 in Norwich. This monument erected at Mystic in
1889 by the State of Connecticut, relocated in 1986 to respect a sacred site of
the 1637 Pequot War."

Appendix P

John Crow (2)
(1606-1634-1686)

---

9.   Crow, John, born 1606 England; came to America in 1634; died 16 January 1686, Hartford, Connecticut; one of the "Founders of Hartford"; married (2) 1645, Elizabeth Goodwin, daughter of Elder William Goodwin of Hartford; their daughter was:

8.   Mehitable Crow, born 1652; died 8 December 1730, Hartford, Connecticut; married Colonel Samuel Partridge, born 15 October 1645, Hartford, Connecticut; died 25 December 1740; buried Hadley, Massachusetts; their daughter was:

7.   Partridge, Mehitable, born 26 August 1675, Hatfield, Massachusetts; died 19 October 1756, Hampton, Massachusetts; married Justice Nathaniel Dwight, born 20 November 1666, England; died 7 November 1711, West Springfield, Massachusetts; their daughter was;

6.   Dwight, Mehitable, born 2 November 1705, Northampton, Massachusetts; died 20 November 1767, Suffield, Connecticut; married Abraham Burbank; their son:

5.   Burbank, Shem Thomas, born 21 May 1736, Suffield, Connecticut; died 31 January 1800, Granville, Massachusetts; married Anna Fitch, born 12 July 1737, Lebanon, Connecticut; their daughter:

4.   Burbank, Anne, born 15 December 1782, Suffield, Connecticut; died 29 March 1872, Albion, Michigan; married Joseph Ackley of Fort Ann, New York; their son:

3.   Ackley, Robert O., born 21 January 1826, Fort Ann, New York; died 17 November 1882, Albion, Michigan; married Lydia Osborn; their daughter:

2.   Ackley, Lydia Elizabeth, born 3 August 1856, Fort Ann, New York; died 13 September 1943, Albion, Michigan; married Crittenden I. Cool; their daughter:

1.   Cool, LaVanchie Margaret, born 11 May 1882, Albion, Michigan; died 11 November 1935, Valparaiso, Indiana; married Charles Robert Looney.

INDEX

E

I

Y

www.ingramcontent.com/pod-product-compliance
Lightning Source LLC
Chambersburg PA
CBHW061335280526
45784CB00001B/24